RECEPTION
HISTORIES

ALSO BY STEVEN MAILLOUX

Interpretive Conventions: The Reader in the Study of American Fiction

Rhetorical Power

RECEPTION HISTORIES

Rhetoric, Pragmatism, and American Cultural Politics

S T E V E N M A I L L O U X

Cornell University Press

Ithaca and London

First published 1998 by Cornell University Press.
First printing, Cornell Paperbacks, 1998.

Printed in the United States of America

Cornell University Press strives to utilize environmentally responsible suppliers and materials to the fullest extent possible in the publishing of its books. Such materials include vegetable-based, low-VOC inks and acid-free papers that are also either recycled, totally chlorine-free, or partly composed of nonwood fibers.

Library of Congress Cataloging-in-Publication Data

Mailloux, Steven.
    Reception histories: rhetoric, pragmatism, and American cultural politics / Steven Mailloux.
        p.   cm.
    Includes bibliographical references and index.
    ISBN 0-8014-3505-6 (cloth: alk. paper).—ISBN 0-8014-8506-1 (pbk.: alk. paper)
    1. English philology—Study and teaching (Higher)—United States. 2. Literature—History and criticism—Theory, etc.   3. Criticism—United States—History—20th century.   4. Rhetoric—Political aspects—United States.   5. Reader-response criticism—United States.   6 Politics and literature—United States. 7. Multiculturalism—United States.   8. Culture conflict—United States.   9. Pragmatism.   I. Title.
    PE68.U5M35   1998
    808'.071'073—dc21   98-10513

Cloth printing   10   9   8   7   6   5   4   3   2   1
Paperback printing   10   9   8   7   6   5   4   3   2   1

For Mary, Roman, and Tess

CONTENTS

PREFACE

This book offers a series of reception histories that engage current debates in critical theory (Part One), rhetorical studies (Part Two), and cultural politics (Part Three). These reception histories present detailed rhetorical accounts of interpretations performed at specific times and places. In each case, I examine how particular tropes, arguments, and narratives contribute to historical acts of interpreting words, texts, traditions, and contexts.

The name I give to my perspective on reception history is "rhetorical hermeneutics," a critical perspective encapsulated in a slogan: rhetorical hermeneutics uses rhetoric to practice theory by doing history. Each section of *Reception Histories* demonstrates how this slogan works in practice and what it means in terms of poststructuralist theory (Part One), nineteenth-century U.S. cultural studies (Part Two), and the contemporary history of curricular reform within the so-called Culture Wars (Part Three).

Part One on rhetorical pragmatism begins by describing the traditions of rhetoric and hermeneutics in which I am working. It then develops a rhetorically-oriented neopragmatism by describing how the Anglo-American pragmatist tradition has read and reread the older Greek Sophists. Chapter 1, "Articulation and Understanding," defines and works out the relations among several key terms in a rhetorical hermeneutics: "rhetoric," "rhetorical theory," "interpretation," and "hermeneutic theory." While arguing for the pragmatic inseparability of rhetoric and hermeneutics, I explore several theoretical problems in the human sciences, including interpretive relativism, cultural incommensurability, and ethnocentric politics. Drawing on Charles Taylor's notions of articulation, understanding, and rationality, I propose a rhetorical pragmatism to address questions of cross-cultural evaluation and communication.

Chapter 2, "The Sophistry of Rhetorical Pragmatism," develops this neopragmatism further through a reception history of Protagoras's man-as-measure dictum within the pragmatist tradition. I begin by looking at readings of Greek sophistry by William James, John Dewey, and especially the "forgotten pragmatist" F. C. S. Schiller. I continue with a discussion of sophistic rhetoric and Protagorean relativism in the recent neopragmatist theories of Richard Rorty and Stanley Fish and conclude by showing how this rhetorical pragmatism and current attacks on it can be viewed as a contemporary restaging of the Plato/Sophist debate.

Chapter 3, "Interpretation and Rhetorical Hermeneutics," uses an analysis of "interpretation" as a way to introduce a redescription of "rhetorical hermeneutics": rhetorical hermeneutics combines rhetorical pragmatism with cultural rhetoric studies. This combination is partly explained through a brief reception history of rhetorical hermeneutics itself. Most of the chapter explains how rhetorical hermeneutics is simultaneously a rhetorical version of neopragmatism when applied to problems in interpretive theory and a rhetorical version of cultural studies when doing reception histories of specific interpretive acts within particular cultural conversations. That is, rhetorical hermeneutics uses rhetoric to practice hermeneutic theory by doing reception studies within cultural history.

Part Two on cultural rhetoric studies moves from explicit theoretical argument to detailed rhetorical history. It presents a series of reception histories that concurrently tell a tale about mid-nineteenth-century New England culture and make an argument about late twentieth-century academic literary criticism. Chapter 4, "Ideological Rhetoric and Bible Politics: Fuller Reading Douglass," offers a rhetorical study of one specific act of interpretation: Margaret Fuller's 1845 review of Frederick Douglass's *Narrative*. I place this interpretive act within the 1840s ideological debates over slavery, abolition, and conflicting interpretations of the Christian Bible. Simultaneously, I contrast this reception history to a less historically oriented reader criticism and suggest a rhetorical approach to questions of ideology critique.

Chapter 5, "Good and Bad Persuasions: Critics Reading Bunyan," begins by focusing on the interpretations of *Pilgrim's Progress* made by early reader-response critics in the 1970s. It then contrasts this more narrowly historical approach to a reception history of *Pilgrim's Progress* influenced by reception aesthetics and recent developments in the history of the book. Chapters 4 and 5 illustrate how reception history can function as a specifically rhetorical form of cultural studies. At the same time, they argue that an earlier reader criticism can be reconceived as a more historically oriented rhetorical inquiry.

Chapter 6, "The Use and Abuse of Fiction: Readers Eating Books," provides a more general example of studying cultural rhetoric. It traces the circulation of a specific trope—reading as eating—within nineteenth-century literary texts (Alcott's *Little Women*, Aldrich's *The Story of a Bad Boy*) and institutional contexts dealing with the regulation of juvenile delinquency (state reformatories) and the uses of fiction (public debates over young adult education). As part of this chapter's performance of a cultural rhetoric study, I show how nineteenth-century debates over the harmful effects of fiction repeat tropes and arguments found in a long intellectual tradition concerned with the uncontrollable dangers of rhetoric—from Plato's *Gorgias* through English translations of Fénelon's *Dialogues on Eloquence*.

In Part Three on rhetorical studies and the Culture Wars, the last two chapters of the book gather together the various strands of the theoretical and historical arguments put forward in Parts One and Two. Here I work out some of the intellectual implications and possible institutional consequences for rhetorical studies within contemporary U.S. higher education.

Chapter 7, "Rhetoric Returns to Syracuse: The Reception of Curricular Reform," begins with a description of the institutional politics behind the development of Syracuse University's new major in English and Textual Studies. I tell this story as a reception history of my own failed attempt, as chair of the Syracuse English Department, to convince my colleagues to use "cultural rhetoric" as an organizing term for reconceptualizing the disciplinary activities usually housed in U.S. English departments. Rhetorical analysis of departmental memos and other exchanges provides a record of how the new major was proposed, negotiated, and finally approved. I then trace the reception of the resulting curriculum within local newspapers, national magazines, and scholarly journals during the so-called Culture Wars of the nineties. Thus, this chapter presents another example of doing reception history as a form of cultural rhetoric studies.

In Chapter 8, "Rhetorical Studies: Future Prospects," I argue for an expanded role for rhetorical studies within the university of the future. I begin with a discussion of the rhetorical politics of naming, so important to the history I told in the previous chapter (where "textual studies" won out over "rhetoric" at Syracuse). I proceed to a rhetorical consideration of Gerald Graff's teaching-the-conflicts model and conclude with a series of suggestions about how cultural rhetoric studies (including rhetorical hermeneutics) can help the academic humanities of today face the intellectual and political challenges of tomorrow.

All these chapters clarify and elaborate the argument I first offered in *Rhetorical Power*. As in that book, "rhetoric" remains the key term throughout *Reception Histories*, and I define it initially as the study of textual effects, of their production and reception. Thus, under such a definition, reader-response criticism can be seen as a contemporary rhetorical perspective on literature as it examines textual effects during reading; while its close neighbor, reception study, is another rhetorical approach focusing on the historical effects of texts for specific reading communities. In doing reception histories, I develop a notion of "cultural rhetoric" as the political effectivity of trope and argument in culture and investigate the relation of cultural rhetoric study to critical theory and other intellectual practices.

Another way to introduce my project is to tell some stories about the invention of rhetoric in ancient Sicily around 467 B.C. One narrative relates that after the deaths of the Syracusan tyrants Gelon and Hieron, Corax and Tisias invented rhetorical theory as a way of teaching citizens how to argue in the courts to regain their confiscated property. In this account, rhetoric is an enabling device for changing the economic and political order. But a second narrative about rhetoric's birth describes Corax as a powerful figure in the retinue of Hieron, and it is said that he invented rhetoric only as a way of maintaining his power in the new republic. Through his rhetorical skills and theories, Corax was able to influence the democratic assembly, guide the direction of the newly organized state, and, for a price, teach others to do the same. According to these two conflicting accounts, then, rhetoric at its legendary origin appears as a theoretical practice *either* for instituting radical change *or* for maintaining traditional power relations.[1]

Alongside these stories, I'd like to place another. In 388 B.C. Plato traveled to Sicily to advise the latest Syracusan tyrant on how to combine philosophy with government. He found nothing to please him in "the tastes of a society devoted to Italian and Syracusan cookery," a society more de-

---

[1] Cicero, *Brutus*, trans. G. L. Hendrickson in *Cicero*, vol. 1 (Cambridge, 1962), p. 49; and "Prolegomena Artis Rhetoricae," in *Prolegomenon Sylloge*, ed. Hugo Rabe (Leipzig, 1931), pp. 24–25. (I am very grateful to Karen Bassi and Jeffrey Carnes for their help in translating this Greek text by an anonymous Christian author of the fourth or fifth century.) Also see D. A. G. Hinks, "Tisias and Corax and the Invention of Rhetoric," *Classical Quarterly* 34 (1940): 67; Stanley Wilcox, "Corax and the *Prolegomena*," *American Journal of Philology* 64 (1943): 1–23; and Vincent Farenga, "Periphrasis on the Origin of Rhetoric," *MLN* 94 (1979): 1033–55.

voted to pleasure and luxury than self-control and goodness.[2] Failing to convert the elder Dionysius to his way of thinking, Plato returned to Athens to found the Academy and write his *Gorgias*. In this dialogue about political justice, Plato coined the term *rhētorikē* and thus invented the theoretical distinction between rhetoric and philosophy, between using language and searching for truth.[3] Prior to Plato, the older Greek Sophists had taught theories of truth and language, philosophy and rhetoric, under the single activity of studying logos. Plato, in contrast, separated rhetoric out from philosophy, much to the eventual disadvantage of the former in favor of the latter.

According to Plato's Socrates, rhetoric is not an art at all; it is merely a knack whose "sum and substance [is] flattery."[4] What part of flattery is rhetoric? It "is an insubstantial image of a part of politics" (463d). Politics, an art dealing with the soul, consists of justice and legislation, while medicine and gymnastics deal with the body. Flattery falsely imitates these four arts of body and soul. As parts of flattery, cosmetics is to gymnastics as sophistry is to legislation, and pastry-cooking is to medicine as rhetoric is to justice (465c). Socrates adds that though the sophist and rhetorician are "distinct in nature, yet, because they are close, they get mixed up in the same places and about the same things" (465c). *Gorgias* was a rhetorical tour de force, masterfully dividing prior unities (rhetoric and philosophy) and collapsing current divisions (rhetoric and sophistry) to the ultimate historical benefit of Platonic philosophy.

These various stories about the origins of rhetorical theory give me most of the topoi for the following chapters of reception history. They highlight historically the theoretical arguments about rhetoric's contemporary relation to interpretation, history, theory, and politics, which I develop especially in Part One. They also introduce some of the recurrent tropes of cultural practice (cooking, eating) that I track in Part Two on cultural rhetoric study. And, more or less coincidentally, the Syracuse settings remind me of the defining intellectual tradition and geographical location of my inquiries. For it is the interpretive history of ancient Syracuse and the material circumstances of a modern Syracuse that have

---

[2] Plato, "The Seventh Letter," in *Phaedrus and the Seventh and Eighth Letters*, trans. and ed. Walter Hamilton (New York, 1973), p. 326.

[3] See Edward Schiappa, "Did Plato Coin *Rhētorikē*?" in his *Protagoras and Logos: A Study in Greek Philosophy and Rhetoric* (Columbia, S.C., 1991), pp. 40–49; and his "*Rhētorikē*: What's in a Name? Toward a Revised History of Early Greek Rhetorical Theory," *Quarterly Journal of Speech* 78 (February 1992): 1–15.

[4] *Gorgias* 463a. The translation is by R. E. Allen in his edition of *The Dialogues of Plato*, vol. 1 (New Haven, Conn., 1984).

contributed so significantly to shaping my ongoing project: tracing the rhetorical paths of thought.

Thanks to everyone who helped me write this book, including those who have never read a word of it. I am grateful to those whose invitations or editorial support led to the writing of earlier versions of several chapters: Wallace Bacon, Michael Hyde, Walter Jost, Frank Lentricchia, James Machor, Thomas McLaughlin, Carolyn Miller, Donald Pease, George Pullman, Thomas Sloane, Isaiah Smithson, and Michael Sprinker. For criticism, suggestions, and miscellaneous other things, thanks to William Andrews, Paul Armstrong, Lindon Barrett, Karen Bassi, Jeffrey Carnes, Michael P. Clark, Stanley Fish, Gerald Graff, Shirley Brice Heath, Patricia Hunter, William Murphy, Spence Olin, Hershel Parker, Louise Wetherbee Phelps, David Plotkin, Dieter Polloczek, Peter Rabinowitz, Richard Rorty, Louise Rosenblatt, Thomas Rosteck, Edward Said, Herbert Simons, Alvin Sullivan, Brook Thomas, Victor Vitanza, Charles Watson, Ross Winterowd, Stephen Yarbrough, and Mas'ud Zavarzadeh. For other kinds of encouragement, I thank Michael R. Clark, Tom Clark, Henry Kirsch, Terry Lyle, Guy Nishida, Bill Stockert, and especially Russ Mailloux, Terri Mailloux, Mary Ann Young, and Nell Mailloux. I am indebted to students in my courses on critical theory and rhetorical studies and to my colleagues in the English and Comparative Literature Department at the University of California, Irvine. I remain grateful for the opportunity to have chaired the English Department at Syracuse University. I particularly wish to thank participants in the Theory Group during my years at Syracuse: Steven Cohan, John Crowley, Jean Howard, Veronica Kelly, Stephen Melville, Felicity Nussbaum, Bill Readings, Bennet Schaber, Linda Shires, Robyn Wiegman, and Tom Yingling. While completing this book, I had the good fortune to be a member of the "Post-National American Studies" Resident Research Group organized by John Rowe and sponsored by the University of California Humanities Research Institute in fall 1996. I am grateful to the UCHRI and the University of California, Irvine, for the material support enabling me to participate in the group and to my fellow members for a most interesting and educational experience.

I owe a special debt to three people who read more of this book more times than anyone: Don Bialostosky, Ed Schiappa, and, as always, Peter Carafiol. Bill Cain also deserves a special thanks along with the contributors to his volume on rhetorical hermeneutics, including Giles Gunn, Robert Holub, Louise Z. Smith, Gregory Jay, Carl Freedman, David Downing, Dale Bauer, William Spurlin, and Michele Sordi.

Earlier versions of several chapters appeared in the following publications: Chapter 1 in *Rhetoric and Hermeneutics in Our Time*, edited by Walter Jost and Michael J. Hyde (Yale University Press, 1997); Chapter 2 in *Rhetoric, Sophistry, Pragmatism*, edited by Steven Mailloux (Cambridge University Press, 1995); parts of Chapter 3 in *Critical Terms for Literary Study*, edited by Frank Lentricchia and Thomas McLaughlin (University of Chicago Press, 1989), in *Text and Performance Quarterly* 11 (July 1991), and in *Reconceptualizing American Literary/Cultural Studies*, edited by William Cain (Garland Press, 1996); Chapter 4 in *Readers in History*, edited by James Machor (Johns Hopkins University Press, 1993); part of Chapter 5 in *Studies in the Literary Imagination* 28 (fall 1995); Chapter 6 in *boundary 2* 17 (spring 1990); part of Chapter 7 in *English Studies/Culture Studies*, edited by Nancy Ruff and Isaiah Smithson (University of Illinois Press, 1994); and parts of Chapter 8 in *Teaching the Conflicts*, edited by William Cain (Garland Press, 1994), and in *Making and Unmaking the Prospects of Rhetoric*, edited by Theresa Enos (Lawrence Erlbaum, 1997). I am grateful to the editors and publishers for permission to reprint this material.

Thanks also to Elizabeth Holmes, Carol Betsch, Kay Scheuer, and everyone else at Cornell University Press who helped turn a manuscript into this book. I am especially grateful (again) to Bernhard Kendler for his valuable advice and unstinting support. I have long understood why other editors call him "an editor's editor."

Finally, and above all, I want to thank Molly Mailloux for the line "Are we being rhetorical yet?" and so much, much more.

STEVEN MAILLOUX

Irvine, California

PART ONE

RHETORICAL
PRAGMATISM

ARTICULATION AND UNDERSTANDING

I should imagine that the name *Hermes* has to do with speech, and signifies that he is the interpreter (*hermēneus*), or messenger, or thief, or liar, or bargainer; all that sort of thing has a great deal to do with language. As I was telling you, the word *eirein* is expressive of the use of speech, and there is an often-recurring Homeric word *emēsato,* which means "he contrived." Out of these two words, *eirein* and *mēsasthai,* the legislator formed the name of the god who invented language and speech, and we may imagine him dictating to us the use of this name. "O my friends," says he to us, "seeing that he is the contriver of tales or speeches [*eirein emēsato*], you may rightly call him *Eiremes.*" And this has been improved by us, as we think, into *Hermes*.

          —Plato, *Cratylus* 407e–408b, trans. Benjamin Jowett

Behind Plato's pseudo-etymology are the various Greek myths that present Hermes as the messenger of the gods, translator of their meanings to humans, interpreter par excellence. Hermes is also, perhaps not surprisingly, the inventor of speech and language, which Socrates describes as intimately connected with interpretation. In addition, this god of interpretation and language is a contriver, a liar, a trickster not to be trusted. That is, Hermes is Plato's archetypal Sophist.

But I am getting ahead of myself. Let me begin again by taking a simple lesson from Plato's derivation of "Hermes," a lesson that forms the thesis of this chapter: I wish to assert the practical inseparability of interpretation and language use and thus of the discourses that theorize those practices, hermeneutics and rhetoric. In developing this rhetorical hermeneutics, I shall address three problems widely debated within the human sciences: interpretive relativism, cultural incommensurability, and ethnocentric politics. Along the way, I will call upon Hermes and his near relations to serve as my guides.[1]

---

[1] Hermes, of course, was also the guide of souls, psychopompos. For fuller discussion of Hermes' mythic roles, see Norman O. Brown, *Hermes the Thief: The Evolution of a Myth* (Madi-

The traditions of both rhetoric and hermeneutics address very practical tasks. Hermeneutics deals with interpretation focused on texts, and rhetoric with figuration and persuasion directed at audiences. "Interpretation" can be defined as the establishment of textual meaning; while "rhetoric" as figurative and suasive force might be characterized as the effects of texts or, more pointedly, as the political effectivity of trope and argument in culture. Interpretation involves the translation of one text into another, a Hermes-like mediation that is also the transformation of one linguistic event into a later one. Rhetoric involves the transformation of one audience into another, which is also a psychogogic translation from one position into a different one. These translating and transforming activities relate to each other historically and theoretically in a complex mixture.

Rhetorical theory is to rhetorical practice as hermeneutics is to interpretation. As practices, rhetoric and interpretation denote both productive and receptive activities. That is, interpretation refers to the presentation of a text in speech—as in oral performance—and the understanding or exegesis of a written text; similarly, rhetoric refers to the production of persuasive discourse and the analysis of a text's effects on an audience. In some ways rhetoric and interpretation are practical forms of the same extended human activity: Rhetoric is based on interpretation; interpretation is communicated through rhetoric. Furthermore, as reflections on practice, hermeneutics and rhetorical theory are mutually defining fields: hermeneutics is the rhetoric of establishing meaning, and rhetoric the hermeneutics of problematic linguistic situations. When we ask about the meaning of a text, we receive an interpretive argument; when we seek the means of persuasion, we interpret the situation. As theoretical practices, hermeneutics involves placing a text in a meaningful context, while rhetoric requires the contextualization of a text's effects.

A rhetorical hermeneutics making the above claims must also admit that the inseparability of rhetoric and interpretation depends on the tropes and arguments used to figure and define the activities it is describing. We can understand this better by examining the traditions that describe these practices. Again, a Platonic text will get us going, a myth about the close Egyptian cousin to our guide Hermes.

When Phaedrus, in the dialogue that bears his name, asks Socrates to answer his own question—"Do you know how you can act or speak about rhetoric so as to please God best?"—the philosopher responds by re-

son, Wis., 1947); Karl Kerényi, *Hermes, Guide of Souls,* trans. Murray Stein (Zurich, 1976); and William G. Doty, "A Lifetime of Trouble-Making: Hermes as Trickster," in *Mythical Trickster Figures,* ed. William J. Hynes and Doty (Tuscaloosa, Ala., 1993), pp. 46–65.

counting an ancient Egyptian legend about the god Theuth (Thoth), who "invented numbers and arithmetic and geometry and astronomy, also draughts and dice, and, most important of all, letters." Presenting the last of these to the god Thamus, Theuth proclaims, "This invention, O king, will make the Egyptians wiser and will improve their memories; for it is an elixir of memory and wisdom that I have discovered." But Thamus chastises the father of writing for thinking he can both produce and judge his own offspring. Instead of aiding one's memory, Thamus argues, writing will discourage its use. "You have invented an elixir not of memory, but of reminding; and you offer your pupils the appearance of wisdom, not true wisdom, for they will read many things without instruction and will therefore seem to know many things, when they are for the most part ignorant and hard to get along with, since they are not wise, but only appear wise."[2]

In his gloss on this myth, Socrates is less concerned with what writing will do to the memory than what it will *not* do for truth. Unlike the spoken word in dialogue, the written text remains powerless to correct its receiver's misreading: "Every word, when once it is written, is bandied about, alike among those who understand and those who have no interest in it, and it knows not to whom to speak or not to speak; when ill-treated or unjustly reviled it always needs its father to help it; for it has no power to protect or help itself" (275e). For Socrates, then, the myth of Theuth is the story of the use and abuse of a new technology; it is about the lack of interpretive and rhetorical controls resulting from written inscription.

But "writing" easily becomes a synecdoche for all textuality, all rhetorical productions open to interpretive reception. For the spoken word is no less written than the one materially inscribed on a tablet. According to Socrates, "the living and breathing word," the word spoken in dialogue, is also the "word which is written with intelligence in the mind of the learner, which is able to defend itself and knows to whom it should speak, and before whom to be silent" (276a). That is, all words are written, inscribed, in one form or another, and the different forms, the different technologies of their production, are part of the rhetorical context in which they are received. As he often is, Plato's Socrates is quite the sophistic rhetorician here as he three times over follows the paths of Hermes and Theuth: in persuasive skill, rhetorical analysis, and clever trickery.[3]

[2] Plato, *Phaedrus*, trans. Harold North Fowler, in *Plato*, vol. 1 (Cambridge, Mass., 1932), 274b–275b, translation slightly revised. Further citations are given in the text.
[3] Thoth, like Hermes after him, was a trickster god. See Patrick Boylan, *Thoth, the Hermes of Egypt: A Study of Some Aspects of Theological Thought in Ancient Egypt* (London, 1922);

Skillfully persuasive, Socrates posits a commonsense distinction between speaking and writing. He then analyzes that distinction in terms of
the different rhetorical contexts speaking and writing enter into: the
context of dialogue increases the probability that the speaker's point will
be made simply because the speaker is there for rhetorical follow-up,
whereas the context of reading without the author's presence contains
no such backing. But what Socrates cleverly ignores in his persuasive contrast is that the speaker's presence guarantees neither that the intended
point will be understood nor, once understood, that it will be accepted.
Any rhetoric, spoken or written, is open to interpretive risk and unex-
pected resistance. In fact, there are contexts in which a written word provides a much higher probability of interpretive success and rhetorical
effectiveness from the author's perspective: contexts in which there is
more time for interpretive activity (for reading slowly or rereading) or in
which the very writtenness of a text testifies to its authority (scriptures or
constitutions).

This rhetorical interpretation echoes Jacques Derrida's deconstructive
reading of the *Phaedrus*: speech is *neither in principle nor in general* more intimate with some originary source or even with itself than writing is.[4] The
distance between a spoken or written word and its producer's intention
is a function of the interpretations made in the rhetorical context of the
word's reception. This theoretical point is illustrated rather ironically in
Plato's myth when Theuth, the creator of writing, loses control of its subsequent evaluation. Thamus challenges Theuth's authority, making arguments against his claim, counterarguments that Socrates appears to
accept. I say "appears" because there are some interesting differences between Thamus's arguments and Socrates' interpretation and extension
of them. Thamus begins his refutation by attacking Theuth's credibility:
"You, who are the father of letters, have been led by your affection to as-
cribe to them a power the opposite of that which they really possess"
(275a). Theuth is unreliable as a judge, Thamus suggests, because his
paternal fondness for his offspring makes his words biased and thus un-
trustworthy. But this attack on Theuth's ethos is exactly the kind of argument Socrates dismisses when he accuses his own listener, Phaedrus, of
questioning the myth just told on grounds that "it makes a difference
who the speaker is" rather than "whether his words are true or not"

---

and Garth Fowden, *The Egyptian Hermes: A Historical Approach to the Late Pagan Mind,* 2d ed.
(Princeton, N.J., 1993), pp. 22–24.

[4] Jacques Derrida, "Plato's Pharmacy," in *Dissemination,* trans. Barbara Johnson (Chicago, 1981), pp. 61–171. Also see Jasper Neel, *Plato, Derrida, and Writing* (Carbondale, Ill.,
1988).

(275c). Against Socrates, then, Thamus claims it *does* make a difference who speaks.

But what of Thamus's words themselves, the arguments he makes directly against Theuth's predictions about the usefulness of writing? Here Socrates does not so much contradict Thamus's arguments as give them a radically different turn, proposing a supplemental meaning that is difficult to ground in the myth. The crucial passage in Socrates' gloss is this: "He who thinks, then, that he has left behind him any art in writing, and he who receives it in the belief that anything in writing will be clear and certain, would be an utterly simple person, and in truth ignorant of the prophecy of Ammon [Thamus], if he thinks written words are of any use except to remind him who knows the matter about which they are written" (275c). The second part of this passage, after "prophecy of Ammon," does state one of Thamus's criticisms of writing—that it will not instruct, only remind the reader—but the first part of the passage is hard to connect with anything Thamus says in the myth. He does complain that writing will encourage false pride among the ignorant, but he does not seem to be worried about the lack of clarity or certainty, reliability or permanence in the writing itself. It is Socrates, not Thamus, who introduces the dangers of interpretive relativism.

A rhetorical hermeneutics can almost agree with Thamus's characterization (though not his evaluation) of reading: readers can only understand what they in some sense already know. This notion of interpretation sounds counterintuitive only when put so baldly. The point is that successful interpretation depends on the interpreter's prior web of beliefs, desires, practices, and so forth. From this perspective shared by several rhetorical and hermeneutic theorists, an interpreter's assumptions are not prejudices that distort understanding but the enabling ground of the process. In *Truth and Method*, for example, Hans-Georg Gadamer argues that "if we want to do justice to man's finite, historical mode of being, it is necessary to fundamentally rehabilitate the concept of prejudice and acknowledge the fact that there are legitimate prejudices."[5] Following Heidegger, Gadamer views prejudices, presuppositions, and fore-understandings as the very condition of interpretation. As Joel Weinsheimer explains, "Understanding is projection, and what it projects are expectations that precede the text." Suitable projection or so-called "objectivity in interpretation consists not in the avoidance of preconception but its confirmation; and arbitrary, inappropriate preconceptions are

---

[5] Hans-Georg Gadamer, *Truth and Method*, 2d ed., rev. trans. Joel Weinsheimer and Donald G. Marshall (New York, 1989), p. 277.

characterized not by the fact that they are preconceptions but only by the fact that they do not work out."[6] Without a reader's preconceptions, interpretation can't even begin. Similarly, Stanley Fish argues that "interpretations rest on other interpretations, or, more precisely, on assumptions—about what is possible, necessary, telling, essential, and so on—so deeply held that they are not thought of as assumptions at all." Or again: "Perception [including reading] is never innocent of assumptions, and the assumptions within which it occurs will be responsible for the contours of what is perceived."[7]

A rhetorical hermeneutics invoking such pragmatist and hermeneutical claims has not yet responded directly to the worries of Plato's Socrates in his gloss on the myth of Theuth. In fact, rhetorical hermeneutics would appear to the foundational Platonist as just another ruse by Hermes' followers, the sophistic rhetoricians. As Socrates puts it in the *Cratylus* before he presents his interpretation of "Hermes": Protagoras, the master Sophist, "says that man is the measure of all things, and that things are to me as they appear to me, and that they are to you as they appear to you. . . . But if Protagoras is right, and the truth is that things are as they appear to anyone, how can some of us be wise and some of us foolish?"[8] Sophistic relativism privileges each person's perceptions (based on that individual's assumptions, beliefs, desires) and thus makes it impossible to judge who is right or wrong, wise or foolish, better or worse. According to Platonists, this is not only ethical relativism but nihilistic solipsism.

We can translate this Platonic charge against the Sophists into the three interconnected problems I have mentioned: relativism, incommensurability, and ethnocentrism. To explore these further, I shall use another Platonic myth, one in which my guide makes only a brief appearance.

In response to a Socratic question, Protagoras tells the story of how Prometheus stole fire and practical wisdom from the gods and gave them to humans for their survival (*Protagoras* 321). But as people began to gather in cities, they could not get along, for they lacked political excellence (*politikē aretē*). Fearing their self-destruction, Zeus sent Hermes (another thief!) to bring reverence and justice to humans that they might join together to govern their cities.

---

[6] Joel C. Weinsheimer, *Gadamer's Hermeneutics: A Reading of "Truth and Method"* (New Haven, Conn., 1985), p. 166.

[7] Stanley Fish, *Doing What Comes Naturally: Change, Rhetoric, and the Practice of Theory in Literary and Legal Studies* (Durham, N.C., 1989), pp. 195, 78.

[8] Plato, *Cratylus*, trans. Benjamin Jowett; rpt. in *Plato: The Collected Dialogues*, ed. Edith Hamilton and Huntington Cairns (Princeton, N.J., 1961), 386a–c.

Hermes asked Zeus how he should impart justice and reverence among men:—Should he distribute them as the arts are distributed; that is to say, to a favoured few only, one skilled individual having enough of medicine or of any other art for many unskilled ones? "Shall this be the manner in which I am to distribute justice and reverence among men, or shall I give them to all?" "To all," said Zeus; "I should like them all to have a share; for cities cannot exist, if a few only share in the virtues, as in the arts. And further, make a law by my order, that he who has no part in reverence and justice shall be put to death, for he is a plague of the State."[9]

Paul Feyerabend used this myth to illustrate one of his theses in defense of relativism: "Laws, religious beliefs and customs rule, like kings, in restricted domains. Their rule rests on a twofold authority—on their *power* and on the fact that it is *rightful* power: the rules are *valid* in their domains."[10] Feyerabend means to suggest that his own form of relativism has nothing to do with no-controls, "anything goes" nihilism. In Feyerabend's reading, Protagoras "believed that there had to be laws and that they had to be enforced" but "that laws and institutions had to be adapted to the societies in which they were supposed to rule, that justice had to be defined 'relative to' the needs and the circumstances of these societies." This does not mean, Feyerabend argues, "that institutions and laws that are valid in some societies and not valid in others are therefore arbitrary and can be changed at will" (44).

Feyerabend goes on to connect his relativist reading of the Prometheus-Hermes myth with Protagoras's *anthrōpos metron* maxim—"Humans are the measure of all things, of those that are that they are; and of those that are not, that they are not"[11]—which Feyerabend interprets as meaning that "the laws, customs, facts that are being put before the citizens ultimately rest on the pronouncements, beliefs and perceptions of human beings and that important matters should therefore be referred to the (perceptions and thoughts of the) people concerned and not to abstract agencies and distant experts" (48). Feyerabend notes the traditional absolutist objection to *anthrōpos metron*: "Good ideas, procedures, laws, according to Plato, are neither popular ideas, procedures, laws, nor things

---

[9] *Protagoras,* trans. Benjamin Jowett; rpt. *The Works of Plato,* ed. Irwin Edman (New York, 1928), 322c–d.

[10] Paul Feyerabend, "Notes on Relativism," in his *Farewell to Reason* (London, 1987), p. 43; further citations are in the text.

[11] For the Greek, see Plato, *Theaetetus,* in *Plato,* ed. Harold North Fowler, vol. 7 (Cambridge, Mass., 1921), 152a.

that are supported by authorities such as kings, wandering bards, or experts; good ideas, procedures, laws are things that 'fit reality' and are true in this sense" (49). There is for the antisophistic objectivist the Standard outside all communities, beyond the finite, transcending the human, to which historical communities are responsible and against which their actions and beliefs can be judged absolutely. In contrast, a rhetorical hermeneutics agrees with Feyerabend in rejecting this Platonic picture and argues that all we have to deal with as situated interpreters are the webs of belief and desire that constitute our rhetorical contexts.

Feyerabend later puts forth another thesis compatible with rhetorical hermeneutics: "For every statement (theory, point of view) that is believed to be true with good reasons *there may exist* arguments showing that either its opposite, or a weaker alternative is true" (74). This thesis (and its stronger version [76]) can also be related to Protagorean sophistry, the (in)famous *dissoi-logoi* fragment: according to Diogenes Laertius, "Protagoras was the first to say that on every issue there are two arguments opposed to each other."[12] The British pragmatist F. C. S. Schiller argued that this maxim fit neatly with *anthrōpos metron* as both emerged from the challenges facing a practicing rhetorician.[13] Feyerabend would no doubt have agreed with Schiller's observation.

Feyerabend, however, develops his argument in an entirely different direction, as he quotes the rhetorical observations made by anthropologist E. E. Evans-Pritchard in his study of the Azande of Central Africa: "Let the reader consider any argument that would utterly demolish all Zande claims for the power of [their] oracle[s]. If it were translated into Zande modes of thought it would serve to support their entire structure of belief. For their mystical notions are eminently coherent, being interrelated by a network of logical ties and are so ordered that they never too crudely contradict sensory experience but, instead, experience seems to justify them."[14] The conclusion Feyerabend draws: "Zande practices are 'rational' because supportable by argument" (74). This appeal to the cultural anthropologist's experience brings us back to the central point

---

[12] Diogenes Laertius, IX.51, trans. Michael J. O'Brien, in *The Older Sophists*, ed. Rosamond Kent Sprague (Columbia, S.C., 1972), p. 4.

[13] F. C. S. Schiller, review of Heinrich Gomperz, *Sophistik und Rhetorik*, Mind 22 (January 1913): 112. For further discussion, see Chap. 2 below. On the interpretive history of Protagoras's texts, see Edward Schiappa, *Protagoras and Logos: A Study in Greek Philosophy and Rhetoric* (Columbia, S.C., 1991). For a study using reception theory, see John Poulakos, *Sophistical Rhetoric in Classical Greece* (Columbia, S.C., 1995); cf. Kathleen E. Welch, *The Contemporary Reception of Classical Rhetoric: Appropriations of Ancient Discourse* (Hillsdale, N.J., 1990).

[14] E. E. Evans-Pritchard, *Witchcraft, Oracles, and Magic among the Azande* (Oxford, 1937), pp. 319–20; quoted in Feyerabend, *Farewell to Reason*, p. 74.

of Feyerabend's essay: the relativism he defends is "not about concepts (though most modern versions of it are conceptual versions) but about human relations. It deals with problems that arise when different cultures, or individuals with different habits and tastes, collide" (83).

This collision is precisely the concern of Charles Taylor's provocative essay "Rationality," which also discusses discussions of the Zande culture.[15] Taylor provides rhetorical hermeneutics with yet another way of formulating the inseparability of rhetoric and interpretation and at the same time allows another run at the question of cultural relativism. In "Rationality," Taylor attempts to establish a framework for making valid crosscultural judgments. He does this in several steps, some of which will prove useful to us here. Taylor argues that descriptions can make appropriate transcultural discriminations. He privileges the description that distinguishes between "theoretical" and "atheoretical" cultures, defining "theoretical" as giving an account from a "disengaged perspective." The ancient Greeks invented this form of theory, where "theoretical understanding is related to rationality" and "rational understanding is linked to articulation." To "articulate," in turn, means to "distinguish and lay out the different features of the matter in perspicuous order" (136–37).

A rhetorical hermeneutics would separate out Taylor's useful claims about the intimate relation between theoretical understanding and explanatory articulation from his more problematic assumptions concerning theory as a disengaged perspective. It would extend the claims for an "inner connection" (137) between *theoretical* understanding (reason) and *practical* articulation (giving persuasive accounts) to all forms of understanding and language use. That is, to say it once again, interpretation (establishing meaning) and rhetoric (troping/arguing) are closely connected and mutually defining practices. And furthermore, this relation of understanding and articulation is duplicated again at the level of theory, with accounts of understanding (hermeneutics) being closely related to those of articulation (rhetoric). As Gadamer puts it, "Hermeneutics may be precisely defined as the art of bringing what is said or written to speech again. What kind of an art this is, then, we can learn from rhetoric."[16]

A rhetorical hermeneutics supports Taylor's attempt to develop an integral relation between understanding and articulation but notes prob-

[15] Charles Taylor, "Rationality," in *Philosophy and the Human Sciences,* vol. 2 of his *Philosophical Papers* (Cambridge, 1985), pp. 134–51; further references are given in the text.
[16] Hans-Georg Gadamer, "Hermeneutics as a Theoretical and Practical Task," in his *Reason in the Age of Science,* trans. Frederick G. Lawrence (Cambridge, Mass., 1981), p. 119.

lems when he brings this model to bear on the question of transcultural comparisons. Taylor uses Peter Winch's essay "Understanding a Primitive Society," which, like Feyerabend's, relies for its examples on Evans-Pritchard's study of the Azande. Winch criticizes the anthropologist for assuming a notion of reality independent of language use. "Evans-Pritchard, although he emphasizes that a member of scientific culture has a different conception of reality from that of a Zande believer in magic, wants to go beyond merely registering this fact and making the differences explicit, and to say, finally, that the scientific conception agrees with what reality actually is like, whereas the magical conception does not."[17]

Now, Winch does want to preserve "the idea that men's ideas and beliefs must be checkable by reference to something independent—some reality," for to abandon such measures would be, he fears, "to plunge straight into an extreme Protagorean relativism" (308).[18] But Winch holds on to "the check of the independently real" by making the measuring act internal rather than external to a culture's language use. "Reality is not what gives language sense," he writes. "What is real and what is unreal shows itself *in* the sense that language has. Further, both the distinction between the real and the unreal and the concept of agreement with reality themselves belong to our language." Accordingly, Winch makes no value judgments in his cross-cultural comparisons and affirms that "a primitive system of magic, like that of the Azande, constitutes a coherent universe of discourse like science, in terms of which an intelligible conception of reality and clear ways of deciding what beliefs are and are not in agreement with this reality can be discerned" (308–9).

Winch argues against making evaluative judgments of incommensurable activities within different cultures and advocates simply describing these cultural differences (and perhaps learning from them). Taylor also recognizes a "plurality of standards of rationality" but disagrees with

[17] Peter Winch, "Understanding a Primitive Society," *American Philosophical Quarterly* 1 (October 1964): 308; further references are given in the text. For other hermeneutic discussions of Winch's essay, see Richard J. Bernstein, *Beyond Objectivism and Relativism: Science, Hermeneutics, and Praxis* (Philadelphia, 1983), pp. 97–107; and Gerald L. Bruns, *Hermeneutics Ancient and Modern* (New Haven, Conn., 1992), pp. 4–8.

[18] This is clearly a different relativism from the one Feyerabend posits in his interpretation of Protagoras. Also see Peter Winch, "Comment," in *Explanation in the Behavioural Sciences*, ed. Robert Borger and Frank Cioffi (Cambridge, 1970), p. 254; and his slightly more developed reading of *anthrōpos metron*, from which he also distances his own position, in Winch, "The Universalizability of Moral Judgments," in *Ethics and Action* (London, 1972), p. 168.

Winch that such recognition disables comparative evaluations between cultures ("Rationality" 151). He proposes instead criteria for making valid transcultural judgments of rationality.

The example Taylor gives is a judgment that a theoretical culture (like his own) is superior to an atheoretical culture (like the Azande's). Taylor does not explicitly defend his judgment by claiming *it* is disengaged. Rather, he argues only that the culture he judges as (in some respects) superior is so because it has developed an activity—theoretical understanding—that is disengaged. "There is," he claims, "an inner connection between understanding the world and achieving technological control which rightly commands everyone's attention, and doesn't just justify our practices in our own eyes" (147). Theoretical understanding leads to the new science, which leads to a technological advance that must be recognized as such by everyone. A theoretical culture is superior to an atheoretical one at least in terms of theoretical understanding, scientific knowledge, and technological progress.

To understand Taylor's argument most generously, we must retrieve another of his notions, that of articulation. One culture is superior to another in terms of articulated reasons. And reasons are exactly what Taylor gives to support his judgment of the superiority of his culture over the Azande's. However, articulation, like understanding, comes from within a cultural position rather than being disengaged from it. Thus, Taylor articulates reasons for why theoretical cultures are superior to atheoretical cultures, but his reasons arise from within his theoretical culture and address an audience within that same culture. If the rhetorical context were different (for example, the Zande context posited by Evans-Pritchard), Taylor's articulations, his good reasons, might completely fail to convince.

At times Taylor seems to acknowledge the inescapably ethnocentric character of his interpretive judgment and its rhetorical support. He notes, for instance, that "there is no such thing as a single argument proving *global* superiority" of one culture over another. There is only local preeminence in terms of one culture's standards, Taylor seems to suggest. "Perhaps the critics are right," he continues, "who hold that we have been made progressively more estranged from ourselves and our world in technological civilization. Maybe this could even be shown as convincingly as the scientific superiority of moderns." Taylor correctly argues that such a rhetorical outcome "would not refute this scientific superiority. It would just mean that we now had two transcultural judgments of superiority; only unfortunately they would fall on different sides" (149–50). We could understand Taylor to be arguing that cross-cultural judgments can be made but acknowledging that which ones are convincing to whom depend on the relevant cultural context.

But Taylor does not simply object to Winch's position on the inappropriateness of making transcultural judgments of incommensurable activities. Apparently still wishing to defend the possibility of non-ethnocentric cross-cultural evaluations, Taylor ends by referring back to the contrast between the beliefs underlying Zande magic and those grounding modern science:

> Both offer articulations, they lay out different features of the world and human action in some perspicuous order. In that, they are both involved in the kind of activity which I have argued is central to rationality. But one culture can surely lay claim to a higher, or fuller, or more effective rationality, if it is in a position to achieve a more perspicuous order than another. (150)

But the question again is: more perspicuous, more persuasively lucid *for whom?* That *rhetorical* matter is always culture-specific: what convinces European scientists and their followers might not convince Zande oracles and theirs. Put another way: Winch is correct in positing a plurality of standards of rationality; against Winch, Taylor is right that such a plurality does not disable cross-cultural evaluations; but against Taylor, a rhetorical hermeneutics argues that such judgments are always ethnocentrically located within the culture making them.[19] Interpretive judgments and rhetorical articulations are woven together *within* a culture's social practices even when the topic of articulated judgment is another culture's practices.

Both Winch and Taylor try to avoid the cruder forms of ethnocentrism, as Taylor writes: "Really overcoming ethnocentricity is being able to understand two incommensurable classifications" (145). But this overcoming is partial at best, for it is our own ethnocentric web of beliefs and desires that gives us interpretive purchase on any object of attention, including the texts or classification systems of another culture. The validity of our interpretations is a function of the rhetorical context in which we argue them: who participates in the conversation, when and where, with

---

[19] But also cf. Taylor on using "the language of perspicuous contrast" to compare cultures: Charles Taylor, "Understanding and Ethnocentricity," in *Philosophy and the Human Sciences*, pp. 116–33; "Comparison, History, Truth," in *Myth and Philosophy*, ed. Frank Reynolds and David Tracy (Albany, N.Y., 1990), pp. 37–55; and "The Politics of Recognition," in *Multiculturalism: Examining the Politics of Recognition*, 2d ed., ed. Amy Gutmann (Princeton, N.J., 1994), pp. 66–73.

what purposes, and so on. Part of the current rhetorical context for academic intellectuals is a widespread belief not only in the possible incommensurability of radically different cultures and alien traditions but also in the authoritative ethos of the rhetorical agents speaking from within those cultures and across those traditions. It is to this theme of otherness and agency that I would now like to turn, again calling on a relative of Hermes.

The Fon of West Africa also have a trickster god, Legba, modeled after the Yoruba's Esu-Elegbara.[20] Legba is a linguistic mediator, the creator of magic, the sponsor of divination, a conniving thief and troublemaker who also restores and reconciles. He is the translator among the Fon gods, who speak different languages, and the messenger from gods to humans, empowering oracles to interpret destiny in the divining process. As inventor of magic, Legba "draws into the open the power of all boundaries, opens passageways to new life, and makes transformation possible even as he stimulates conflict," writes Robert Pelton. He "lives where separate worlds meet and can move back and forth between them, yet he cannot substitute one for the other." Legba is the Hermes-like deceiver, who translates and transforms. He is a "living limen," a passageway to the other, who "relentlessly enlarges the scope of the human."[21]

If transcultural judgments are always cross-cultural translations, then such interpretations are liminal acts opening up a space in which boundaries are transformed yet paradoxically maintained even as they are crossed. Boundaries are crossed in interpretation when one culture becomes the conversational topic or interpretive object of another; boundaries are maintained as the interpretive act in its rhetorical exchanges figures and persuades within the context of the interpreting culture; and boundaries are moved as interpretation changes the shape—trivially or dramatically—of the culture in which the interpretation is produced and received. To understand an act within a foreign culture, the differences must be found in the margins of our own. A completely other would be unintelligible. But as the marginal comes into focus or even moves toward the center, the boundaries of our horizons can shift and even be expanded by the other within. Another way of putting this: as we

---

[20] "Esu's most direct Western kinsman is Hermes," writes Henry Louis Gates, Jr., in his survey and interpretation of the "divine trickster figure," who in passing from Africa to the New World functions as "the figure of formal language use and its interpretation"; see Gates, *The Signifying Monkey: A Theory of African-American Literary Criticism* (New York, 1988), pp. 5, 8, 35.

[21] Robert D. Pelton, *The Trickster in West Africa: A Study of Mythic Irony and Sacred Delight* (Berkeley, Calif., 1980), pp. 84, 88, 108–9.

interact with other communities, traditions, cultures, we can reweave our webs of belief to take account of the other, and we do this more or less successfully from differing points of view within and outside our own groups.

When Christian missionaries first visited the Fon of Dahomey, they interpreted Legba as the primitive disguise for Satan. In fact, they cited one of the Fon creation myths in support by reading it as a corrupted version of the Adam and Eve story. But the Fon were not persuaded by this interpretation:

> The story the missionaries tell about the fruit does not exist here. That Legba gave this fruit, that we do not know. . . . But the missionaries, when they heard our name of Adanhu and Yewa, said our gods and theirs were all the same. They tried to teach us the rest about the beginning of man and woman, but the Dahomeans [the Fon] do not agree. They say this is not their story. They know nothing about Legba trying to give fruit.[22]

Here we have an act of resistance to an ethnocentric reading, an example of the Fon's assertion of rhetorical agency and interpretive power. A rhetorical hermeneutics takes account of both the missionaries' interpretation and the Fon's rhetorical opposition. It also attempts to make theoretical sense of these historical events as interrelated acts of understanding and articulation.

In the course of this chapter, I have tried to show how hermeneutics and rhetoric are intertwined and how viewing understanding as articulation contributes to clarifying the theoretical problems of relativism, incommensurability, and ethnocentrism. Let me now sum up and extend a few of these points. I have referred to the inescapability of ethnocentrism but also to a cruder form of ethnocentric activity. Such usages assume that our webs of vocabularies, beliefs, and desires constitute both the power and limits of our rhetorical and interpretive acts. We are agents within and because of our enculturation. I thus agree with Richard Rorty that to see ethnocentrism as "an inescapable condition" is to make ethnocentricity "roughly synonymous with 'human finitude.'"[23] That is, we

[22] Fon storyteller, "The First Humans: Missionary Version of Legba Rejected," in *Dahomean Narrative: A Cross-Cultural Analysis,* ed. Melville J. Herskovits and Frances S. Herskovits (Evanston, Ill., 1958), p. 151.

[23] Richard Rorty, "Introduction: Antirepresentationalism, Ethnocentrism, and Liberalism," in *Objectivity, Relativism, and Truth,* vol. 1 of his *Philosophical Papers* (Cambridge, 1991), p. 15. For some pragmatist criticisms of Rorty's pragmatist notion of ethnocentrism, see

are never not in a particular culture with a particular form of life or set of practices. Such a situation does not disable but grounds interpretation and evaluation of actions both inside and outside one's culture. A particular ethnos—the particular shape of one's finitude, its time and place, its network of beliefs and desires—provides the historical context in which judgments are made and supported.

A rhetorical hermeneutics claims that this cultural context cannot be completely transcended but can be slowly and significantly changed. Ethnocentrism is with us always, but its shape can be transformed. A belief within the Western intellectual's ethnos now includes a prohibition on forcefully imposing one's beliefs on other cultures. To borrow Rorty's somewhat ironic formulation, some of us in the West have become "sufficiently leisured and civilized . . . to substitute . . . conversation with foreigners for conquest of them."[24] Our particular form of ethnocentrism explicitly privileges verbal persuasion over physical violence, rhetoric over war, both among groups within our own culture and between our culture and others. Thus, a rhetorical hermeneutics claims simultaneously that all cultures are ethnocentric and that a particular culture might distinguish more or less acceptable forms of ethnocentric activity. A particular ethnos might—and ours does—establish an ethnocentric continuum from "physical conquest" through "cultural imperialism" to "respectful understanding," a continuum that can be used to justify the condemnation of cruder forms of ethnocentric behavior toward other cultures.

We might see the historical development of this continuum within our culture and the embrace of its expansion by a significant segment of academic intellectuals as forming the context for the philosophical and anthropological debates over incommensurability. The notion of incommensurability provides a rhetorical resource for explaining or justifying many of the newer stances taken along the ethnocentric continuum. As I have developed it here, "incommensurability" refers not to an absolute inability to translate between cultures, not to an impervious obstacle blocking the articulated understanding of one culture by another. Rather, to posit incommensurability means accepting that in order to make sense of an alien culture's actions, those actions, including speech acts, must be placed in their own contexts of vocabularies, beliefs, and desires—contexts that may be extremely different, radically other than our own. Thus,

---

Giles Gunn, *Thinking across the American Grain: Ideology, Intellect, and the New Pragmatism* (Chicago, 1992), pp. 94–116.

[24] Rorty, "Solidarity or Objectivity?" in *Objectivity*, p. 25.

"incommensurability" is an interpretive category enabling us to deal with competing modes of intelligibility and communication within and outside our own cultural communities.

This take on incommensurability challenges the view that one culture can be so different from another that cross-cultural communication is in principle doomed from the start. Instead, as Rorty argues, "our form of life and the natives' [in another culture] already overlap to so great an extent that we are already, automatically, for free, participant-observers, not *mere* observers" of that culture. Moreover, "this overlap in effect reduces the intercultural case to an intracultural one—it means that we learn to handle the weirder bits of native behavior (linguistic and other) in the same way that we learn about the weird behavior of atypical members of our own culture."[25]

But "incommensurability" is also a shorthand for rhetorically explaining why agents from different cultures fail to communicate or make sense of one another's acts. It is a way of describing the historical scene of two actors in interpretive and rhetorical trouble. It marks a strategy for establishing the grounds for how to proceed, what advice to give: Try harder with interpretive translation or give up and go bilingual; continue the attempt to translate a set of alien terms into your own idiom or learn the other community's language.

Whatever the interpretive process of intra- and intercultural exchanges, the rhetorical outcome depends on how different agents reweave their beliefs and practices as a result of the exchanges. This reweaving constitutes what we call learning. What Evans-Pritchard wrote of the Azande applies to actors in other cultures as well: "In this web of belief every strand depends upon every other strand, and a Zande cannot get out of its meshes because this is the only world he knows. The web is not an external structure in which he is enclosed. It is the texture of his thought and he cannot think that his thought is wrong. Nevertheless, his beliefs are not absolutely set but are variable and fluctuating to allow for different situations and to permit empirical observation and even doubts."[26] The web is rewoven through interpretation and persuasion, and thus change takes place. This view of articulated understanding ap-

---

[25] Rorty, "Inquiry as Recontextualization: An Anti-dualist Account of Interpretation," in *Objectivity*, p. 107. Rorty is here developing the argument he finds in Donald Davidson's "Radical Interpretation," in his *Inquiries into Truth and Interpretation* (Oxford, 1984), pp. 125–39. For a relevant sorting out of several theoretical positions, see the chapter "Rationality, Relativism, the Translation and Commensurability of Cultures" in Stanley Jeyaraja Tambiah, *Magic, Science, Religion, and the Scope of Rationality* (Cambridge, 1990), pp. 111–39.

[26] Evans-Pritchard, *Witchcraft*, pp. 194–95.

plies both within and between different cultural communities. As Rorty puts it, "To say that we must work by our own lights, that we must be eth- nocentric, is merely to say that beliefs suggested by another culture must be tested by trying to weave them together with beliefs we already have."[27] Rhetorical hermeneutics helps to show how this is so as it argues for the pragmatic intimacy of understanding and articulation both within cul- tures and between them.

[27] Rorty, "Solidarity," p. 26. For an alternative pragmatist account of rhetorical prob- lems treated here, see Peter Carafiol, *The American Ideal: Literary History as a Worldly Activity* (New York, 1991), pp. 162–66; and his "'Who I Am': Ethnic Identity and American Liter- ary Ethnocentrism," in *Criticism and the Color Line: Desegregating American Literary Studies*, ed. Henry B. Wonham (New Brunswick, N.J., 1996), pp. 43–62.

CHAPTER **2**

THE SOPHISTRY OF
RHETORICAL PRAGMATISM

One of the things for which Plato has been most applauded by those modern schools which pique themselves on counting him among their precursors, is the warfare which he is supposed to have made on a skeptical philosophy, attributed, totally without evidence, to the Sophists generally, and considered as one of the means by which they demoralized the Greeks.
—John Stuart Mill, "Grote's Plato" (1867)

The Socratic quest [for truth] has been replaced by the relativism of the sophists. Having cast out Zeus, Whirl is king; we again hear Protagoras' assertion that man is the measure of all things—indeed that there are as many different standards of measure as there are classes or even individuals.
—John Silber, *Straight Shooting: What's Wrong with America and How to Fix It* (1989)

Jacques Derrida has warned against a too easy restaging of the battle between Plato and the Sophists. "We must try not to reduce modern conflicts to this opposition," he says. "We have, of course, to refer to these Greek situations because they are part of our heritage, but some essential things have changed, and we have to take these changes into account." Derrida's historicist admonitions are a needed caution against the polemical reductiveness of today's Culture Wars, and he properly counsels us not to equate the late twentieth-century cultural scene with that of Greece in the fifth century B.C. However, might it still be possible to respond to Derrida's call for an "accurate analysis . . . of what is inherited, but also of what is new in our culture" without completely accepting his claim that for such analyses "the battle between Plato and the sophists is not pertinent enough"?[1] What, for example, should we make of self-

[1] Gary A. Olson, "Jacques Derrida on Rhetoric and Composition: A Conversation," *Journal of Advanced Composition* 10, no. 1 (1990): 17.

proclaimed versions of Platonism and sophistry, whose rhetorical presence in contemporary debates testifies to their ongoing (im)pertinence?[2]

In this chapter, I will address these questions as I examine two overlapping contexts of reception: the current revival of American pragmatism and revaluations of sophistic rhetoric within the humanities. The so-called rhetorical turn in the human sciences has in some disciplines become a more specific rehabilitation of Greek sophistry. Since Plato, the older Sophists have often been condemned as subjectivists and skeptics, unscrupulous traders in opinion rather than knowledge, rhetorical mercenaries who taught their clients to disregard objective truth in making the weaker case appear to be the stronger. Especially during the last decade, revisionist interpreters have vigorously challenged this traditional negative view of the Sophists. Indeed, Susan Jarratt and Victor Vitanza have gone so far as to suggest that we are presently within a Third Sophistic.[3] Whether this is the case or not, sophistic rhetoric is certainly undergoing a renaissance of interest, illustrated most notably in the publication of several important revisionist books in the 1990s.[4]

As notable as the return of sophistic rhetoric, there has also been a significant renewal of American pragmatism. Again, this revival is interdisciplinary, centered in the neopragmatist writings within contemporary philosophy and literary studies.[5] Though most conspicuous in these two disciplines, pragmatism is also being intensely discussed in such

[2] For a very different argument for the cultural relevance of Plato and the Sophists, see Barry Cooper, "Plato and the Media," in *Public Policy and the Public Good*, ed. Ethan Goodman (New York, 1991), pp. 15–28; and for an argument about what might be termed the continuing *philosophical* pertinence of Platonism and sophistry, see Jacques Derrida, "Plato's Pharmacy," in *Dissemination*, trans. Barbara Johnson (Chicago, 1981), pp. 61–171.

[3] Victor J. Vitanza, "Critical Sub/Versions of the History of Philosophical Rhetoric," *Rhetoric Review* 6 (fall 1987): 45.

[4] See, for example, Susan C. Jarratt, *Rereading the Sophists: Classical Rhetoric Refigured* (Carbondale, Ill., 1991); Edward Schiappa, *Protagoras and Logos: A Study in Greek Philosophy and Rhetoric* (Columbia, S.C., 1991); Joseph Margolis, *The Truth about Relativism* (Cambridge, Mass., 1991); Barbara Casson, *L'effect sophistique* (Paris, 1995); Victor J. Vitanza, *Negation, Subjectivity, and the History of Rhetoric* (Albany, N.Y., 1997); and Steven Mailloux, ed., *Rhetoric, Sophistry, Pragmatism* (Cambridge, 1995). Other sophistic revivals have been declared in the last hundred years, but there has usually been less emphasis on the importance of the rhetoric/philosophy combination within sophistry. See, for example, Charles Trinkaus, "Protagoras in the Renaissance: An Exploration," in *Philosophy and Humanism: Renaissance Essays in Honor of Paul Oskar Kristeller*, ed. Edward P. Mahoney (New York, 1976), pp. 190–91, n. 1.

[5] See, for example, work in philosophy by Richard Bernstein, Nancy Fraser, Joseph Margolis, Richard Rorty, Charlene Haddock Seigfried, and Cornel West; and for literary studies, see Peter Carafiol, Stanley Fish, Giles Gunn, Ihab Hassan, Frank Lentricchia, Richard Poirier, Louise Rosenblatt, Barbara Herrnstein Smith, and W. J. T. Mitchell, ed., *Against Theory: Literary Studies and the New Pragmatism* (Chicago, 1985).

fields as American studies, political science, historiography, speech communication, composition, law, and religious studies.[6]

Despite the enormous growth of publications on rhetoric, on pragmatism, and most recently on Greek sophistry, discussion has only just begun concerning the relationship between American pragmatism and sophistic rhetoric. In this chapter I develop further the perspective of rhetorical pragmatism by examining the various ways pragmatism, rhetoric, and sophistry intersect in their theoretical and political implications. Contemporary neopragmatism can be viewed as a postmodernist reception of sophistic rhetoric, and it is as such that its advocates and opponents demonstrate the continuing relevance of the struggle between Platonism and sophistry. Connected to that conflict are several questions: How do the pragmatist and rhetorical turns in academic disciplines relate to recent issues in a wider cultural politics outside the university? Is neopragmatism an antitheory irrelevant to any specific political program; is it a reactionary defense of traditional institutions; or is it a justification for radical democratic reforms? Is pragmatism, like sophistry, open to the Platonic charge of relativism? Does rhetorical pragmatism thus lead to political quietism, because it provides no objective basis for ethical choice; or to social anarchy, because it provides justification for *any* political choice? In dealing with these questions, I will put forward a notion of rhetorical pragmatism that will be taken up again in explaining rhetorical hermeneutics in the following chapter.

PRAGMATISTS READ PROTAGORAS

Linkages between sophistry and pragmatism actually began early in the present century. Jean Bourdeau titled his 1907 journalistic critique of a new philosophical movement "Une sophistique du pragmatisme"; William James translated the following passage from it as a typical misunderstanding of his position:

> Pragmatism is an Anglo-Saxon reaction against the intellectualism and rationalism of the Latin mind. . . . Man, each individual man, is the measure of things. He is able to conceive none but relative truths, that is to

---

[6] For one example, see Michael Brint and William Weaver, eds., *Pragmatism in Law and Society* (Boulder, Colo., 1991); and for a more extensive interdisciplinary bibliography, see Mailloux, *Rhetoric, Sophistry, Pragmatism*. Also see Russell B. Goodman, ed., *Pragmatism: A Contemporary Reader* (New York, 1995) and Louis Menand, ed., *Pragmatism: A Reader* (New York, 1997).

say, illusions. What these illusions are worth is revealed to him, not by general theory, but by individual practice.[7]

James uses this passage to illustrate the misrepresentation of pragmatism as ignoring "the theoretic interest,"[8] but he might also have commented on how it typifies, in its reference to Protagoras's *anthrōpos metron* doctrine, a related misreading of pragmatism (and of Greek sophistry) as skeptical relativism.[9] In another essay collected in *The Meaning of Truth*, James does cite the accusation that pragmatism is akin to relativistic sophistry. Here he notes that among the "most formidable-sounding onslaughts" against pragmatism is the charge that "to make truth grow in any way out of human opinion is but to reproduce that protagorean doctrine that the individual man is 'the measure of all things,' which Plato in his immortal dialogue, the *Theaetetus*, is unanimously said to have laid away so comfortably in its grave two thousand years ago."[10] I will have occasion later to take up this attack on pragmatic and sophistic "relativism," but for now let me describe in more detail some general interpretations of "pragmatism" and "sophistry" circulating in the cultural conversation at the turn of the century.

The 1902 *Dictionary of Philosophy and Psychology*, edited by James Mark Baldwin, includes entries by three of the founders of pragmatism: James, C. S. Peirce, and John Dewey. Under "Pragmatism," Peirce emphasizes its antimetaphysical "maxim for attaining clearness of apprehension: 'Consider what effects, that might conceivably have practical bearings, we conceive the object of our conception to have. Then, our conception of these effects is the whole of our conception of the object.'" Under the same entry, James extends this methodological maxim toward a pragmatic notion of truth, defining pragmatism as the "doctrine that the whole 'meaning' of a conception expresses itself in practical consequences, consequences either in the shape of conduct to be recommended, or in

---

[7] William James, *The Meaning of Truth* (1909; rpt. Cambridge, Mass., 1975), p. 113, n. 4, translating from Jean Bourdeau, "Une sophistique du pragmatisme," *Journal des Débats*, October 19, 1907.

[8] James, *The Meaning of Truth*, p. 111.

[9] According to Protagoras, "of all things the measure is man, of things that are that they are, and of things that are not that they are not" (Plato, *Theaetetus* 152a, trans. Michael J. O'Brien, in *The Older Sophists*, ed. Rosamond Kent Sprague [Columbia, S.C., 1972], p. 19). Though I retain the traditional translation of *anthrōpos* as "man" when directly quoting from specific English texts throughout this chapter, I use the term "human-measure" to refer to Protagoras's famous maxim; see the argument for more inclusive language in Schiappa, *Protagoras and Logos*, p. 131, n. 4.

[10] James, *The Meaning of Truth*, pp. 141–42.

that of experiences to be expected, if the conception be true; which consequences would be different if it were untrue, and must be different
from the consequences by which the meaning of other conceptions is in
turn expressed."[11]

Later, pragmatists would support such controversial notions as: Truth
is what works; truth is the expedient in the way of thinking; truth is war-
ranted assertability.[12] These slogans invited the charge of skeptical relativism against pragmatist epistemology; but in 1902 the *Dictionary* entry
"Relativity of Knowledge" makes no mention of pragmatism. It does remark on Protagorean sophistry, however, as G. E. Moore explains that
the term "relativity of knowledge"

> is now commonly applied to the theory of Protagoras, expressed in the
> famous saying . . . 'man is the measure of all things.' This theory seems
> to have been based on the obvious fact that the same object may appear
> different to different men at the same time, or to the same man at dif-
> ferent times. It is from this fact that Protagoras appears to have drawn
> the contradictory conclusion that all our beliefs may be not partially,
> but wholly untrue, as is implied in his stating his theory with regard to
> all things. (*Dictionary* 451)

Moore attributes a radical skepticism to *anthrōpos metron*, viewing it as a
complete rejection of all knowledge claims. Another *Dictionary* entry extends this charge to sophistry in general: "In ancient philosophy, the
Sophists may be said to be the first definitely to raise the epistemological
question, by their skeptical impeachment of the possibility of truth or
universally valid statement."[13]

In "Presocratic Philosophy," James H. Tufts alludes to the ethical complaint traditionally made against this sophistic epistemology. Commenting from within the individualistic, subjectivist interpretation of the human-measure doctrine, Tufts writes: "Individualism is . . . the prevailing
note [of sophistry], and this found expression in the saying attributed to
Protagoras, 'Man is the measure of all things,' which is the classic formu-

---

[11] *Dictionary of Philosophy and Psychology*, ed. James Mark Baldwin (New York, 1901–2),
vol. 2, p. 321; further references to this volume will be cited in the main text as *Dictionary*.

[12] See William James, "Pragmatism's Conception of Truth," in *Pragmatism: A New Name
for Some Old Ways of Thinking* (1907; rpt. Cambridge, Mass., 1975), pp. 95–113; John Dewey,
"A Short Catechism Concerning Truth" (1910) and "The Problem of Truth" (1911), rpt.
The Middle Works, vol. 6, ed. Jo Ann Boydston (Carbondale, Ill., 1978), pp. 3–68: and
Dewey, *Logic: The Theory of Inquiry* (1938), rpt. *The Later Works*, vol. 12, ed. Boydston (Car-
bondale, Ill., 1986).

[13] A[ndrew] S[eth] P[ringle-]P[attison], "Epistemology," in *Dictionary*, vol. 1, p. 333.

lation for the doctrine of relativism. It is not known that Protagoras himself applied his principle to ethics. He developed it rather with reference to sense perception." Tufts notes that Plato depicts only younger Sophists as "maintaining that 'might is right,' or that laws are merely the invention of the 'many weak' against the 'natural law'" (*Dictionary* 336).

Tufts, Dewey's coauthor on the *Ethics* (1908), precedes his explanation of Protagorean relativism with a more general description of the Sophists, who

> represent a shifting of the centre of interest and study from the cosmos to man, and an emergence of science from closed schools or societies into public discussion. The growing democracy made knowledge valuable to the citizen as well as to the scholar. Teachers of every subject, and especially teachers of rhetoric, found eager hearers. The study of the art of persuasion, especially upon political themes, led naturally to the study of politics itself. (*Dictionary* 336)

Rhetoric and its crucial relation to politics play no role, however, in the few direct references Dewey himself makes to the Sophists in his contributions to the *Dictionary*. Under "Nihilism," for example, he claims that

> the first pure nihilist in philosophic theory was also the last, viz. the Sophist Gorgias of Leontini, who is reported to have taught: (1) that nothing exists; (2) that if anything did exist it would be unknowable; (3) if it existed and were knowable it could not be communicated. (*Dictionary* 177)

Dewey's reference to Protagoras is more qualified. Under "Sensationalism," he mentions the traditional elaboration on the human-measure doctrine: "Some of the Sophists (Protagoras, in particular, to all appearance) applied the conception of Heraclitus, that all is becoming, in such a way as to give validity, on the side of the knowing process, only to that which is in itself changing and partakes of motion, viz. sense." Then Dewey adds parenthetically, "But this may be merely the Platonic interpretation in *Theaetetus*" (*Dictionary* 516).

It is, of course, the "Platonic interpretation" of the Sophists and rhetoric more generally that remains the intellectual backdrop against which the associations between pragmatism and sophistic rhetoric are made at both the beginning and end of the twentieth century. Dewey considered Plato his "favorite philosophic reading" and once remarked, "Nothing could be more helpful to present philosophizing than a 'Back to Plato' movement; but it would have to be back to the dramatic, restless, cooperatively inquiring Plato of the *Dialogues*, trying one mode of attack after another to see what it might yield; back to the Plato whose highest flight of metaphysics always terminated with a social and practical turn, and not to the artificial Plato constructed by unimaginative commentators who treat him as the original university professor."[14] If Dewey rejects the interpretive history that finds in Plato an "all-comprehensive and overriding system,"[15] he does not necessarily accept the traditional Platonic condemnation of the Sophists. Still, his attitude toward the Sophists, especially Protagoras, appears more fluid than his unchanging admiration for Plato.[16]

Though he does distance himself somewhat from a sensationalist reading of *anthrōpos metron* by attributing it to Plato's interpretation in the *Theaetetus*, Dewey appears to accept the traditional association between subjectivism and sophistry in another 1902 *Dictionary* entry. In "Realism," he claims that the problem in one of its aspects "goes back to Socrates, who asserted that the object of knowledge (and hence the true, the certain, the real) was the universal, endeavoring in this way to overcome the subjectivism of the Sophists" (*Dictionary* 422). Later in the decade, however, Dewey provides a very different view of the Sophists, both in the attitude and the argument of his interpretation.

In his 1907 syllabus for a course called "History of Education," Dewey explains that the Sophists "present for the first time in the history of Europe a class of professional teachers separate from other interests and callings. . . . Many of the sophists were what would now be termed humanists; aiming, by teaching literature and other social studies, to make the Greek states more conscious of their common language, literature and religion, and thereby to bring them into more friendly relations with each other." Among their other accomplishments, Dewey notes that the Sophists attempted "to train effective speakers and writers, involving the theory of persuasion and argument" and that they called "attention to the training in the arts relating to statesmanship . . . thus introducing the topics of political science and political economy." In his syllabus, Dewey also observes that "even the saying that 'Man is the measure of all things'

---

[14] John Dewey, "From Absolutism to Experimentalism" (1930), rpt. *The Later Works*, vol. 5, ed. Jo Ann Boydston (Carbondale, Ill., 1984), pp. 154–55.

[15] Dewey, "From Absolutism to Experimentalism," p. 154.

[16] See John P. Anton, "John Dewey and Ancient Philosophies," *Philosophy and Phenomenological Research* 25 (June 1965): 477–99; Frederick M. Anderson, "Dewey's Experiment with Greek Philosophy," *International Philosophical Quarterly* 7 (1967): 86–100; and J. J. Chambliss, *The Influence of Plato and Aristotle on John Dewey's Philosophy* (Lewiston, N.Y., 1990).

was probably not meant in an individualistic sense, but rather was intended to emphasize the value of culture and civilization of humanity as against barbarism and animal nature."[17]

Dewey thus seems to modify his 1902 reading of the Sophists as nihilistic and subjectivist and to move to a more positive evaluation by 1907, a change that rejects the individualistic interpretation of *anthrōpos metron* and endorses a communal meaning for that Protagorean doctrine. During this five-year period, Dewey reviewed a book by the British pragmatist, F. C. S. Schiller.[18] It is in the work of Schiller during the first years of the twentieth century that we find the clearest connections made between Anglo-American pragmatism and sophistic rhetoric.

Like Dewey, William James reviewed Schiller's *Humanism*, published in 1903, calling its author pragmatism's "most vivacious and pugnacious champion."[19] In the introduction to his book, Schiller argues that pragmatic humanism has "affinities with the great saying of Protagoras, that *Man is the Measure of all things*. Fairly interpreted, this is the truest and most important thing that any thinker ever has propounded." Schiller proceeds to take the first of his many swipes at Plato's antirelativist critique of Protagoras: "It is only in travesties such as it suited Plato's dialectic purpose to circulate that [the human-measure dictum] can be said to tend to skepticism; in reality it urges Science to discover how Man may measure, and by what devices make concordant his measures with those of his fellow-men."[20]

Here we have Schiller's first suggestion of the pragmatist link he sees between Protagorean sophistry and sophistic rhetoric. He strongly rejects the traditional Platonic reading of Protagoras, denying its claim that the *anthrōpos metron* doctrine inevitably leads to radical skepticism about

[17] John Dewey, "History of Education" (1907), rpt. *The Later Works*, vol. 17, ed. Jo Ann Boydston (Carbondale, Ill., 1990), pp. 183–84.

[18] However, even hedged claims for Schiller's influence on Dewey must be tempered by Dewey's later acknowledgment of indebtedness to other sources, e.g., Alfred Benn's reading of the Sophists. See John Dewey, "The 'Socratic Dialogues' of Plato" (1925), rpt. *The Later Works*, vol. 2, ed. Jo Ann Boydston (Carbondale, Ill., 1984), p. 124n; and cf. Alfred William Benn, *The Philosophy of Greece* (London, 1898), chap. 5, "The Diffusion of Culture: Humanists and Naturalists."

[19] William James, "Humanism," *Nation* 78 (March 3, 1904): 175–76; rpt. James, *Essays, Comments, and Reviews*, ed. Frederick H. Burkhardt, Fredson Bowers, and Ignas K. Skrupskelis (Cambridge, Mass., 1987), p. 551. Today, Schiller is pragmatism's most forgotten major figure. See Reuben Abel, *The Pragmatic Humanism of F. C. S. Schiller* (New York, 1955), p. 3; Kenneth Winetrout, *F. C. S. Schiller and the Dimensions of Pragmatism* (Columbus, Ohio, 1967), p. 6; and Herbert L. Searles and Allan Shields, preface to *A Bibliography of the Works of F. C. S. Schiller* (San Diego, 1968), p. iv.

[20] F. C. S. Schiller, *Humanism: Philosophical Essays* (London, 1903), p. xvii.

the human ability to know the truth. In direct opposition to this negative, skeptical interpretation, Schiller reads Protagoras as arguing positively for the human origin of truth and thus affirming, not rejecting, mankind's ability to know it. There is only a hint here of Schiller's individualistic take on the human-measure dictum, his belief that Protagoras meant individual men as well as mankind as a group. But Schiller does make quite explicit even in this passing remark that the truth claims advanced by men, the measures asserted by individuals, must be negotiated among other men. It is the task of sophistic rhetoric to investigate and theorize how this rhetorical process takes place, to establish what rhetorical "devices make concordant [one man's] measures with those of his fellow-men."

In his 1907 essay "From Plato to Protagoras," Schiller develops his earlier comments and clearly demonstrates how his humanism is both sophistic and pragmatist.[21] His first extended discussion of the Sophists begins and ends with Athenian cultural politics. Following Grote and Gomperz, Schiller finds the origins of sophistry in the political situation of Greece in the fifth century B.C.[22] "The rise of democracies rendered a higher education and a power of public speaking a *sine qua non* of political influence—and, what acted probably as a still stronger incentive—of the safety of the life and property, particularly of the wealthier classes" (31). And it was the Sophists—"university extension lecturers hampered by no university"—who "professed to supply this great requisite of practical success" (31). Young men of the upper classes paid for sophistic lessons in rhetoric, which they hoped would gain them honor in the democratic assemblies and protection in the public courts.

The political context of sophistic education resulted in "a great development of rhetoric and dialectic" (31–32), and the Sophists grew wealthy from their professional success with already rich and prospectively famous (or economically nervous) clients. Schiller points out that "this sophistic education was not popular with those who were too poor or too niggardly to avail themselves of it, *i.e.* with the extreme democrats and the old conservatives; it was new, and it seemed to bestow an unfair and undemocratic advantage on those who had enjoyed it" (32). Schiller's brief remarks on the contradictory (democratic *and* undemocratic) ori-

[21] Schiller, "From Plato to Protagoras," in his *Studies in Humanism* (London, 1907), pp. 22–70; page citations in this and the next three paragraphs refer to this essay, which is a revised version of Schiller's review essay "Plato and His Predecessors," *Quarterly Review* 204 (1906): 62–88.

[22] See George Grote, *History of Greece* (London, 1847–56), vol. 8, chap. 67; and Theodor Gomperz, *Greek Thinkers: A History of Ancient Philosophy*, vol. 1, trans. Laurie Magnus (London, 1905), chap. 5.

gins of sophistic rhetoric foreshadow recent debates over the ideological affiliations of neosophistry and the political consequences of rhetoric more generally.[23] He clearly identifies rhetoric with democracy—only in such a political structure could sophistic rhetoric develop—but recognizes, at least in passing, that rhetoric could serve undemocratic interests when rhetorical education was restricted by socioeconomic privilege.

Schiller explains other reasons for attacks on the Sophists in ancient Athens, particularly "the jealous polemic directed by the philosophers (especially by Plato) against rival teachers" (32). He turns then to "the great idea of Protagoras, the greatest of the Sophists. . . . His famous dictum that 'man is the measure of all things' must be ranked even above the Delphic 'Know thyself,' as compressing the largest quantum of vital meaning into the most compact form" (33). To prove his case, Schiller takes up the conflicted history of interpreting the human-measure maxim. Postponing specific discussion of Plato's reading, Schiller notes that past interpreters of "man is the measure of all things" have disagreed over whether "man" refers to individual men or to mankind as a whole. Schiller suggests the either/or choice has simply been a mistake repeated throughout the maxim's interpretive history. "Protagoras may well have chosen an ambiguous form in order to indicate both the subjective and the objective factor in human knowledge and the problem of their connexion" (33). That is, according to Schiller, Protagoras intended both the subjective interpretation of the dictum—individual men are the measure of all things—and the objective interpretation—mankind in general is the measure. Furthermore, the double meaning itself points up the epistemological problem of how to get from one aspect to the other, from the subjective perceptions and assertions of one man to the "objective truth, in some sense 'common' to mankind" (34). In other words, Schiller asks, "what . . . is the transition from subjective truth for the individual to objective truth for all?" (34–35).

It is here that Schiller takes up the Platonic criticism of Protagoras through a counterreading of the *Theaetetus*, specifically Protagoras's defense (*Theaetetus* 165e–168c). The details of Schiller's reading are interesting and worthy of attention, especially as he develops them in later essays in *Studies in Humanism* and his 1908 pamphlet *Plato or Protagoras?* But for my purposes here only one point need be noted: Schiller's *rhetorical*

<hr/>

[23] On the contested relationship between sophistic rhetoric and democratic ideology, see, for example, John Poulakos, "Sophistical Rhetoric as a Critique of Culture," in *Argument and Critical Practice*, ed. Joseph W. Wenzel (Annandale, Va., 1987), pp. 97–101; Edward Schiappa, "Sophistic Rhetoric: Oasis or Mirage?" *Rhetoric Review* 10 (fall 1991): 9–10; and Jarratt, *Rereading the Sophists*, pp. 98–107.

answer to the question of how to account for "subjective" and "objective" aspects of truth, of how to move from individual assertions to shared, communal knowledge. Schiller writes, "For if there is a mass of subjective judgments varying in value, there must ensue a selection of the more valuable and serviceable, which will, in consequence, survive and constitute growing bodies of objective truth, shared and agreed upon by practically all" (38). Schiller characterizes this selection process as rhetorical when he points out that "it is still possible to observe how society establishes an 'objective' order by coercing or cajoling those who are inclined to divergent judgments in moral or aesthetic matters" (38). Thus, for Schiller's Protagoras, the pragmatic character of truth—its value or usefulness—merges with and is completed by the rhetorical politics of society, its coercions and cajoleries, its threats and persuasions.

In other places, Schiller works out the details of this rhetorical pragmatism and its relations to Protagorean sophistry. For example, in "The Ambiguity of Truth" he argues that past philosophers, including Plato, often equivocated between two very different meanings for the term— truth as claim and truth as validity.[24] Schiller explains how the two usages are rhetorically related: a truth-claim is made from a particular position and then it is either refuted or sustained as valid in a particular historical community. Though Schiller usually gives this rhetorical process more of an individualistic slant, his account always makes clear the social situatedness of the truth-establishing process, arguing that individual truth-claims struggle to receive social recognition, and they do so successfully when the rhetor's audience finds the claims useful. That is, persuasion results from the pragmatic efficacy of the arguments employed.

Schiller refers to this discussion of truth's ambiguity in his most explicit argument for the intimate connection between pragmatic sophistry and rhetorical practice, a review of Heinrich Gomperz's *Sophistik und Rhetorik*.[25] Schiller agrees with Gomperz that "*all* the opinions of the Sophists were relative to, and derivative from, their professional ideal of 'effective speaking'" and then links one such opinion—the human-measure dictum—with Protagoras's "rhetorical technique of arguing both sides of a case" (111–12).[26] Truth-claims are relative to persons, and different persons might thus understandably make different arguments about the same topic. As Schiller paraphrases Gomperz, "all as-

[24] Schiller, *Studies in Humanism*, pp. 144–46.
[25] F. C. S. Schiller, review of Heinrich Gomperz, *Sophistik und Rhetorik*, *Mind* 22 (January 1913): 115n; page citations in the rest of this paragraph refer to this review.
[26] "Protagoras was the first to say that on every issue there are two arguments opposed to each other" (Diogenes Laertius, IX.50, trans. in Sprague, *The Older Sophists*, p. 4).

sertions, however 'contradictory,' that are really made . . . are true, in the
sense that there really is something in the situation which provokes different minds so to formulate their various estimates" (112). However, he
disagrees with Gomperz that an "enormous paradox" vitiates the views of
Protagoras, whose relativism declared all views true but whose dogma-
tism preferred his own over others (114). Schiller sees nothing paradox-
ical in this Protagorean sophistry, for assertions can all be relatively true
but still not equally valuable or socially validated. He explains:

> No one who had spent his life [like Protagoras] in teaching others how
> to argue cases, could well fail to observe that there was always something
> to be said on both sides, and that to say it well it was necessary to pay
> some attention to the structure of language, the logical concatenation
> of thoughts, and the persuasiveness of rhetoric. Nor could he fail to
> note that the most various views were in fact held to be true, and that so-
> cial assent had quite as great powers in making them effectively 'true' as
> effectively 'just'. But neither could he allow, whether as an expert
> teacher or as a sensible and practical man, that all these conflicting
> views were in fact of equal value. (115)

Thus, it is through a pragmatic appeal to experience that Schiller affirms both Protagoras's human-measure dictum and his two-arguments
teaching.

There are other places in the work of F. C. S. Schiller where a sophistic rhetorical pragmatism emerges, but I will end this section by referring
again to the less explicitly rhetorical of Schiller's fellow pragmatists. In
their reviews of *Humanism*, both James and Dewey pick out Schiller's
pragmatist reading of Protagoras for special attention. James writes,

> The ancient phrase, "man the measure of all things," was, it is true, orig-
> inally used skeptically: the human view was by Protagoras contrasted
> with a possible superhuman view which would be truer. But this con-
> temporary humanism [of Schiller's] is so radical that it "falls on t'other
> side," and creates a new standard of sincerity and veracity. There is no
> possible superhuman view, it seems to say, to act as a reductive and
> falsifier of "merely human" truth.

James then adds his own emphasis to Schiller's interpretation of *anthrōpos
metron*:

> Experiences are all; and all experiences are immediately or remotely
> continuous with each other. As surely as we have thoughts, so surely are

some of them superior. They are *experienced* as superior—other way of "being" superior there is none. And the experience consists not in their copying independent archetypes of "reality," but solely in the fact of their *succeeding better*, and connecting themselves more satisfactorily with the residuum of life. Truth, in short, lives in the actually felt relations between experiences themselves.[27]

According to James, Schiller's humanistic pragmatism transforms the Protagorean maxim from a negative, skeptical critique of transcendental theories of "superhuman" knowledge into a positive pragmatist theory of "merely human," experiential truth.

Dewey's review of *Humanism* also cites Schiller's interpretation of the human-measure dictum; but rather than remarking on its past skeptical readings, he focuses instead on its present usefulness in answering the charge of solipsism made against pragmatist thought. Like James, Dewey praises Schiller for emphasizing the pragmatic attitude toward experience and quotes approvingly Schiller's remark that humanism is "content to take human experience as the clue to the world of human experience, content to take Man on his own merits. . . . To remember that Man is the measure of all things, *i.e.*, of his whole experience world, and that if our standard measure be proved false all our measurements are vitiated."[28] Dewey then takes such passages as a clear answer to critics who "with one voice have acclaimed [Schiller's] point of view as subjective, irretrievably so, as individualistic, as solipsistic. When Mr. Schiller remarks that if Man as the standard measure be proved false all further measurements are thereby vitiated, he has, to my mind, answered the critics by anticipation. The standpoint cannot fairly be labelled as per the above, unless the human nature which is taken as furnishing the key and clue to human experience be purely subjective, be enclosed within an exclusively psychical individuality."[29] Dewey thus rejects the charges of Schiller's critics and goes on to deny in typical pragmatist fashion any "hypothetic universality which exists not in everyday concrete human nature, as observation and description, history and analysis reveal that human nature," a hypothetic universality "which exists only in projections which are the special monopoly of philosophy."[30]

---

[27] James, "Humanism," p. 552.

[28] Schiller, *Humanism*, p. xx, quoted in Dewey's review, *Psychological Bulletin* 1 (September 1904): 335–40; rpt. Dewey, *The Middle Works*, vol. 3, ed. Jo Ann Boydston (Carbondale, Ill., 1977), p. 313.

[29] Dewey, rev. of *Humanism*, p. 313.

[30] Dewey, rev. of *Humanism*, p. 314.

NEOPRAGMATISM AS POSTMODERN SOPHISTRY

At the end just as at the beginning of the century, pragmatism and sophistic rhetoric intersect in the claims of their advocates and the objections of their detractors. Richard Rorty, perhaps today's most influential neopragmatist, summarizes his antifoundationalist critique of traditional epistemology by juxtaposing "conversational" and "confrontational" explanatory models:

> We can think of knowledge as a relation to propositions, and thus justification as a relation between the propositions in question and other propositions from which the former may be inferred. Or we may think of both knowledge and justification as privileged relations to the objects those propositions are about. . . . If we think of knowledge in the second way, we will want to get behind reasons to causes, beyond argument to compulsion from the object known, to a situation in which argument would be not just silly but impossible, for anyone gripped by the object in the required way will be *unable* to doubt or to see an alternative. To reach that point is to reach the foundations of knowledge.[31]

This search for foundations has been the goal of philosophy since Plato. In contrast, to think of knowledge in the first, antifoundationalist way is to "think of 'rational certainty' as a matter of victory in argument rather than of relation to an object known," to accept that "our certainty will be a matter of conversation between persons, rather than a matter of interaction with nonhuman reality," to see no "difference in kind between 'necessary' and 'contingent' truths" but only "differences in degree of ease in objecting to our beliefs." In short, Rorty argues, we shall "be where the Sophists were before Plato brought his principle to bear and invented 'philosophical thinking': we shall be looking for an airtight case rather than an unshakable foundation."[32] Rorty's pragmatist reading of the Sophists places something akin to rhetoric at the center of their philosophy, or, better, makes sophistic philosophy and rhetoric indistinguishable.[33]

[31] Richard Rorty, *Philosophy and the Mirror of Nature* (Princeton, 1979), p. 159.

[32] Rorty, *Philosophy and the Mirror of Nature*, pp. 156–57. I will return to Rorty's rhetorical pragmatism in Chap. 3.

[33] Rorty himself refrains from using the term "rhetoric" in describing his pragmatist project in order to avoid reinstating the logic/rhetoric opposition he sees Dewey as having rejected. (Personal communication.) Cf. Gary A. Olson, "Social Construction and Composition Theory: A Conversation with Richard Rorty," *Journal of Advanced Composition* 9 (1989): 3; and "Discussion entre Jean-François Lyotard et Richard Rorty," *Critique* 41 (May 1985): 584.

Susan Haack, one of Rorty's severest philosophical critics, has compared this "most radical of contemporary self-styled neo-pragmatists" with the "uncompromisingly revolutionary" F. C. S. Schiller. She notes that "in a spirit, no doubt, of deliberate provocation, Schiller likens his views to those of Protagoras." Haack goes on to claim that "the affinity of Rorty's and Schiller's conceptions of pragmatism" is not due to Schiller's direct influence but is perhaps "the result rather of Rorty's (mis)reading James much as Schiller did."[34] Given James's positive review of Schiller's *Humanism* and his approving comments in *Pragmatism*, Haack should say much more about exactly how Schiller gets James wrong.[35] Be that as it may, a full response to Haack's charge against Schiller's "revolutionary, relativistic humanism" (653) involves some of the same arguments I will mount against similar charges emerging from the cultural right and left against contemporary rhetorical pragmatism.

Let me note in passing, however, the peculiar way Haack's specialist philosophical critique gets picked up in a more interdisciplinary venue and then is problematically related to various pieces of popular culture. In *The American Scholar*, Tibor Machan conjoins Haack's Schillerian version of Rorty with a complaint about the relativistic attitude toward truth he attributes to "the current multicultural movement, according to which the Western way of thinking is simply one among several equally valid options." He concludes his case against Rortian pragmatism by associating Haack's description of it with fragments from the mass media: "Hadn't you heard, truth is irrelevant, it is only information that counts today" (a CEO in Michael Crichton's *Disclosure*) and "What is a lie when every man has his own truth?" (a character in the television program *Homicide*).[36] Though this clever juxtapositioning doesn't amount to much as a coherent philosophical or sociological argument, it does illustrate a significant rhetorical phenomenon I wish to explore in later chapters: the transformation of specialized professional discourse into popular culture citations, or more generally, the migration of various tropes,

---

[34] Susan Haack, "Pragmatism," in *The Blackwell Companion to Philosophy*, ed. Nicholas Bunnin and E. P. Tsui-James (Oxford, 1996), pp. 653–54. Further references to this article are given in the main text.

[35] Haack does have more to say about James in her "Can James's Theory of Truth Be Made More Satisfactory?" *Transactions of the Charles S. Peirce Society* 20, no. 3 (1984): 269–78; and about Rorty and James in chap. 9 of her *Evidence and Inquiry: Towards Reconstruction in Epistemology* (Oxford, 1993). Rorty responds to this chapter in *Rorty and Pragmatism: The Philosopher Responds to His Critics*, ed. Herman J. Saatkamp, Jr. (Nashville, 1995), pp. 148–53.

[36] Tibor Machan, "Indefatigable Alchemist: Richard Rorty's Radical Pragmatism," *The American Scholar* 65 (summer 1996): 423–24.

arguments, and narratives throughout different sites within a cultural conversation.

Another neopragmatist, this one speaking from legal and literary theory, tells a story similar to Rorty's about sophistic rhetoric. Stanley Fish reminds us that "the quarrel between philosophy and rhetoric survives every sea change in the history of Western thought, continually presenting us with the (skewed) choice between the plain unvarnished truth straightforwardly presented and the powerful but insidious appeal of 'fine language,' language that has transgressed the limits of representation and substituted its own forms for the forms of reality." Fish goes on to point out that "there have always been friends of rhetoric, from the sophists to the anti-foundationalists of the present day," and he recapitulates several of their arguments. Among those rhetorical defenses, he repeats that of the Sophists: "The chief accusation . . . is that rhetoricians hold 'the probable (or likely-seeming, plausible) in more honour than the true' (*Phaedrus*, 267a). The sophist response is to assert that the realm of the probable—of what is likely to be so given particular conditions within some local perspective—is the only relevant realm of consideration for human beings."

Fish details this position of sophistic rhetorical pragmatism: "The argument [for rhetoric] is contained in two statements attributed famously to Protagoras. The first declares the unavailability (not the unreality) of the gods: 'About gods I cannot say either that they are or that they are not.' And the second follows necessarily from the absence of godly guidance: 'Man is the measure of all things, of the things that are that they are, and of the things that are not that they are not' (quoted in Plato, *Theaetetus*, 152a)." Fish then draws the antiskeptical conclusion: "This is not to say that the categories of the true and good are abandoned, but that in different contexts they will be filled differently and that there exists no master context (for that could only be occupied by the unavailable gods) from the vantage point of which the differences could be assessed and judged." Or as he pragmatically puts it in another place: "To the accusation that rhetoric deals only with the realms of the probable and contingent and forsakes truth, the sophists and their successors respond that truth itself is a contingent affair and assumes a different shape in the light of differing local urgencies and the convictions associated with them."[37]

---

[37] Stanley Fish, *Doing What Comes Naturally: Change, Rhetoric, and the Practice of Theory in Literary and Legal Studies* (Durham, N.C., 1989), pp. 478–81.

Fish makes many other useful points in his demonstration of neo-pragmatism's intersection with sophistic rhetoric, but the following is most helpful in moving to the final topic of this chapter:

> The [sophistic] result is to move rhetoric from the disreputable periph-ery to the necessary center: for if the highest truth for any man is what he believes it to be (*Theaetetus*, 152a), the skill which produces belief and therefore establishes what, in a particular time and particular place, is true, is the skill essential to the building and maintaining of a civilized society. In the absence of a revealed truth, rhetoric is that skill, and in teaching it the sophists were teaching "the one thing that mattered, how to take care of one's own affairs and the business of the state."[38]

From his neopragmatist perspective, Fish draws our attention to a point made again and again in the revisionist histories of sophistic rhetoric, its indissoluble link to the realm of politics. What has become central in contemporary debates over critical theory, political philosophy, and ed-ucational policy are the questions of whether there are any necessary po-litical consequences to rhetoric or pragmatism or sophistry and whether the structural or constitutive bonds between rhetorical pragmatism and cultural politics have any specific ideological content.

There are in fact many different theoretical and political issues buried in these two questions. To get at a few of the most important ones, let me quote some antirhetorical attacks recently emanating from the cultural right. In *Tenured Radicals: How Politics Has Corrupted Our Higher Education*, Roger Kimball entitles one chapter "The New Sophistry" and includes as an epigraph the saying attributed to Thrasymachus in Plato's *Republic*: "What I say is that 'just' or 'right' means nothing but what is to the inter-est of the stronger party."[39] Near the end of the chapter, Kimball writes in full polemical heat:

> There was a time when one studied rhetoric to equip oneself to employ its resources effectively for the sake of truth and justice and to inoculate oneself against rhetoric's seductive charms. For Professor Fish, however, rhetoric is all there is. This has always been the contention of profes-sional rhetoricians, from the time of sophists such as Thrasymachus, Cal-

[38] Fish, *Doing What Comes Naturally*, p. 480, quoting William K. Guthrie, *The Sophists* (Cambridge, 1971), p. 193.
[39] Roger Kimball, *Tenured Radicals* (New York, 1990), p. 142; further references to this book are cited in the text.

licles, and Protagoras, down to contemporary sophists such as Rorty, Fish, and their many disciples. Plato rightly condemned rhetoric as a "shadow play of words" that was concerned with semblance, not reality. (164)

Kimball condemns Fish's "deliberate attempt to supplant reason by rhetoric, truth by persuasion, using the simple device of denying that there is any essential distinction to be made between them" (164). He concludes by charging that Fish's "recent work illustrates the extent to which academic literary studies have abandoned the most elementary distinctions of taste, judgment, and value. It is one of the clearest symptoms of the decadence besetting the academy that the ideals that once informed the humanities have been corrupted, willfully misunderstood, or simply ignored by the new sophistries that have triumphed on our campuses" (165).

Behind Kimball's diatribe are the traditional charges against sophistic relativism and nihilism we have already seen. Kimball accurately reports one of Fish's responses to such charges: "Does might make right? In a sense the answer I must give is yes, since in the absence of a perspective independent of interpretation some interpretive perspective will always rule by virtue of having won out over its competitors."[40] But Kimball fails to note Fish's further neopragmatist explanation, in which he answers the nihilism charge by denying, then rhetoricizing, its assumption of an absolute opposition between unprincipled preference and universal principle. In a particular historical context, one person's principles may be another's illegitimate preferences and there is no arhetorical, disinterested way to characterize such a dispute. Fish elaborates his sophistically pragmatist point:

In the (certain) event that some characterization will prevail (at least for a time) over its rivals, it will do so because some interested assertion of principle has managed to *forcefully* dislodge other (equally interested) assertions of principle. It is in this sense that force is the sole determinant of outcomes, but the sting is removed from this conclusion when force is understood not as "pure" or "mere" force (phenomena never encountered) but as the urging (perhaps in the softest terms) of some point of view, of some vision of the world complete with purposes, goals, standards, reasons—in short, with everything to which force is usually opposed in the name of principle.[41]

---

[40] Fish, *Doing What Comes Naturally*, p. 10, quoted in Kimball, *Tenured Radicals*, p. 161.
[41] Fish, *Doing What Comes Naturally*, p. 12.

In other words, it is only through contextualized suasive force that this or some other preferred principle or principled preference carries the rhetorical day.

It is not surprising that Kimball remains unconvinced by this bit of sophistic rhetoric and fails to give more of Fish's supporting argument. What is surprising about Kimball's antirhetorical polemic, however, is the appeal he himself makes to rhetorical power: Fish's "position is far from convincing," Kimball declares (161); and then after giving part of Fish's rhetorical response to the usual charge of relativist self-contradiction, Kimball asks, with no sense of apparent self-contradiction in his own argument, "But is his response convincing?" (162). Whether we think Kimball presents the "new sophistries" fairly or not, surely his own bottom-line appeal to suasive force must give us pause in such an unqualified condemnation of sophistic rhetoric.

More consistent in carrying out his antirhetorical attack is Dinesh D'Souza in *Illiberal Education: The Politics of Race and Sex on Campus*. He too associates neopragmatism and poststructuralist thought more generally with being on the wrong side of the contest between Plato and the Sophists. Fish and his like-minded colleagues are guilty of fostering a "fashionable sophistry" among their students, but "when [students] discover, at places like Duke [where Fish was chair of the English Department], that there is no wisdom to be found, their adolescent rebelliousness turns anarchic and nihilistic." Against such sophistry, D'Souza quotes Plato's Socrates in the *Euthydemus* characterizing "the temperament of mind that was equally applicable to the Sophists of his day as to the Duke critics in ours. 'Mastery of this sort of stuff would by no means lead to increased knowledge of how things are, but only to the ability to play games with people, tripping them up and flooring them with different senses of words, just like those who derive pleasure and amusement from pulling stools from under people when they are about to sit down, and from seeing someone floundering on his back.'"[42]

Unfortunately, D'Souza answers a useful pedagogical question—What are the effects of teaching a specific theory?—with a priori philosophical answers: According to D'Souza's Plato, the ancient and postmodern Sophists are guilty of corrupting the youth because their antifoundationalist theories necessarily lead to nihilism and anarchy. In contrast, the response of a thoroughgoing rhetorical pragmatist would be to examine historically and locally how such teaching affects students in the

---

[42] Dinesh D'Souza, *Illiberal Education* (New York, 1991), pp. 189–90, translating from *Euthydemus* 278b–c.

short and long term and (the much easier task) to reject the Platonic framework that equates principles and standards with the ahistorical, transcendental, and absolutely foundational rather than with the historical, contextual, and rhetorically negotiated.

The right is not alone in its objections, for the cultural left has also challenged the dangers of rhetorical pragmatism and postmodern sophistry. Take for example one such attack, *Beyond Aesthetics*, in which Stuart Sim condemns current postmodernisms for rejecting the metanarratives that have traditionally grounded radical politics. He argues that such antifoundationalism leads necessarily to restricting political activity to local interventions based on individualistic "little narratives." Alluding to Jean-François Lyotard's agonistic postmodernism, Sim declares: "Tending your own little narrative, agonistically or otherwise, looks very much like a conservative tactic to keep change to a manageable minimum within the confines of a comfortable *status quo*."[43] He connects the rise of postmodern antifoundationalism with the "current revival of interest in rhetoric" (97). Indeed, it is precisely this rhetorical interest that is causing many of the intellectual and political problems.

Sim admits that "the move into rhetoric is a characteristic one for the antifoundationalist to make, and it need not be seen as reprehensible" (86). However, noting that "rhetoric can hardly be viewed as neutral," that "it is always in the service of an ideological position," Sim goes on to ask, "what are the conditions under which a given rhetoric gains plausibility?" His worried answer: the "personal charisma" of the rhetor becomes most important within contexts of the postmodern "collapse of grand narrative authority and of foundations" (93–94). Then Sim gets to his real problem with rhetorical antifoundationalism: "Not everyone will misuse rhetoric, but some will, some always do. It was to avoid such an outcome that foundationalism was devised" (94). Here we see played out once again the traditional conflict between philosophy and rhetoric, between Plato and the Sophists. Or as Sim himself puts it: "The spectre that [foundationalism] set out to exorcise was the spectre of clever, and possibly unscrupulous, language-game theorists (the sophists are always with us) exploiting the innocent and unwary" (94).

The problem with Sim's version of antisophistry is that it begs all the important questions, at least from a sophistic rhetorician's point of view. Rhetoric does not self-evidently stand condemned because it is always partisan *if*, as a postmodern sophist might argue, such partisanship is in fact

---

[43] Stuart Sim, *Beyond Aesthetics: Confrontations with Poststructuralism and Postmodernism* (Toronto, 1992), p. 90; further references to this book are cited in the text.

unavoidable in philosophy or any other language game. Rhetoric is not necessarily disreputable because it is constantly deployed ideologically *if* there is no ahistorical, neutral space outside all ideologies. Charisma and emotional appeal do at times influence an argument's success, but in most rhetorical contexts they are so intimately interwoven with logical rigor, evidentiary support, appeal to precedent, shared paradigms, and so forth that it makes only foundationalist sense to try and separate them out and condemn them as illegitimate. And, yes, it would be nice to have theoretical, transcendental protection against the use and abuse of all historical instruments, including rhetoric, but no such theory or metanarrative seems to have worked, and now in the "postmodern condition" all such foundations are more and more often being called into question.[44]

Nevertheless, the pragmatic jury might still be out on at least one of the questions Sim poses: Who is the greater political danger, the foundationalist or the antifoundationalist? "The risk we run when we ditch [foundationalism] unceremoniously is that we expose all the world's vulnerable little narratives, not so much to a tyrannical grand narrative, as to the verbally fluent, charisma-based narrative" that tends "to want to deflect individuals from connecting with those narratives rooted in a belief in collective action and a desire for radical socio-economic change" (94). A pragmatic rhetorician must grant that *in specific times and places* perhaps an appeal to foundationalism might work "to limit the abuse of language power" (94), as so many antirhetorical philosophers have declared it should be allowed to do always and everywhere. The problem is, of course, that you can't know beforehand when those specific contexts will arise, and instead you must rhetorically negotiate each and every new situation.

The rhetorical pragmatist would go further, however, and argue that for the most part it is better to keep the issue of foundationalism versus antifoundationalism logically separate from the issue of reactionary versus progressive politics. Given the right rhetorical circumstances, any philosophy can be appropriated by any politics.[45] Just as fanatic abso-

---

[44] The rhetorical conflict between Platonism and sophistry has been and continues to be played out in a myriad of ways in contemporary cultural politics, but I have limited myself here to only a few of the more telling examples. I will return in Part Three to this conflict as it is restaged in relation to university curriculum reforms and the Culture Wars.

[45] This point has been made most effectively by Gerald Graff in several discussions of what he calls the "fallacy of overspecificity": see, for example, Graff, "The Pseudo-Politics of Interpretation," *Critical Inquiry* 9 (March 1983): 602–5; and "Co-optation," in *The New Historicism*, ed. H. Aram Veeser (New York, 1989), pp. 174–75.

lutists can argue for murder or for love and self-proclaimed relativists can be altruistically tolerant or irresponsibly indifferent, foundationalism and antifoundationalism guarantee no specific political consequences. It is not that theory never has any consequences; at certain times in certain places it has very real rhetorical effects.[46] Convincing someone of a particular grand narrative or a particular theory of human nature might indeed result in changing a life or transforming the world. But not every politics needs a grand narrative or requires an essentialist theory of humanity. Collective action to change society, affirm cultural values, or reform higher education requires some agreement and a measure of solidarity. It requires a lot of give-and-take in rhetorical negotiation. It cannot be guaranteed by either rhetoric or philosophy, by rhetorical pragmatism or foundationalist theory. However, some of us working in the pragmatist tradition think that at this historical moment a strategic emphasis on the first term in each of these pairs might enhance the effectiveness of progressive political activity in and outside our academic institutions.

True, rhetorical pragmatism does call into question traditional foundationalist supports for political projects. But this is not a debilitating problem if, as Rorty argues, deep philosophical justifications are unnecessary for state legitimation or revolutionary activity, for reactionary conservatism or radical democracy.[47] And true, rhetorical pragmatism claims no necessary, logical connection to any particular political ideology. But still, with its tropes of dialogue and conversation, with its arguments for rhetorical exchange, with its narratives of interpretive debates as the only way to establish truth, sophistic rhetorical pragmatism can promote and be promoted by democratic forms of political organization. How such a historical connection is developed depends on the particular circumstances in which the development takes place. I share the hope most recently articulated by Giles Gunn:

> While pragmatic criticism advocates no particular policies, it does possess a specifiable politics. It is a politics distinguished by the democratic preference for rendering differences conversable so that the conflicts

[46] For the debate over theoretical consequences, see Mitchell, *Against Theory*; my *Rhetorical Power* (Ithaca, 1989), chap. 6; and Jonathan Arac and Barbara Johnson, eds., *Consequences of Theory* (Baltimore, 1991).

[47] Richard Rorty, "The Priority of Democracy to Philosophy," in his *Objectivity, Relativism, and Truth* (Cambridge, 1991), pp. 175–96.

they produce, instead of being destructive of human community, can become potentially creative of it; can broaden and thicken public culture rather than depleting it.[48]

[48] Giles Gunn, *Thinking across the American Grain: Ideology, Intellect, and the New Pragmatism* (Chicago, 1992), p. 37. The political hope I am expressing here is supported by several recent critiques and developments of neopragmatism: see Nancy Fraser, *Unruly Practices: Power, Discourse, and Gender in Contemporary Social Theory* (Minneapolis, 1989), chap. 5; Cornel West, *The American Evasion of Philosophy: A Genealogy of Pragmatism* (Madison, Wis., 1989); John Clifford, "The Neopragmatic Scene of Theory and Practice in Composition," *Rhetoric Review* 10 (fall 1991): 100–107; David Theo Goldberg, *Racist Culture: Philosophy and the Politics of Meaning* (Oxford, 1993), chap. 9; and Charlene Haddock Seigfried, *Pragmatism and Feminism: Reweaving the Social Fabric* (Chicago, 1996).

INTERPRETATION AND
RHETORICAL HERMENEUTICS

I am, in the deepest sense, a translator. I go on translating, even if I must but translate English into English.
—Kenneth Burke, letter to Malcolm Cowley, 4 June 1932

When I think back on all the crap I learned in high school,
It's a wonder I can think at all.
The lack of education hasn't hurt me none.
I can read the writing on the wall.
—Paul Simon, "Kodachrome"

Reading words on walls. Explicating poems in classrooms. Making sense of dreams from the gods. Reading, explicating, making sense: these are three names given to the activity of interpretation. In English, "interpret" has most often meant "to expound the meaning of (something abstruse or mysterious); to render (words, writings, an author, etc.) clear or explicit; to elucidate; to explain" (*OED*). But an earlier sense of the verb was "to translate," and so interpretation is also "the action of translating; a translation or rendering of a book, word, etc." (*OED*). The word "interpretation" itself derives from the Latin, *interpretatio*, meaning not only "the action of expounding, explaining" but also "a translation, rendering." In Latin rhetoric, *interpretatio* referred to "the explanation of one word by another, the use of synonyms." *Interpretatio* was formed on *interpres*: "an intermediary, agent, go-between" and "an interpreter of foreign languages, translator."[1] In its etymology, then, "interpretation" conveys the sense of a translation pointed in two directions simultaneously: *toward* a text to be interpreted and *for* an audience in need of the interpretation. That is, the interpreter mediates, Hermes fashion, between

[1] *Oxford Latin Dictionary*, ed. P. G. W. Glare (Oxford, 1982), p. 947.

the translated text and its new rendering *and* between the translated text and the audience desiring the translation.

It is the heritage of these two etymological senses—translation *of* a text and translation *for* an audience—that we might try to capture in a heuristic definition: "interpretation" is "acceptable and approximating translation."[2] Each term here provokes additional questions: (1) Approximating *what*? (2) Translating *how*? and (3) Acceptable *to whom*? For the next few pages, we can use these questions to organize our discussion of interpretation and work toward a clearer understanding of its rhetorical aspects.

INTERPRETATION

Approximating *what*? Translation is always an approximation, which is to say that interpretation is always directed. It is always an approximation of something; it is always directed *toward* something: situations, actions, gestures, graffiti, poems, novels, dreams, etc. Such objects of interpretation we can call "texts." Ultimately anything can be viewed as a text, anything can be interpreted: walls, letters on walls, even poems about letters on wall, such as this one by Emily Dickinson:

> Belshazzar had a Letter—
> He never had but one—
> Belshazzar's Correspondent
> Concluded and begun
> In that immortal Copy
> The Conscience of us all
> Can read without its Glasses
> On Revelation's Wall—

If we think of interpreting as the translation of texts, then this is clearly a text requiring translation. In fact, here we have two texts in need of interpreting: Dickinson's poem and the "Letter . . . on Revelation's Wall" to which the poem refers. Just as the words of the "Letter" are missing, so too are some of the usual textual markers in the poem, like traditional

---

[2] See my *Interpretive Conventions: The Reader in the Study of American Fiction* (Ithaca, 1982), p. 144.

punctuation. Dickinson's idiosyncratic dashes do give us some guidance but not much.

The poem itself translates a biblical story. In chapter 5 of the Book of Daniel, Belshazzar, king of the Chaldeans, holds a feast using sacred vessels taken from the Jewish temple at Jerusalem. During the feast, a hand appears and writes on the wall the words "Mene, Mene, Tekel, Upharsin." The king cannot interpret the writing, nor can any of his advisors. The problem of reading, making sense of texts, thus becomes foregrounded in the story. Daniel is summoned for help, and he ends up interpreting the "Letter" from the "Correspondent," God: "This is the interpretation of the thing: Mene, God hath numbered thy kingdom, and finished it. Tekel, Thou art weighed in the balances, and art found wanting. Peres, Thy kingdom is divided, and given to the Medes and Persians."

The three words written on the wall refer literally to three measures of weight: a mina, a shekel, and two half minas. Daniel interprets the message by punning off these words: the first resembles a Hebraic verb meaning "numbered," the second "weighed," and the third "to divide." He uses these verbal puns to interpret the message as an accusation and a prophecy. And in the chapter's final lines the prophecy of punishment is indeed fulfilled: "In that night was Belshazzar the king of the Chaldeans slain. And Darius the Median took the kingdom." Here we have an interpretation made in the context of political oppression and presented as a consequence of the oppressor's moral iniquity: Israel had been conquered, the Jews enslaved, and now their religious vessels desecrated. The reading of the wall-writing both advertises the king's crime and announces his punishment.[3]

It is possible that Dickinson meant her poem to serve as a similar announcement. Adding the inscription, "Suggested by our Neighbor," she sent it to her brother, probably after the 1879 Lothrop scandal in Amherst. This local affair involved newspaper reports of a father's physical cruelty to his daughter and resulted in a libel suit filed against the *Springfield Republican* by Reverend C. D. Lothrop, the accused father. The court found against Lothrop in April, and Dickinson may have been commemorating the occasion with this poem. From this biographical perspective, the poem refers to the judgment made by the court, which found Lothrop guilty of patriarchal oppression.[4]

[3] For the biblical story and its exegesis, see "The Book of Daniel" in George A. Buttrick et al., eds., *The Interpreter's Bible* (New York, 1956), vol. 6, pp. 418–33.
[4] For the texts of Dickinson's poems quoted in this chapter, see *The Poems of Emily Dickinson*, ed. Thomas H. Johnson, 3 vols. (Cambridge, Mass., 1958). On the Lothrop trial, see

More generally, Dickinson's poem takes the biblical tale and makes it into an allegory for the conscience "of us all," through which God points out and warns us about our sins, giving each of us our own private "Letter." This allegorizing of the poem translates the literary text, which itself translates a biblical story into a poem. Just as the poem approximates— is directed toward—the Biblical story, so too does my interpretation approximate the poem.

Now there are various ways to take the question—What does interpretation approximate?—and develop it into a hermeneutic theory, a general account of how readers make sense of texts. For example, we could say that the words of my reading approximately translate those of the poem and that Daniel's words approximately translate those on the wall. Such a formalist theory could go on to claim that what determines our interpretations is what they approximate, the words on the page. A different theoretical approach argues that what is approximately translated—for example, by Dickinson's reader and by Daniel—is, ultimately, the author's intention. Such an intentionalist theory could go on to claim that interpretations are constrained by the intention behind or in the words.[5] Dickinson in the poem and God in the letter intended a meaning that the interpreter must decipher to read the text correctly. Both formalist and intentionalist theories attempt to provide a foundation for constraining the interpretive relationship between reader and text. Often, such theories not only claim to *describe* how interpretation takes place but to *prescribe* how it should take place. These foundationalist theories present themselves as both general accounts of making sense and specific guides to correct interpretations. Antifoundationalism charges that such philosophical guarantees are theoretically incoherent or otherwise problematic and fail to make good on their claims in actual interpretive practice.[6]

Jay Leyda, *The Years and Hours of Emily Dickinson* (New Haven, 1960), vol. 2, esp. pp. 245–50, 257–59, 310.

[5] On formalist and intentionalist theories, see Section II of Sanford Levinson and Steven Mailloux, eds., *Interpreting Law and Literature* (Evanston, Ill., 1988), esp. pp. 37–42.

[6] Tom Rockmore provides a working definition of "foundationalism" and usefully unpacks its constitutive tropes: "Foundationalism" refers to "the assumption that 'there are secure foundations, that is a firm, unshakable basis, on which to erect any edifice of knowledge.' Knowledge, from this angle of vision, is understood as like a building or structure that reposes directly on a conceptual underpinning. For both a building and the theory of knowledge, if the underpinnings of the edifice can be made secure, then nothing can shake the higher stories" (Rockmore, introduction to *Antifoundationalism Old and New*, ed. Rockmore and Beth J. Singer [Philadelphia, 1992], p. 6). For other recent accounts of foundationalism and antifoundationalism, see Evan Simpson, ed., *Anti-Foundationalism and Practical Reasoning: Conversations between Hermeneutics and Analysis* (Edmonton, Alta., 1987); my

Translating *how?* Our second question moves away from the *object* of interpretation—the text and its sense—to the *activity* of interpreting—the process of sense-making. In reading the Dickinson poem above, I provided two kinds of interpretive approaches, both grounded in a theory of author's intention: historicizing and allegorizing. In the former approach, I suggested that Dickinson intended to refer specifically to Rev. Lothrop getting a well-deserved public humiliation. In the latter, I suggested that Dickinson intended a more universal message about the conscience of us all. It is not necessary to choose between these two complementary meanings, but it is important to recognize the contrasting methods used to arrive at these different interpretations. In historicizing I used a strategy of placing the text in the historical context of its production. In allegorizing I followed a strategy that assumes poetry can refer to a second, more universal level of meaning beyond its particular historical reference. These reading strategies or interpretive conventions provide a way of describing the process of interpretation rather than its textual object. They are ways of characterizing how interpretive translation takes place. They emphasize what the reader contributes to interpretation rather than what the text gives the reader to interpret.[7]

We have now seen displayed several different strategies for interpreting texts. For example, Daniel uses puns or verbal resemblances to read the writing on the king's wall, and I earlier used etymologies to explore meanings for "interpretation" itself. Methods or strategies of making sense are associated with various theories of how interpretation does or should take place. Above I connected historicizing and allegorizing a text's meaning with intentionalist theories of interpretation. Punning and etymologizing are as often associated with formalist theories of interpretation as they are with intentionalist approaches. All these strategies—historicizing, allegorizing, punning, and using etymologies—can be restated as rules for correct interpretation. That is, certain interpretive conventions become in certain contexts the privileged way of making sense of texts. Identifying puns may be acceptable for interpreting ancient and contemporary graffiti but not for reading constitutions. Allegorizing may be appropriate for poetry and scripture but not for legislated statutes. For these supposedly more straightforward legal texts, the-

---

Rhetorical Power (Ithaca, 1989), chap. 1; and Hugh J. Silverman, ed., *Questioning Foundations: Truth/Subjectivity/Culture* (New York, 1993).

[7] See Jonathan Culler, *Structuralist Poetics* (Ithaca, 1975); Mailloux, *Interpretive Conventions*; and Peter J. Rabinowitz, *Before Reading: Narrative Conventions and the Politics of Interpretation* (Ithaca, 1987).

ories of *neutral principles* are often proposed as ways to guarantee that interpreters resist more literary methods of making sense.[8]

Theories of neutral principles posit rules for guaranteeing correct interpretations, e.g., formalist rules for looking at "the words on the page" or intentionalist rules for respecting authorial purposes. These rules or interpretive principles are presented as neutral in the sense that they are viewed as capable of being applied in a disinterested manner safe from personal idiosyncrasy or political bias. Antifoundationalism rejects the possibility of such "neutral principles" and questions whether constitutions are in fact inherently more straightforward than literary texts and whether interpretive theories can actually constrain readings or avoid political entanglements. To approach these issues more closely, let us now turn to our third question: Acceptable *to whom?*

In *Adventures of Huckleberry Finn* the boy narrator and Jim, the runaway slave, are separated in the fog while traveling down the Mississippi River. Despairing after a night-long search, Jim gives Huck up for dead and, exhausted, falls into a troubled sleep. Meanwhile, Huck finds his way back to the raft, and, after Jim awakes, Huck plays a rather insensitive trick on his companion, convincing him that the pain and horrors of the night before never really happened. It was all just a dream. Jim then says "he must start in and ' 'terpret' it, because it was sent for a warning." After Jim presents a wild translation of the dream that wasn't a dream, Huck tries to clinch the joke by responding: "Oh, well, that's all interpreted well enough, as far as it goes, Jim . . . but what does *these* things stand for?" as he points to the leaves, rubbish, and smashed oar, all evidence of the previous night's catastrophe. Now one way to view Jim's dream interpretation is to see it as a rather laughable misreading. This is Huck's view and the view he wants his readers to share so that they get the joke on Jim.

But Huck's request for another interpretation, not of the dream but of the proof that there was no dream, produces a more serious response that makes Huck's joke backfire.

> Jim looked at the trash, and then looked at me, and back at the trash again . . . [H]e looked at me steady, without ever smiling, and says:
> "What do dey stan' for? I's gwyne to tell you. When I got all wore out wid work, en wid de callin' for you, en went to sleep, my heart wuz mos' broke bekase you wuz los', en I didn' k'yer no mo' what become er me en de raf'. En when I wake up en fine you back agin, all safe en soun',

---

[8] Herbert Wechsler, "Toward Neutral Principles of Constitutional Law," *Harvard Law Review* 73 (1959): 1–35.

de tears come en I could a got down on my knees en kiss' yo' foot I's so thankful. En all you wuz thinkin 'bout wuz how you could make a fool uv ole Jim wid a lie. Dat truck dah is *trash*; en trash is what people is dat puts dirt on de head er dey fren's en makes 'em ashamed."

If we saw Jim's dream interpretation as a misreading, we certainly see nothing wrong with his allegorical reading of the trash. We get the point and so does Huck, as he writes that Jim then "got up slow, and walked to the wigwam, and went in there, without saying anything but that. But that was enough. It made me feel so mean I could almost kissed *his* foot to get him to take it back." Twain turns the incident into another episode in Huck's struggle with his racist upbringing when he has the boy write further: "It was fifteen minutes before I could work myself up to go and humble myself to a nigger—but I done it, and I warn't ever sorry for it afterwards, neither."[9] Interpreting this passage, readers recognize how Huck's apology undercuts his continuing racial prejudice, how his respect and affection for Jim work to undermine his society's ideology of white supremacy.

If you agree that Jim misread the "dream" but convincingly interpreted the "trash," if you agree with my reading of these readings and with my interpretation of the final passage, then we are agreeing on what to count as a correct interpretation for these various texts. Correct interpretations are those that are considered accurate, valid, acceptable. But acceptable to whom? One answer is suggested by another Dickinson poem:

> Much Madness is divinest Sense—
> To a discerning Eye—
> Much Sense—the starkest Madness—
> 'Tis the Majority
> In this, as All, prevail—
> Assent—and you are sane—
> Demur—you're straightway dangerous—
> And handled with a Chain—

This poem is about how correct interpretations are established, how sense-making is defined as right or wrong, sense or nonsense, sanity or madness. Read literally, it simply states that sense or meaning is in the eye of

---

[9] Mark Twain, *Adventures of Huckleberry Finn*, ed. Walter Blair and Victor Fischer (Berkeley, Calif., 1985), pp. 104–5. See my *Rhetorical Power*, chap. 3, for an extended rhetorical analysis of Twain's novel as an ideological performance within post-Reconstruction debates over "the Negro problem"; also see Peter Messent, "Racial Politics in *Huckleberry Finn*," chap. 5 of his *Mark Twain* (New York, 1997), pp. 86–109.

the beholder, rather than in the object beheld. The poem suggests further that the majority of interpreters determine what counts as sense. Of course, the point of the poem does not end there. Dickinson is not simply describing the conditions of "correct" interpreting—majority rules—but is sarcastically protesting against that fact. Thus the poem rewrites the question—To whom are correct interpretations acceptable?—as a problem about the politics of interpretation, about a reading's status within the power relations of a historical community. These questions point us away from the exchange between interpreter and text and toward that between interpreter and interpreter—that is, from the hermeneutic problem of how text and reader interact to the *rhetorical* problem of how interpreters interact with other interpreters in trying to argue for or against different meanings. For rhetorical hermeneutics, these two problems are ultimately inseparable.

When we move from foundationalist theories about reading texts to the rhetorical politics of interpretive disputes, we do not abandon the issues raised by my original three heuristic questions. In one sense, we will simply be broadening our area of concern. When we focus only on the text, an author's intention, or a reader's interpretive conventions, as we have done, there is a strong tendency to view interpretation as a private reading experience involving only an independent text (and author) and an individual reader. Many foundationalist theories give in to this temptation and compound the mistake by completely ignoring the sociopolitical context in which interpretation takes place. By focusing on interpretive rhetoric in later chapters, we will see more exactly how interpretation functions repeatedly as a politically interested act of persuasion.

In the cases of reading discussed earlier, I hinted at this politics of interpretation whenever I noted how an interpretive act took place within the context of power relations in a historical community. For example, we saw how Daniel's reading of the wall-writing functioned within a national situation of political oppression and then how Dickinson's poem translated this biblical story into a new context involving the politics of family and gender. Similarly, Jim's dream interpretation and Huck's reactions play a part in Mark Twain's commentary on the politics of race in nineteenth-century U.S. culture. In each of these cases, interpretation takes place in a political context and each interpretive act relates directly to the power relations (whether of nation, family, gender, class, or race) involved in that context.

However, what is not quite as clear in these examples is how interpretation itself can be politically interested, how claims for a reading are always direct attempts to affect power relations through coercion or persuasion. These effects can be subtle and microscopic as in cases where students ask a teacher to explain a line of poetry and she convinces them to accept a particular reading. The effects become more obvious when there are radical disagreements over interpretations, when the correct reading is in actual dispute. At such times, the least persuasive interpretation loses out. Indeed, in some extreme cases of interpretive controversy, Dickinson seems to be right:

> 'Tis the Majority
> In this, as All, prevail—
> Assent—and you are sane—
> Demur—you're straightway dangerous—
> And handled with a Chain—

Most situations involving interpretive disagreement do not result in such blatant suppression of dissent. However, a poem protesting a majority's tyranny over an individual dissenter does foreground what is always the case: any interpretive dispute involves political interests and consequences.

Old news in some intellectual quarters, such general claims remain empty without detailed illustrations of how they apply in specific historical contexts. In the next chapter, I provide an extended example of this rhetorical politics: pro- and antislavery interpretations of the Christian Bible in the 1840s. This interpretive dispute involved not only readings of Scripture but also theories for reading it. We can conclude our brief look at "interpretation" by quoting some of this hermeneutic theory from Reverend William Graham's *The Contrast; or, The Bible and Abolitionism: an Exegetical Argument*:

> Abolitionism assumes to demonstrate . . . that the relation of master and slave is a gross sin—a violation of the laws of our being. From this, it follows, by necessary consequence, that no book authorizing this relation can come from God. The Christian Abolitionist denies that this relation is authorized by the Bible and adopts a system of exegetical rules that make the Scriptures teach according to his theory.[10]

---

[10] William Graham, *The Contrast; or, The Bible and Abolitionism: An Exegetical Argument* (Cincinnati, 1844), pp. 39–40.

Instead of using "the strict laws of interpretation" (40), abolitionists adopt a hermeneutic theory to suit their political ideology, and in so doing they reject the obvious meanings of the Bible. For these biased readers, scriptural evidence supporting slavery is interpreted out of existence. For them,

> Abraham's "servants, bought with his money," are religious converts, and *eved* and *doulos*, instead of meaning slave, mean in fact only hired servant. The effect of such a mode of interpreting the Scriptures is obvious. Men learn to believe that the Bible is an unintelligible book. It ceases to speak to the heart and conscience with divine authority. The writing upon the wall may be from God, but the impression is according to their confidence in the interpreter. (40)

Having the wrong hermeneutic theory leads to relativism and interpretive distortion, according to Graham. But, from the perspective of rhetorical hermeneutics, what counts as the right theory, the legitimate "laws of interpretation," is not independent of one's ideological position in the political and religious debates. That is, the biblical interpretation and its hermeneutic justification are part of the same rhetorical configuration. Indeed, a hermeneutic theory provides no guarantees for correctly interpreting Scripture or any other text, though it does provide additional argumentative strategies for making one's case.[11] Doing rhetorical hermeneutics means writing rhetorical histories of such interpretive debates, focusing on the use of theory in rhetorical practice and on the practice of theory in doing history.

Why Rhetorical Hermeneutics?

Rhetorical hermeneutics *uses rhetoric to practice theory by doing history*. The rest of the chapter explains why and how this is so. The present section outlines the rhetorical context of critical theory and academic disciplines in the 1980s to account for why a rhetorical hermeneutics was proposed in the first place, and the final section describes its major theoretical claims by responding to specific objections to its arguments.

Rhetorical hermeneutics is the theoretical practice that results from the intersection between rhetorical pragmatism and the study of cultural rhetoric. Thus, one way of explaining rhetorical hermeneutics is to define

---

[11] See my *Rhetorical Power*, "Conclusion: The ABM Treaty Interpretation Dispute."

the latter two modes of inquiry more fully and then describe how the overlap between them constitutes a rhetorical approach to specific historical acts of cultural interpretation.[12]

In the 1980s cultural studies became an influential outgrowth of several interdisciplinary projects in the human sciences. In his mid-decade essay "What Is Cultural Studies Anyway?" Richard Johnson began his answer, "Cultural studies is now a movement or a network. It has its own degrees in several colleges and universities and its own journals and meetings. It exercises a large influence on academic disciplines, especially on English studies, sociology, media and communication studies, linguistics and history." Johnson went on to address the problems of institutionalization and definition, offering his own view of the interdisciplinary field: "For me cultural studies is about the historical forms of consciousness or subjectivity, or the subjective forms we live by, or, in a rather perilous compression, perhaps a reduction, the subjective side of social relations."[13] Other quite different definitions of cultural studies also circulated in the eighties, but a certain consensus began to emerge. As Vincent Leitch commented near the end of the decade, "During the eighties, advocates of cultural studies influenced by poststructuralist thought advanced the argument that a pure pre-discursive, pre-cultural reality or socioeconomic infrastructure did not exist: cultural discourse constituted the ground of social existence as well as personal identity. Given this 'poetic,' the task of cultural studies was to study the conventions and representations fostered by the whole set of cultural discourses."[14]

[12] I return here to the definition of "interpretation" presented in Chap. 1—"the practice of establishing textual meaning"—and note again that I am using the term "hermeneutics" in its broad sense to refer to "theories of interpretation." A powerful influence on recent hermeneutics has been the German hermeneutical tradition, ably described in Richard E. Palmer, *Hermeneutics: Interpretation Theory in Schleiermacher, Dilthey, Heidegger, and Gadamer* (Evanston, Ill., 1969). Also, working within Heideggerian hermeneutics and very influential on my own rhetorical hermeneutics is Hubert L. Dreyfus, *What Computers Can't Do: The Limits of Artificial Intelligence*, rev. ed. (New York, 1979); also see Dreyfus and Paul Rabinow, *Michel Foucault: Beyond Structuralism and Hermeneutics*, 2d ed. (Chicago, 1983). For several more recent discussions of topics related to rhetorical hermeneutics, see George Pullman, ed., "Reconfiguring the Relation of Rhetoric/Hermeneutics," special issue of *Studies in the Literary Imagination* 28 (fall 1995); and Walter Jost and Michael J. Hyde, eds., *Rhetoric and Hermeneutics in Our Time* (New Haven, Conn., 1997).

[13] Richard Johnson, "What Is Cultural Studies Anyway?" *Social Text*, no. 16 (winter 1986/87): 38, 43.

[14] Vincent B. Leitch, *American Literary Criticism from the Thirties to the Eighties* (New York, 1988), p. 404. For other overviews of cultural studies in the 1980s, see Judith Newton and Deborah Rosenfelt, eds., *Feminist Criticism and Social Change: Sex, Class, and Race in Literature and Culture* (New York, 1985); Tania Modleski, ed., *Studies in Entertainment: Critical Approaches to Mass Culture* (Bloomington, Ind., 1986); Cary Nelson and Lawrence Grossberg, eds., *Marxism and the Interpretation of Culture* (Urbana, Ill., 1988); Lynn Hunt, ed., *The New*

Cultural studies as an academic movement had varying effects on disciplines in the humanities and social sciences. In English departments, for example, cultural studies helped expand the discipline's subject matter to include nonliterary as well as literary texts and also cultural genres such as film and television and social practices more generally. In the new English and Textual Studies major at Syracuse University, a predominantly cultural studies approach replaced the usual coverage model of literary historical periods. Instead of focusing exclusively on literature organized into periods such as Medieval, Renaissance, Victorian, and so on, the ETS major takes as its subject matter a variety of cultural texts and organizes their study through different modes of inquiry—historical, theoretical, and political. Courses offered during the first full year of the ETS curriculum (1990–91) included in the history group Introduction to Reception Aesthetics (Cases in American Culture), Introduction to Literary History—1700 to Contemporary (English Romantic Writers), and Studies in Periodization and Chronology (The American 1890s); in the theory group, Introduction to Semiotic Theories of Representation (Film Theory), Studies in Hermeneutics (Interpreting Law and Literature), Studies in Psychological Theories of Representation (Feminism and Psychoanalysis), Studies in Semiotics (Hearing and Textuality), Studies in Theory of Genre (Epistolarity and the Novel), and Studies in Cultural Theories of Representation (Eurocentrism, Postcoloniality, Revolution); and in the politics group, Introduction to Feminisms (Politics, Culture, Theory), Studies in Feminisms (Gender and the Culture of Television), and Studies in Sexualities (Power, Gender, and Shakespeare).[15] Most of these sample courses indicate the influence of recent cultural studies on the new Syracuse major and suggest some of the ways that an interdisciplinary cultural studies movement can change the shape of a traditional discipline.

A specifically *rhetorical* form of cultural studies begins by rethinking this contemporary interdisciplinary approach in terms of a rhetorical framework with a vocabulary of terms such as "cultural conversation," "textual effects," "tropes," "arguments," etc. In such a reconceptualization, "culture" gets defined as "the network of rhetorical practices that

---

Cultural History (Berkeley, Calif., 1989); H. Aram Veeser, ed., *The New Historicism* (New York, 1989); and Patrick Brantlinger, *Crusoe's Footprints: Cultural Studies in Britain and America* (New York, 1990).

[15] For full descriptions of these courses and the ETS major, see *The English Newsletter: Undergraduate News from the English Department, Syracuse University* 1, no. 1 (March 1990) and no. 2 (November 1990). I discuss the production and reception of this major in Chap. 7.

are extensions and manipulations of other practices—social, political, and economic."[16] Rhetoric is not simply an expression or reflection of "deeper" historical forces, whether psychological, social, political, or economic. Rather, rhetorical practices are (at least partly) constitutive of these other historical categories. A rhetorically oriented cultural studies, then, describes and explains past and present configurations of rhetorical practices as they affect each other and as they extend and manipulate the social practices, political structures, and material circumstances in which they are embedded at particular historical moments.

A cultural rhetoric studies might, for example, interpret the function of a trope like "reading as eating" within a particular historical community during a specific historical period. How, for instance, was the trope tied to arguments about children reading fiction in the United States during the second half of the nineteenth century? How did the tropes and arguments about reading fiction relate to cultural narratives about "moral degeneracy" and "juvenile delinquency"? How did this cultural rhetoric of reading (its tropes, arguments, and narratives) circulate within different social institutions such as the family, the factory, the church, the primary school, the state reformatory, and the university and within different discourses such as popular novels, religious treatises, professional studies of child rearing, newspaper editorials and literary reviews, and political speeches about censorship? How did the figurative meaning of such tropes as "reading as eating" or "critical reading as mental discipline" get literalized in proposals to establish physical exercise classes alongside required courses in studying literature within state reformatories for juvenile delinquents in the 1880s? And how did this cultural rhetoric of reading get deployed differently according to gender in children's literature and in reformatories for male and female adolescents?[17]

---

[16] Mailloux, *Rhetorical Power*, p. 165.

[17] See Chap. 6, below, on the cultural rhetoric of "eating books" and (mis)using fiction. There are many related examples of rhetorically oriented cultural studies in such disciplines as symbolic anthropology, speech communication, cultural history, and interpretive sociology, and one could cite a growing number of proposals and examples of related approaches from contemporary literary studies influenced by poststructuralist theory. The genealogies of Michel Foucault and Edward Said stand behind some of the most interesting studies of cultural rhetoric—see Foucault, *Discipline and Punish: The Birth of the Prison*, trans. Alan Sheridan (New York, 1977), and *Power/Knowledge: Selected Interviews and Other Writings, 1972–1977*, ed. Colin Gordon (New York, 1980); Said, *Orientalism* (New York, 1978), and *The World, the Text, and the Critic* (Cambridge, Mass., 1983); and my *Rhetorical Power*, chap. 5. And, of course, there's always Kenneth Burke; for a useful recent collection, see Burke, *On Symbols and Society*, ed. Joseph R. Gusfield (Chicago, 1989). For additional bibliography and discussion, see Thomas Rosteck, "Cultural Studies and Rhetorical Stud-

Questions of this kind focus most projects in cultural rhetoric studies and put into play such working definitions of rhetoric as "the political effectivity of trope and argument in culture."[18]

Rhetorical hermeneutics is a form of cultural rhetoric studies that takes as its topic specific historical acts of interpretation within their cultural contexts. But before expanding this description, I need to present rhetorical hermeneutics as a theoretical stance toward interpretation, a position related to the rhetorical pragmatism introduced in the previous chapters. There are several ways of characterizing rhetorical pragmatism of the 1980s: a recent form of antifoundationalist historicism; a poststructuralist instance of sophistic rhetoric; a rhetoricized version of contemporary neopragmatism. The last of these descriptions is especially useful for my current purposes.

Arguably, Richard Rorty was the most influential neopragmatist during the eighties. His *Philosophy and the Mirror of Nature* set the stage for a significant revival of North American pragmatism in philosophy and other related disciplines.[19] Here I will use one of Rorty's essays as a synecdoche for the rhetorical aspects of his whole anti-Philosophical project.

To provide another rhetorical perspective on and from neopragmatism, we can start with a quotation from early in Rorty's article "Is Derrida a Transcendental Philosopher?":

> On my view, the only thing that can displace an intellectual world is another intellectual world—a new alternative, rather than an argument against an old alternative. The idea that there is some neutral ground on which to mount an argument against something as big as 'logocentrism' strikes me as one more logocentric hallucination. I do not think that demonstrations of 'internal incoherence' or of 'presuppositional relationships' ever do much to disabuse us of bad old ideas or institutions. Disabusing gets done, instead, by offering us sparkling new ideas, or utopian visions of glorious new institutions. The result of genuinely original thought, on my view, is not so much to refute or subvert our

---

ies," *Quarterly Journal of Speech* 81 (August 1995): 386–421; and Rosteck, ed., *At the Intersection: Cultural Studies and Rhetorical Studies* (New York, 1998).

[18] Mailloux, *Rhetorical Power*, p. xii.

[19] As explained in Chap. 2, above. See Richard Rorty, *Philosophy and the Mirror of Nature* (Princeton, 1979); and for recent commentary and detailed bibliographies, see Alan R. Malachowski, ed., *Reading Rorty: Critical Responses to "Philosophy and the Mirror of Nature" (and Beyond)* (Oxford, 1990), and Herman J. Saatkamp, Jr., ed., *Rorty and Pragmatism: The Philosopher Responds to His Critics* (Nashville, 1995).

previous beliefs as to help us forget them by giving us a substitute for them.[20]

This passage strikes me as an especially rich example of rhetorical pragmatism. Among the rhetorical points made are two on argumentation that Rorty makes again and again throughout his writings in the eighties. First is the antifoundationalist point that there is no transcendental ground, no Archimedian standpoint beyond all argumentation, beyond all rhetoric, from which truth-claims can be adjudicated. And second is the nominalist, Wittgensteinian point that propositional argumentation does not bring about persuasion or conversion between two different paradigms or language games.

In developing the first, antifoundationalist claim, Rorty rejects the "specifically *transcendental* project—a project of answering some question of the form 'what are the conditions of the possibility of . . . ?'—of, for example, experience, self-consciousness, language or philosophy itself." Rorty admits "that asking and answering that question is, indeed, the mark of a distinct genre"—foundationalist philosophy—but argues that "it is a thoroughly self-deceptive question. The habit of posing it—asking for noncausal, nonempirical, nonhistorical conditions—is the distinctive feature" of the Kantian tradition. "The trouble with the question is that it looks like a 'scientific' one, as if we knew how to debate the relative merits of alternative answers, just as we know how to debate alternative answers to questions about the conditions for the *actuality* of various things (e.g., political changes, quasars, psychoses). But it is not" (210).

Instead of continuing the Kantian foundationalist tradition in philosophy, Rorty wants to redescribe the rhetorical strategies and purposes of this philosophical genre, abandon some of its projects, and move philosophy in a different direction with new self-definitions. As traditionally viewed within the genre, transcendental projects are treated as if one could argue over their alternative proposals in some common vocabulary:

> If one thinks of writers like Hegel, Heidegger, and Derrida as digging down to successively deeper levels of noncausal conditions—as scientists dig down to ever deeper levels of causal conditions (molecules behind tables, atoms behind molecules, quarks behind atoms . . .)—then the hapless and tedious metaphilosophical question "How can we tell

[20] Rorty, "Is Derrida a Transcendental Philosopher?" *Yale Journal of Criticism* 2 (spring 1989): 208–9; further references to this essay are given in the text.

when we have hit bottom?" is bound to arise. More important, so will the question "Within what language are we to lay out arguments demonstrating (or even just making plausible) that we have *correctly* identified these conditions?" (212).

When and how can the philosophical conversation end and how could we recognize the conclusion? "The latter question causes no great embarrassment for physicists, since they can say in advance what they want to get out of their theorizing. But it *should* embarrass people concerned with the question of what *philosophical* vocabulary to use, rather than with the question of what vocabulary will help us accomplish some specific purpose (e.g., splitting the atom, curing cancer, persuading the populace)" (212). Rorty argues that there is no transcendental ground with a common vocabulary from which to carry out a comparison between theories of ontological conditions of possibility and that we should be thinking of vocabularies as tools to accomplish rhetorical purposes instead of searching for the ultimate vocabulary beyond all others.

The point of foundationalist philosophy is to end all conversation by proposing the final argument, the all-encompassing system, the ground of grounds. Some think Derrida has found this with notions like *différance*, but Rorty sees such notions as "merely abbreviations for the familiar Peircean-Wittgensteinian anti-Cartesian thesis that meaning is a function of context, and that there is no theoretical barrier to an endless sequence of recontextualizations" (212). That is, foundationalist theory (or any other kind) cannot guarantee an end to the sequence of counterarguments. There is always the possibility of arguing against, of proposing new tropes, of offering a conflicting story, of putting forward a different context. Though, we might add, there is not always the probability that a particular rhetorical move of this kind will occur or will work within historically situated debates. Often a story becomes standard, an argument goes unchallenged, an ideology comes to dominate a historical community, and in those rhetorical contexts, the sequence of recontextualizations temporarily stops. Rorty's point is that no foundationalist theory can ever guarantee permanent closure to debate or ensure beforehand even a temporary consensus.

For Rorty, it would be better to redescribe transcendental philosophical projects not as making arguments that can be adjudicated in a common vocabulary but as proposing different worlds with different rhetorical structures. "For my purposes, the important place to draw a line is not between philosophy and non-philosophy but rather between topics

which we know how to argue about and those we do not. It is the line between the attempt to be objective—to get a consensus on what we should
believe—and a willingness to abandon consensus in the hope of trans-
figuration" (210). In distinguishing between "argumentative problem-
solvers like Aristotle and Russell and oracular world-disclosers like Plato
and Hegel" (211), Rorty seems to be making the rhetorical point that
we should recognize a distinction between two uses of language: one
(problem-solving) that argues among different positions with a common
or overlapping vocabulary within the same (philosophical) world; and
another (world-disclosing) that cannot argue across different worlds because there is not a common or significantly overlapping vocabulary and
not enough shared argumentative criteria among the different (philosophical) positions, which themselves establish new vocabularies and criteria for problem solving.

This leads to the second point concerning the initial passage quoted
above, which addresses the question of refuting versus forgetting previous beliefs in displacing an intellectual world. Rorty draws a distinction
between the suitability of argumentation within paradigms and the un-
suitability of argumentation between paradigms. We know how to argue
within a paradigm, he says, but we do not know how to argue across different paradigms; and, further, argumentation is completely irrelevant
to changing position from one paradigm to another. I think Rorty here
overstates the rhetorical case. The conversion to a new paradigm is often
dependent upon the weakening of the old, and the weakening of the old
paradigm includes refutation through propositional argumentation. Indeed, the combination of refutation within an old vocabulary and the offering of an attractive new vocabulary is exactly what Rorty himself is so
good at. His rhetorical strategies include both maneuvers.

Rorty at times seems to agree with this point when he writes: "Argumentation requires that the same vocabulary be used in premises and
conclusions—that both be part of the same language-game. Hegelian
Aufhebung is something quite different. It is what happens when we play
elements of an old vocabulary off against each other in order to make us
impatient for a new vocabulary. But that activity is quite different from
playing old beliefs against other old beliefs in an attempt to see which
survives. An existing language-game will provide 'standard rules' for the
latter activity, but *nothing* could provide such rules for the former" (213).
Rorty could be seen as describing here two kinds of propositional argumentation: One that argues for the self-contradiction, incoherence, or
inadequacy of the old vocabulary (pushing us toward the new) and one

that argues for one belief over the other within old vocabularies. It appears that Rorty wants to say that propositional argumentation applies only to the latter activity. But in both instances such argumentation is part of making a case: for a new world or an old belief. In each, argumentation is the means to a rhetorical end, not an end in itself.

Rorty could, I suppose, preserve his point by weakening his claim for a rigid distinction between the two rhetorical activities of problem solving within an old vocabulary and problem problematizing leading to a new vocabulary. That is, solving problems and disclosing a new world are two radically different rhetorical goals, but the means to achieve these goals can share rhetorical strategies, including propositional argumentation. But instead Rorty chooses to emphasize the rhetorical consequences of two very different kinds of philosophy: "We should . . . recognize that the writers usually identified as 'philosophers' include both argumentative problem-solvers like Aristotle and Russell and oracular world-disclosers like Plato and Hegel—both people good at rendering public accounts and people good at leaping in the dark" (211). And he goes on, "I object to the idea that one can be 'rigorous' if one's procedure [as world-discloser] consists in inventing new words for what one is pleased to call 'conditions of possibility' rather than playing sentences using old words off against each other. The latter activity is what I take to constitute argumentation. Poetic world-disclosers like Hegel, Heidegger and Derrida have to pay a price, and part of that price is the inappropriateness to their work of notions like 'argumentation' and 'rigor'" (211). Rorty agrees with Habermas in a "nominalist, Wittgensteinian rejection of the idea that one can be nonpropositional and still be argumentative" (212). Perhaps this is true, but one can be nonpropositional and still be persuasive or rhetorical.

We can end this gloss on Rorty's essay with another of his rhetorical pragmatist points: "The practice of playing sentences off against one another in order to decide what to believe—the practice of argumentation—no more requires a 'ground' than the practice of using one stone to chip pieces off another stone in order to make a spear-point" (217, n. 16). Similarly, we might say that interpretive arguments over texts need no general hermeneutic foundations, no theoretical description of interpretation in general that provides ahistorical prescriptions for achieving correct meanings. Interpretive arguments get their work done within the historical clash of opinion. Even from this brief sketch of Rorty's views and their implications, it is easy to see why rhetoricians in speech communication, literary studies, and other disciplines have cited his neopragmatism as further evidence of the (latest) return of rhetoric to the humanities.[21]

Rhetorical hermeneutics is the intersection of rhetorical pragmatism and cultural rhetoric studies. Just as rhetorical pragmatism rejects the notion of foundationalist philosophy, rhetorical hermeneutics attempts to move critical theory from general theories about the interpretive process to rhetorical histories of specific interpretive acts.[22] As hermeneutic theory becomes rhetorical history, the focus moves from pragmatist antifoundationalism to studies of cultural rhetoric. But in rhetorical hermeneutics the claim is that a rhetorical analysis of a particular historical act of interpretation *counts as* a specific piece of rhetorically pragmatic theorizing about interpretation. Thus, rhetorical hermeneutics uses rhetoric to practice theory by doing history.

Such a project takes an historical act of interpretation—for example, the Concord (Massachusetts) Library's banning of *Adventures of Huckleberry Finn* in March 1885—and attempts to do a rhetorical analysis of the

[21] See, for example, Janet Horne, "Rhetoric after Rorty," *Western Journal of Speech Communication* 53 (summer 1989): 247–59; Robert E. Smith III, "Reconsidering Richard Rorty," *Rhetoric Society Quarterly* 19 (fall 1989): 349–64; John Trimbur and Mara Holt, "Richard Rorty: Philosophy without Foundations," in *The Philosophy of Discourse: The Rhetorical Turn in Twentieth-Century Thought*, ed. Chip Sills and George H. Jensen (Portsmouth, N.H., 1992), vol. 1, pp. 70–94; and essays in Steven Mailloux, ed., *Rhetoric, Sophistry, Pragmatism* (Cambridge, 1995). My own rhetorical pragmatism has been significantly influenced by the work of Stanley Fish, Walter Michaels, and Steven Knapp. See my *Rhetorical Power*, chap. 6; Fish, *Doing What Comes Naturally: Change, Rhetoric, and the Practice of Theory in Literary and Legal Studies* (Durham, N.C., 1989); and W. J. T. Mitchell, ed., *Against Theory: Literary Studies and the New Pragmatism* (Chicago, 1985).

[22] I will not here analyze in detail the historical connections between epistemology (theories of knowledge) and hermeneutics (theories of interpretation), but only say that the two enterprises have traditionally figured their projects in structurally similar ways and have developed analogous arguments within their theoretical debates; for example, both enterprises ask theoretical questions about a relation between subjects and objects (knower and world, reader and text), have proposed variations on realist and idealist answers to these questions, and have framed those answers in similar vocabularies of conditions or constraints (in terms, for example, of what counts as true knowledge about reality or what counts as a correct interpretation of a text). For hermeneutic treatments of the relation between knowledge and interpretation, see Hans-Georg Gadamer, *Truth and Method*, 2d ed., rev. trans. Joel Weinsheimer and Donald G. Marshall (New York, 1989), pp. 220–24, 254–64, 505–6; and E. D. Hirsch, Jr., *The Aims of Interpretation* (Chicago, 1976), pp. 146–58. Also see debates in epistemic rhetoric: Robert L. Scott, "On Viewing Rhetoric as Epistemic: Ten Years Later," *Central States Speech Journal* 27 (winter 1976): 258–66; Richard A. Cherwitz and James W. Hikins, *Communication and Knowledge: An Investigation in Rhetorical Epistemology* (Columbia, S.C., 1986); and Robert L. Scott, "Rhetoric Is Epistemic: What Difference Does That Make?" in *Defining the New Rhetorics*, ed. Theresa Enos and Stuart C. Brown (Newbury Park, Calif., 1993), pp. 120–36. Recent obituaries for epistemic rhetoric strike me as a bit premature.

cultural conversation in which that act participated. One might investigate why the issue of the "Negro Problem" played no role in the 1880s reception of Mark Twain's novel, a novel that twentieth-century readers have found deeply implicated in the cultural politics of race. How did Samuel Clemens's public persona as a humorist affect interpretations and evaluations of *Huckleberry Finn*; that is, in what way is any 1885 reading of the novel more significant as an event in the evolving cultural reception of Mark Twain than as a part of some purely literary reception of *Huckleberry Finn* (whatever that would mean)? How was the Concord Library committee's reading of the novel connected to debates over the "Bad Boy Boom" of the mid-1880s, anxieties over gang juvenile delinquency and the negative effects of reading crime stories and dime novels?[23] For rhetorical hermeneutics, this reception study provides an instance of interpretive theory as a form of rhetorical history. Unlike foundationalist theories, rhetorical hermeneutics focuses on the rhetorical histories of specific interpretive acts and makes no transcendental claims for its theoretical observations and the historical narratives it tells about interpretation.

OBJECTIONS TO RHETORICAL HERMENEUTICS

Every theory is defined quite specifically by the tropes and arguments it uses to state and defend its claims. Rhetorical hermeneutics is no exception. In this section I place the arguments of rhetorical hermeneutics in relation to those of its best critics as a way of further explaining its theoretical positions.

In "History and Epistemology: The Example of *The Turn of the Screw*," Paul Armstrong mounts a vigorous critique of rhetorical hermeneutics as part of his own proposed epistemology of interpretive conflict.[24] Armstrong begins by presenting a fair summary of the rhetorical turn in hermeneutics: "Some contemporary critics have suggested that history offers a way out of the impasses of epistemology. . . . [I]f the inability of epistemology to legislate correctness means that different communities

---

[23] See my *Rhetorical Power*, chap. 4. For a rhetorical analysis of the novel's later reception history, see Jonathan Arac, *"Huckleberry Finn" as Idol and Target: The Functions of Criticism in Our Time* (Madison, Wis., 1997).

[24] Paul B. Armstrong, "History and Epistemology: The Example of *The Turn of the Screw*," *New Literary History* 19 (winter 1988): 693–712; rpt. Armstrong, *Conflicting Readings: Variety and Validity in Interpretation* (Chapel Hill, N.C., 1990), pp. 89–108. Further references are to the book version, cited as *Conflict* in the main text.

can regard different kinds of argumentation as persuasive, then perhaps we should study concretely the various rhetorical practices in which interpreters have engaged instead of attempting to define absolutely what a right reading must look like. This maneuver would turn epistemology into a historical issue by asking how ways of seeing are institutionalized in discursive practices" (*Conflict* 89). So far so good. But then Armstrong adds that for such a theory "historical study seems to offer a means of avoiding irreconcilable epistemological disputes."Armstrong then (rightly) asserts his strong opposition to any "hope" that historical study represents a guaranteed solution to interpretive disagreement (*Conflict* 89–90).

The problem here is that Armstrong has confused foundationalist theories of knowledge (called collectively "epistemology") and historical claims about how knowledges are generated, contested, revised, etc. (generalizations we can call "epistemologies"). That is, rhetorical hermeneutics does call into question the usefulness of disputes within "epistemology" but then itself puts forward histories of conflicts among competing knowledge claims. Rhetorical hermeneutics avoids epistemological debates (e.g., between textual realism and readerly idealism) by setting their questions aside (e.g., refusing to ask "Does the text or the reader determine interpretation?"). But it does not try to avoid "irreconcilable epistemological disputes," as Armstrong asserts; rather, it attempts to take such historical disputes as a rhetorical focus of study. Again: rhetorical hermeneutics rejects foundationalist theories of epistemology which attempt to prescribe correct interpretations in general, but it does not avoid addressing historical debates over particular epistemic claims.

Armstrong similarly confuses foundationalist epistemology with historical epistemologies in his critique of Rorty's neopragmatism. Again he clearly summarizes his opponent's position: Rorty rejects philosophy as the "'most basic' discipline" whose responsibility it is to establish foundations for judging the knowledge-claims of other disciplines.[25] "In a multiple world of conflicting practices of thinking and speaking, it makes no sense to try to promulgate laws for how the mind should work, because to do so would be to propose only another manner of interpreting and talking about the world, not the way to end all ways. Consequently, Rorty advises, in order to come to grips with certain perpetually vexing philosophical problems, one should not try to develop an improved model of mind but should examine the historical record to see how they arose" (*Conflict* 92). Defining "epistemology" as the "project of learning more about what we could know and how we might know it better by

[25] Rorty, *Philosophy and the Mirror of Nature*, p. 132.

studying how our mind worked,"[26] Rorty advocates the abandonment of epistemology as a philosophical project. Here Armstrong strongly disagrees, arguing that "Rorty's call for the demise of epistemology is self-contradictory because a theory of knowledge is implicit in his description of disciplines as diverse, changing conversations" (*Conflict* 92–93).

But again it is a question of what is meant by "epistemology" or "theories of knowledge." Rorty rejects foundationalist theory but not all reflection about knowledge claims. Indeed, as Armstrong points out, Rorty is constantly making rhetorical generalizations and telling conversational stories about how disciplines produce knowledge. Armstrong has simply missed Rorty's theoretical point. Another way of putting this: we can answer Armstrong's charge of self-contradiction against Rorty by using his own analysis of "theory," a term that has "a variety of meanings" (*Conflict* 91). Armstrong notes two current definitions: (1) "'theory' as the general activity of reflecting on the characteristics of literature and the implications of critical practice" and (2) "local 'theories' about the assumptions and aims that should guide interpretation" (*Conflict* 91). The first kind of theory gives us descriptions and the second prescriptions. What Armstrong does not mention is that foundationalist theory (including epistemology) combines these two forms: it attempts to move from general descriptions to specific prescriptions, for example, from how the interpretive process works in general to how it should work in particular to produce correct interpretations. Rorty does not reject theory as reflection on practice, but he does advocate abandoning foundationalist theory in philosophy (epistemology). Thus, Rorty's call for "the demise of [foundationalist] epistemology" does not contradict his continuing concern with questions of knowledge production, his continuing theoretical reflection on the rhetorical practices of disciplines.

I should note, however, that for Rorty "reflection" is a problematic term for characterizing the kind of philosophy he advocates. He writes that "in its unobjectionable sense, 'theory' just means 'philosophy.' One can still have philosophy even after one stops arguing deductively and ceases to ask where the first principles are coming from." That is, even when one rejects foundationalist theory—"the attempt to get outside practice and regulate it" from the ground of transcendental first principles—one can continue to do a form of theory. "I take 'literary theory,' as the term is currently used in America, to be a species of philosophy, an attempt to weave together some texts traditionally labeled 'philosophical'

---

[26] Rorty, *Philosophy and the Mirror of Nature*, p. 137, quoted in Armstrong, *Conflict*, p. 92.

with other texts not so labeled," e.g., poems, novels, literary criticism.[27] Rorty resists characterizing this as a reflective practice, arguing that this philosophical activity "is not exactly what Mailloux calls 'metapractice (practice about practice),' for that term suggests a vertical relationship, in which some practices are at higher levels than others."[28]

Indeed, I would argue (and would seem to agree more with Armstrong than Rorty here) that in certain rhetorical situations, particular practices are on a "higher level" both in the sense that the topic of one practice can be another practice (interpretive disputes as the topic for theoretical practices such as rhetorical hermeneutics and epistemologies of interpretive conflict) *and* in the sense that at particular historical moments certain practices are privileged over others. Perhaps this is just to argue that the trope of spatial levels is still useful in characterizing the rhetorical activity of theoretical practice despite its traditional associations with foundationalist theory.

But in Armstrong's critique there are theoretical issues at stake more significant than whether he understands Rorty's view of epistemology or whether he agrees with my characterization of theory as practice about practice. These issues involve what Armstrong takes to be the major failing of Rorty's neopragmatism and my rhetorical hermeneutics. One issue concerns his questions: "Are there no 'enduring constraints on what can count as knowledge' (*Mirror* 9), as [Rorty] argues, or are there transhistorical tests for validity? Is it sufficient to regard interpretive standards as totally internal to the community, or should we preserve some notion of otherness as the object to which interpreters are responsible and at which their various conversations aim, even if this otherness can vary radically according to how it is construed?" (*Conflict* 93).

To answer these questions, Armstrong does a reception history of Henry James's *Turn of the Screw*. This move from theory to history is exactly what a rhetorical hermeneutics advocates, but Armstrong somehow believes his study refutes rhetorical hermeneutics and rhetorical pragmatism more generally. There are several reasons for this (I think) mistaken conclusion. Armstrong seems to reject Rorty's attack on epistemology at least partly because it entails a theoretical displacement of the confrontation model of subject and object with a conversation model of disputes among reading subjects. Armstrong agrees that "accurate representation" is not useful as a model for describing understanding and sees as more useful

---

[27] Rorty, "Philosophy without Principles," in Mitchell, *Against Theory*, p. 136.

[28] Rorty, "Philosophy without Principles," p. 136; quoting Mailloux, "Truth or Consequences: On Being Against Theory," in Mitchell, *Against Theory*, p. 71.

a notion of "variable conversations concerned with shifting, often incommensurable problems" for explaining the reception of James's story. However, he argues that the "history of this work shows as well that the process of validation has certain constant forms across different communities and that validation cannot be collapsed into social agreement because it entails a *responsibility to otherness*" (*Conflict* 93, my emphasis). He implies that Rorty overemphasizes conversation and social agreement to such an extent that he loses all "transhistorical tests for validity" such as "a responsibility to otherness."

But rhetorical pragmatism claims that interpretive disputes and social agreements (and disagreements) are *about* otherness—of texts, of disputants, of cultures. A rhetorical hermeneutics, for instance, argues that in most cases of literary reception, each of the disputants is holding the other responsible to the text; it is just that, as Armstrong himself admits, what counts as a relevant or significant part of the text is exactly what is under dispute. "Attempts to mediate or resolve such conflicts by pointing to what is really there in the text extend the debate instead of stopping it" (*Conflict* 94).

But this rhetorical point can also be applied to the question of a text's "otherness" or difference. That otherness cannot serve as a transhistorical test for interpretive validity when the makeup of the text, its identifiable otherness, and responsibility to that difference are all more or less at stake in particular historical debates over a text's interpretation. It is not that rhetorical pragmatism denies the relevance of a text's otherness to an interpretive debate; it is just that often otherness or difference is exactly what the debate is about and thus it cannot be a "transhistorical test" of a particular side's interpretive claims. This is not to say that charging your opponent with failing to respect the text's otherness might not be a very effective rhetorical strategy. It is to say that such a charge must be made to stick in a particular rhetorical context. Respecting difference is a historically specific activity quite relevant to interpretive disputes over texts today, and thus any rhetorical analysis of how contemporary textual interpretation functions must take such a factor into account.

Armstrong provides some insightful comments on the rhetoric of interpretive disputes in his reception analysis of *The Turn of the Screw*. He notes how "if, as Rorty claims, different partners in a discussion may not see eye to eye because they are concerned about different problems, such divergences occur because the interpreters have conflicting beliefs about what the object is and how best to engage it" (*Conflict* 95). In another place he observes, "An antagonist in hermeneutic conflict not only has the option of questioning the opposing community's assumptions and procedures but also may attempt to create embarrassing anomalies for it by pointing to textual details that its readings have not yet accounted for. On the other hand, however, these details are not simply empirical facts, for an interpreter may defend the validity of his or her reading by assimilating anomalous evidence through ingenious hypotheses that the opponent refuses to accept" (*Conflict* 99). Armstrong makes these and other useful theoretical/historical observations in the course of his reception study of *The Turn of the Screw* and thus provides a skillful example of using rhetoric to practice theory by doing history; that is, his study is a convincing instance of rhetorical hermeneutics.

Yet Armstrong takes his history and commentary to be a refutation, not a confirmation of rhetorical hermeneutics. Why? Again the problem is partly a matter of definition: Armstrong takes my agreement with Rorty to mean an abandonment of all historical, epistemological questions rather than a plea for setting aside the foundationalist questions of epistemology. But our differences (misunderstandings?) go deeper than assumed definitions. As Armstrong notes, a rhetorical hermeneutics proposes that "the way to answer the realist/idealist question 'Is meaning created by the text or by the reader or by both?' is simply not to ask it."[29] Against this view, Armstrong argues, "The dispute about *The Turn of the Screw* suggests that the 'realist/idealist question' cannot be bypassed in the history of reception but turns up there again when critics with incompatible beliefs give incommensurable readings to 'the facts of the text'" (*Conflict* 101).

However, again, Armstrong has missed my point if he thinks I disagree with him. I am certainly not saying that "realist" and "idealist" theories of interpretation never play a role in specific historical debates over texts (they do), nor am I saying that as an historian I won't be pointing to texts and assumptions as a way of telling a story about a text's reception and the debates that make it up. It is just that talking about a critic who appeals to foundationalist theories is not an instance of *doing* foundationalist theory. And to argue a specific history for a text's reception or to suggest tips on how to do such histories is not to put forward a realist or idealist epistemology. A rhetorician has no problem with arguing about facts and for heuristics, as long as "facts" are not taken to be noninterpretive givens and as long as "rules" are only seen as proposals to "try doing it this way."

[29] Mailloux, "Rhetorical Hermeneutics," *Critical Inquiry* 11 (1985): 628; rev. and rpt. in Mailloux, *Rhetorical Power*, p. 14; quoted by Armstrong, *Conflict*, p. 100.

To bypass the "realist/idealist question" means simply to refrain from doing foundationalist epistemology.[30]

But in doing historical reception studies, does rhetorical hermeneutics claim to escape the historical problem of its own rhetorical situation? Is rhetorical hermeneutics guilty of ignoring its *own* history and rhetoric when it describes a particular example of interpretive conflict over a particular text? This seems to be what Armstrong suggests when he follows his description of rhetorical hermeneutics with objections that history "does not provide a neutral ground" and that history is itself a "hermeneutic construct" (*Conflict* 90). Is he implying that rhetorical hermeneutics denies these claims? But how could it? Rhetorical hermeneutics rejects foundationalist theory precisely because that theory attempts to place itself outside history and rhetoric in order to describe and prescribe interpretation in general. Any theoretical practice (including rhetorical hermeneutics) is within history as it reflects upon history, within rhetoric as it tropes and argues over interpretations and their histories. There is no ahistorical, nonrhetorical "neutral ground" from which historical arguments can be made. My history of *Huckleberry Finn*'s 1885 reception is an interpretive argument made within the rhetorical situation of the 1980s. It would be self-contradictory for a rhetorician to claim otherwise.

And this same rhetorical, historical embeddedness holds true for the therapeutic *theoretical* claims I am making as well. Another critic, Dieter Freundlieb, takes me to task when I propose that "textual realism" and "readerly idealism" have led to dead ends in epistemology and when I suggest a rhetorical turn to history be taken instead. He writes: "Mailloux thinks he can simply describe the institutional history of literary criticism and explain why realism and idealism seemed attractive to those who subscribed to them without himself engaging in any questions of epistemological validity. The philosophical naivety of Mailloux's move is astounding. He believes that normative questions of historical accuracy and interpretive validity can be dealt with adequately by adopting the position of the epistemologically disengaged historian who can discuss these issues as purely rhetorical moves in a sequence of factual events."[31] Astounding or not, the claim of rhetorical hermeneutics is that there are no standards for "epistemological validity" available if by "standards"

---

[30] See my "The Turns of Reader-Response Criticism," in *Conversations: Contemporary Critical Theory and the Teaching of Literature*, ed. Charles Moran and Elizabeth F. Penfield (Urbana, Ill., 1990), pp. 38–54.

[31] Dieter Freundlieb, "Semiotic Idealism," *Poetics Today* 9, no. 4 (1988): 837; further references are in the text.

one means the ahistorical criteria proposed by various realisms and idealisms throughout the history of epistemology. There are, of course, historically specific "standards" (traditions for argumentative appeal) accepted within particular communities, disciplines, discourses, and so on, but these are local, contingent, rhetorical constructs, which have all the force of such constructs, which is all the force needed for interpretive debate and knowledge production to take place.[32]

But, again, the claim here is not that rhetorical hermeneutics assumes an "epistemologically disengaged historian" even when the rhetorical historian is telling an institutional story about literary criticism and its relevant hermeneutic theories. Such stories are always told by an "engaged" historian—that is, an historian embedded, in this case, in the very history he is attempting to articulate. The only "disengagement" is with the foundationalist questions of epistemology, *not* with the history of interpretive disputes, conflicting theoretical arguments, and changing epistemological assumptions. Thus, rhetorical historians must take all of these into account even as they realize (and at certain moments foreground) their own rhetorical situations in writing the histories they write. Freundlieb is correct in his speculation that I assume my own institutional story of the old New Criticism is "nothing but further rhetoric" (838). But for a practitioner of rhetorical hermeneutics to accept this characterization (without the derogatory "nothing but") is not the fatal admission Freundlieb takes it to be. Rather it is the simple conclusion that follows from taking seriously that there is no escape from rhetoric and history into some transcendental realm from which the past can be heard speaking itself through a chronicler beyond all rhetoric.

Though I argue that it is desirable to use rhetoric to practice theory by doing history, I am not claiming that theory and history never form part of separate disciplinary language games. Contemporary theory, as metapractice about practice, continues philosophical arguments with long traditions. Giles Gunn, a fellow pragmatist, raises one such argument in challenging me to define more clearly the hermeneutic relation between past and present:

> The main issue for interpretation, it seems to me, has to do with the density and opacity of that dimension known as the historical, a density and opacity which involves at the very least, I would think, some sort of interpretive traffic—if not, in addition, some kinds of interpretive nego-

[32] This is, of course, the rhetorical lesson many readers take from Thomas S. Kuhn, *The Structure of Scientific Revolutions*, 2d ed. (Chicago, 1970).

tiations—between our by-whatever-means excavated and reconstructed sense of that prior historical moment and our by-whatever-means intuited and elaborated sense of our own contemporary moment.[33]

I am taken with Gunn's metaphors of interpretive traffic and negotiation between past and present. In one pragmatic sense, this traffic always goes on no matter what; it defines doing history as such and describes the dynamic but delimited process during which new truth is established about past, present, or future. As James puts it, "New truth is always a go-between, a smoother-over of transitions. It marries old opinion to new fact so as ever to show a minimum of jolt, a maximum of continuity."[34] Historical truth results from a requisite traffic between old opinion and new experiences: facts, desires, contradictions, reflections, and so forth. This formulation might not at first seem to coincide with what Gunn means by traffic between past and present, but I suggest returning to his carefully chosen phrases quoted above: he refers to traffic and negotiation "between our by-whatever-means excavated and reconstructed sense of that prior historical moment and our by-whatever-means intuited and elaborated sense of our own contemporary moment." True to our shared pragmatist premises, Gunn here makes no suggestion of some raw and unmediated past or some pure and immediate present that carry on an exchange. Thus, I think he might accept my theoretical restatement of his point. But if he does, then it seems that I cannot help but do history the way he recommends. That is, his prescription of what should be done turns into a description of what's always done.

However, there is another sense in which the past and present can be negotiated: when an interpreter explicitly compares past and present meanings, for example, the readings of *Huckleberry Finn* made in 1885 and 1995. Gunn raises the issue of relativism precisely in relation to this problem of evaluative comparison. Rhetorical hermeneutics, Gunn argues, associates "with a view of experience that, while acknowledging the historicity of all interpretive acts, including its own, in effect denies the possibility of critically comparing and evaluating them. We are thus left hermeneutically with the spectacle of history as a conflict (where there isn't a consensus) of interpretations among which it is impossible, from what I can tell, to adjudicate." I wish to disassociate rhetorical hermeneu-

---

[33] Giles Gunn, "Approaching the Historical" in *Reconceptualizing American Literary/ Cultural Studies: Rhetoric, History, and Politics in the Humanities*, ed. William E. Cain (New York, 1996), p. 60.
[34] William James, *Pragmatism: A New Name for Some Old Ways of Thinking* (1907; rpt. Cambridge, Mass., 1975), p. 35.

tics from at least certain versions of this relativism and claim instead that interpreters can make valid comparisons and evaluate which reading is a more persuasive interpretation of the text in question. Not only do I believe in the superiority of my reading of the rhetorical context of *Huckleberry Finn*'s reception, I also think my own interpretation of *Huckleberry Finn* (in chapter 3 of *Rhetorical Power*) is a correct reading of the novel. I can thus say that, though I understand why certain 1885 readers could read the novel as being primarily or most significantly about bad boys (i.e., I am persuaded by my historical explanation), I believe *Huckleberry Finn* is more importantly about race relations in post-Reconstruction America (i.e, I am persuaded by my textual reading). A rhetorical hermeneutics simply acknowledges that such evaluations take place within present assumptions and practices; yet this recognition does not change one's belief in the truth of one's own historical and textual interpretations.

Now, such rhetorical pragmatist claims about our hermeneutic situation do not mean that we are somehow trapped once and for all within an unchanging web of present beliefs and practices. It's just that past events, including rhetorical acts, can only be encountered in our present. James articulates the implications of this pragmatist truth for doing explanations in general: Any new idea adopted as the true one "preserves the older stock of truths with a minimum of modification, stretching them just enough to make them admit the novelty, but conceiving that in ways as familiar as the case leaves possible. An *outrée* explanation, violating all our preconceptions, would never pass for a true account of a novelty" (*Pragmatism* 35). Again, this does not mean change is impossible, only that it is evolutionary, not revolutionary. Explaining the past, interpreting texts, talking with other people: all these rhetorical activities can have significant consequences for a particular person or group; but "the most violent revolutions in an individual's beliefs leave most of his [or her] old order standing" (*Pragmatism* 35). Rhetorical hermeneutics attempts to chart specific historical instances of how these changes take place through reading and to have these explanations and their implications count as instances of hermeneutic theorizing.

PART TWO

CULTURAL RHETORIC STUDY

4

Ideological Rhetoric
and Bible Politics:
Fuller Reading Douglass

The poem is the transaction that goes on between reader and text.
—Louise M. Rosenblatt (1968)

Every reading is transactional. You run with what you have, and you become something else.
— Gayatri Chakravorty Spivak (1989)

As historical acts of reading, interpretations can themselves be read within the rhetorical context of their production and reception. That context might be troped as a cultural conversation of readers, which in this chapter will include 1845 readers of several kinds of texts: slaves' songs, the Christian Bible, northeastern U.S. secular and religious newspapers, philosophical treatises on morality, and slave narratives. An act of reading is precisely the historical intersection of the different cultural rhetorics for interpreting such texts within the social practices of particular historical communities. In analyzing Margaret Fuller's 1845 reading of Frederick Douglass's *Narrative*, I will illustrate this theoretical claim as I simultaneously tell a different story, that of reader-response criticism and reception aesthetics during the last two decades. This second, metacritical narrative will situate my own rhetorical interpretation of Fuller by showing how an earlier reader-response criticism gets transformed into what I am calling rhetorical hermeneutics.

Reader-response criticism of the 1970s claimed to challenge the formalist theory and practice of New Critical interpretations. Its institutional rhetoric advocated that talk about readers in the process of reading replace talk about literary texts as self-enclosed objects. The Affective Fallacy was declared a fallacy, as several forms of reader talk promoted a range of psychological and social models for interpretation—subjective, transactive, phenomenological, semiotic, affective stylistic, structuralist poetic. Each marked its difference from a text-centered formalism by using a reader vocabulary, but the particular names each gave to "the reader" also distinguished the radically different approaches metacritically lumped together under the name "reader-oriented criticism." Readers were actual, ideal, implied, intended, educated, informed, competent, inscribed; there were mock readers, superreaders, narratees, implied audiences, interpretive communities, literary competencies, reading conventions. As different as their conceptions of reading were, the various forms of 1970s reader talk all tended to deemphasize or completely ignore the act of reading as a historical and political activity.[1]

In the 1980s this situation changed. Pressured by various feminist, Marxist, New Historicist, and other sociopolitical criticisms, reader-oriented theory and practice turned more and more to the historical context and the political aspects of readers reading. Also important in this transformation of readerly approaches was the influence of the reception aesthetics proposed by Hans Robert Jauss. Jauss's reception theory had been introduced into the United States during the first wave of the new reader-response criticism, primarily through his "Literary History as a Challenge to Literary Theory," published in *New Literary History* in 1970. But unlike the phenomenological reader criticism of his University of Constance colleague Wolfgang Iser,[2] Jauss's historically oriented reception theory did not receive book-length treatment in English until the 1982 publication of his *Toward an Aesthetic of Reception* and his *Aesthetic Experience and Literary Hermeneutics*, volumes 2 and 3 in the University of Minnesota's widely acclaimed series "Theory and History of Literature."[3]

---

[1] For more on reader-response criticism, especially its inclusions and exclusions, see Vincent B. Leitch, *American Literary Criticism from the Thirties to the Eighties* (New York, 1988), pp. 211–37; my "The Turns of Reader-Response Criticism," in *Conversations: Contemporary Critical Theory and the Teaching of Literature*, ed. Charles Moran and Elizabeth F. Penfield (Urbana, Ill., 1990), pp. 38–54; Philip Goldstein, *The Politics of Literary Theory* (Tallahassee, Fla., 1990), pp. 100–146; and Peter J. Rabinowitz, "Other Reader-Oriented Theories," in *The Cambridge History of Literary Criticism*, vol. 8, ed. Raman Selden (Cambridge, 1995), pp. 375–403. For the best introduction to reader criticism of the seventies, see Jane P. Tompkins, ed., *Reader-Response Criticism: From Formalism to Post-Structuralism* (Baltimore, 1980).

[2] See Wolfgang Iser, *The Implied Reader: Patterns of Communication in Prose Fiction from Bunyan to Beckett* (Baltimore, 1974), and *The Act of Reading: A Theory of Aesthetic Response* (Baltimore, 1978). Also see Brook Thomas, "Reading Wolfgang Iser or Responding to a Theory of Response," *Comparative Literature Studies* 19 (1982): 54–66; and my *Interpretive Conventions: The Reader in the Study of American Fiction* (Ithaca, 1982), chap. 2.

[3] Besides these two books, also see Robert C. Holub, *Reception Theory: A Critical Introduction* (London, 1984); Hans Robert Jauss, *Question and Answer: Forms of Dialogic Understanding*, trans. and ed. Michael Hays (Minneapolis, 1989); and Louise Z. Smith, "Beyond the

In contrast to various forms of reader talk that focused on a fictional-ized reader represented in the text or an ideal reader implied by the text or an actual reader today reading the text, Jauss's reception aesthetics advocated talking about past historical readers within their specific horizons of expectations. Such talk could develop critical analyses and stories of reading open to a range of factors usually ignored in most reader-oriented criticism, factors constituted by social, political, and economic categories including race, age, gender, ethnicity, nationality, religion, sexuality, and class. This talk about historical acts of reading was strongly encouraged by changes within related institutional practices: the turn to history within theoretical accounts of textual interpretation and the attention to politics within historical analyses of intertextuality. That is, theory talk went historical and historical talk went political. Both combined with reception aesthetics to give reader criticism a more explicitly historical orientation.[4]

There are various ways to trouble the neat narrative I have just told about reader-response criticism. One could point to various places where reader critics of the early seventies did deal with history.[5] Or one could argue that the alleged turns to history and politics in academic criticism and theory were much more complicated than here represented, and, of course, they were. Still, I think my story does have a certain heuristic value, making more visible the changes in the rhetorical context (primarily in institutional discourses) that have occurred in the academic talk about readers reading since the heyday of reader-response theory during the seventies.

And however we have arrived at our present juncture, the current talk about historical acts of reading provides a welcome opportunity for more explicit consideration of how reading is historically contingent, politically situated, institutionally embedded, and materially conditioned; of how reading any text, literary or nonliterary, relates to a larger cultural politics that goes well beyond some hypothetical private interaction between an autonomous reader and an independent text; and of how our particular views of reading relate to the liberatory potential of literacy

---

'Imaginary Museum': Interested Readings, Interesting Tropes," in *Reconceptualizing American Literary/Cultural Studies: Rhetoric, History, and Politics in the Humanities*, ed. William E. Cain (New York, 1996), pp. 83–98.

[4] See James L. Machor, ed., *Readers in History: Nineteenth-Century American Literature and the Contexts of Response* (Baltimore, 1993).

[5] See, for example, Stanley Fish's early claim about the "radically historical" nature of his critical method in Fish, "Literature in the Reader: Affective Stylistics," *New Literary History* 2 (autumn 1970), rpt. in Tompkins, *Reader-Response Criticism*, p. 87. Also see Iser, *Act of Reading*, chap. 3, on the "pragmatics of literature" and the historical "repertoire" within the text.

and the transformative power of education. All these questions about the act of reading encouraged reader-response criticism to move more actively in historical and political directions. My own version of this move has led to a focus on the cultural rhetoric in which readings are presented, circulated, adopted, and contested. This rhetorical focus provides simultaneously a development of reader-oriented criticism, a perspective on recent hermeneutic theory, and an approach within contemporary cultural studies.

Using Rhetoric to Practice Theory by Doing History

Here is one historical act of reading: Margaret Fuller's 1845 review of *The Narrative of the Life of Frederick Douglass, an American Slave.*[6] Fuller begins her review by reading the reception of Douglass's public speaking performances: "Frederick Douglass has been for some time a prominent member of the Abolition party. He is said to be an excellent speaker—can speak from a thorough personal experience—and has upon the audience, beside, the influence of a strong character and uncommon talents." She first identifies the radical position of Douglass by placing him as an abolitionist and then describes the rhetorical power of his ethos as an orator: he speaks from the direct knowledge of personal experience, and he conveys the powerful impression of integrity and unusual ability. She then praises Douglass's book for being as "affecting" as his oratory.

> He has had the courage to name the persons, times and places, thus exposing himself to obvious danger, and setting the seal on his deep convictions as to the religious need of speaking the whole truth. Considered merely as a narrative, we have never read one more simple, true, coherent, and warm with genuine feeling. It is an excellent piece of writing, and on that score to be prized as a specimen of the powers of the Black Race, which Prejudice persists in disputing.

By noting the risk Douglass takes as a fugitive slave, Fuller presents the act of publication as itself further proof of the rhetor's strong character and figures this act as officially sealing his narrative with the emblem of an explicitly *religious* motive in "speaking the whole truth."

---

[6] *New-York Daily Tribune*, 10 June 1845, p. 1. All quotations from Fuller in the next few paragraphs are from this page, and later references are cited in the text as *Tribune*.

Fuller then explains why she reads the *Narrative* as an example of literary skills that race prejudice refused to acknowledge. Her argument at this point gets entangled in the ideological rhetoric of what George Fredrickson has called "romantic racialism"[7]: the belief, in Fuller's words, that

> the African Race had in them a peculiar element, which, if it could be assimilated with those imported among us from Europe, would give to genius a development, and to the energies of character a balance and harmony, beyond what has been seen heretofore in the history of the world. Such an element is indicated in their lowest estate by a talent for melody, a ready skill at imitation and adaptation, an almost indestructible elasticity of nature.

Fuller sees these qualities in some black authors' writings that are "glowing with plastic life and fertile in invention," and she claims "the same torrid energy and saccharine fulness may be felt in the writings of this Douglass, though his life, being one of action or resistance, was less favorable to *such* powers than one of a more joyous flow might have been."

Later in her review Fuller takes up Douglass's life of "action or resistance" as it is rhetorically presented in the *Narrative*. Specifically, she reads Douglass's critique of Southern Christianity against the background of the interpretive controversies being widely reported in the secular and religious press. Here is this part of her review in full: In contrast to William Lloyd Garrison, the radical abolitionist whose words introduce the volume,

> Douglass himself seems very just and temperate. We feel that his view, even of those who have injured him most, may be relied upon. He knows how to allow for motives and influences. Upon the subject of Religion, he speaks with great force, and not more than our own sympathies can respond to. The inconsistencies of Slaveholding professors of religion cry to Heaven. We are not disposed to detest, or refuse communion with them. Their blindness is but one form of that prevalent fallacy which substitutes a creed for a faith, a ritual for a life. We have seen too much of this system of atonement not to know that those who adopt it often

---

[7] George M. Fredrickson, *The Black Image in the White Mind: The Debate on Afro-American Character and Destiny, 1817–1914* (New York, 1971), chap. 4. Bell Gale Chevigny applies Fredrickson's term to Fuller's review in Chevigny, *The Woman and the Myth: Margaret Fuller's Life and Writings* (Old Westbury, N.Y., 1976), p. 340.

began with good intentions, and are, at any rate, in their mistakes worthy of the deepest pity. But that is no reason why the truth should not be uttered, trumpet-tongued, about the thing. "Bring no more vain oblations"; sermons must daily be preached anew on that text. Kings, five hundred years ago, built Churches with the spoils of War; Clergymen today command Slaves to obey a Gospel which they will not allow them to read, and call themselves Christians amid the curses of their fellow men.

Fuller concludes this part of her reading, "The Kingdom of Heaven may not at the beginning have dropped seed larger than a mustard-seed, but even from that we had a right to expect a fuller growth than can be believed to exist, when we read such a book as this of Douglass." The review as a whole ends with a long extract from the *Narrative*, an extract that Fuller introduces as "a suitable answer to the hacknied argument drawn by the defender of Slavery from the songs of the Slave."

Why did Fuller emphasize the religious implications of Douglass's *Narrative* in her review? Why did her historical act of reading argue for this interpretation of Douglass's text? Did Fuller misread Douglass? A psychological reader-response critic might reject the third question as inappropriate and go on to answer the first two questions in terms of a psychobiography of Fuller. A phenomenological or semiotic reader-critic might accept all three questions and put forward either an analysis of the implied reader constructed by the *Narrative* or of the codes assumed by it and compare Fuller's review to that reader or those codes. Other seventies forms of reader talk would use related but different notions, such as an intended informed reader or a generally shared literary competence, as a basis for answering the questions.

A rhetorical hermeneutics answers instead with another question: What counts as convincing evidence for addressing these issues? Certainly not a foundationalist theory that first describes a decontextualized model of an idealized reader interacting with a self-sufficient text and then prescribes comparing this ideal interaction with Fuller's reading of Douglass. But if rhetorical hermeneutics rejects such ahistorical theories of correct interpretation, it does not reject the notion of misreading. Rather this rhetorical antifoundationalism claims that questions of interpretive validity are rhetorically negotiated in every particular case, not in general through the proscriptions of a foundationalist theory but specifically through particular rhetorical transactions over historically situated topics. In fact, a rhetorical hermeneutics argues that theoretical questions about reading and misreading, about correct interpretations of past and present texts, are never effectively answered in general hermeneutic terms. It advocates instead a turn away from such grand theorizing about interpretation and a turn toward rhetorical histories of specific interpretive acts. Hermeneutic theory becomes rhetorical history.

Such a rhetorical hermeneutics, then, delays answering the question about Fuller misreading Douglass and first asks why Fuller reads Douglass the way she does. My rhetorical answer to this new question presents Fuller's interpretive act as historically located within the cultural conversation of 1845 "Bible politics,"[8] and such an answer helps demonstrate my claim that rhetorical hermeneutics uses rhetoric to practice theory by doing history.

The *Narrative*'s Rhetoric of Reading

A rhetorical history of Fuller's interpretation can start with the long *Narrative* extract she uses to end her review. A part of Douglass's rhetoric of reading, this extract deals with the way proslavery ideologues misinterpreted the songs of slaves. Like many reader-response critics today, Fuller here shows how the text she is reading itself thematizes the problem of reading. The reader-in-the-text strategy appeals to the authority of the text, an appeal that is prominent in most attempts to argue an interpretation. Such a rhetorical move implies nothing about an ahistorical theory of independent texts, but it does suggest much about historically arguing a case on a particular topic of interpretation.

In the extract Fuller gives, Douglass makes a convincing argument that proslavery ideologues misread the meaning of the slaves' happy-sounding songs when they interpret them as evidence of slave contentment. He puts

[8] I take this phrase from the title of an 1845 lecture by the Christian abolitionist Gerrit Smith, in which he cited scriptural passages to urge men to vote for antislavery candidates. Since by 1845 Garrison viewed the U.S. Constitution as a proslavery document, he rejected any participation in the voting process and thus criticized Smith's citation of the Bible as "useless." See "Bible Politics," *The Liberator*, 14 November 1845, p. 183. This is only one of several political controversies over how to interpret and use the Bible, which I will be describing as constitutive of the rhetorical context of Fuller's review. In adapting the phrase "Bible politics" to refer to debates over slave literacy and scriptural defenses of slavery, I am modifying and extending the 1840s usage of the term, which referred primarily to campaigning and voting in national elections and working within traditional party politics. See Aileen S. Kraditor, *Means and Ends in American Abolitionism: Garrison and His Critics on Strategy and Tactics, 1834–1850* (New York, 1969); and cf. James Brewer Stewart, "Abolitionists, the Bible, and the Challenge of Slavery," in *The Bible and Social Reform*, ed. Ernest R. Sandeen (Philadelphia, 1982), pp. 31–57.

forward a counterinterpretation that reads the songs as an ironic expression of the slaves' suffering and sadness. In arguing against the racist interpretation of the songs, Douglass's historical act of reading enters into
a debate within the ongoing controversy over domestic slavery in the
United States. That is, Douglass's interpretation is not simply an interaction with the songs but part of a rhetorical transaction with others engaged
in the rancorous struggle over making interested sense of slaves' experiences. Indeed, every act of reading is a reading rhetorically transacted.

Fuller introduces Douglass's reading of slave songs as a "suitable answer" to the "defender of Slavery" (*Tribune* 1).[9] But though she also comments on the author's "powers of observation" in the passage, Fuller does
not highlight an interesting fact about the rhetorical location of Douglass's "answer" and "observation." Douglass does identify two positions
from which the slave songs can be read: from inside the slave's experience and from outside that viewpoint. These are the two reading positions suggested by Fuller's brief introductory comment: Douglass's insider's stance corrects the proslavery outsider's view. But actually Douglass
represents himself as occupying a third position, which is neither insider
nor outsider but a combination of the two, and in telling how he reads
the songs he suggests additional positions from which historical acts of
(mis)reading occur.

Slaves of the out-farms, the extract begins, deemed it a high privilege
to be selected as messengers to "the Great House Farm" at the center of
the plantation. These slaves would sing "wild songs, revealing at once the
highest joy and the deepest sadness." The songs often contained "words
which to many would seem unmeaning jargon, but which, nevertheless,
were full of meaning to [the slaves] themselves." Later, Douglass voices
his astonishment that some people in the North misread these slaves'
songs "as evidence of their contentment and happiness." Rather than
simply declare himself an insider who reads the songs correctly, however,
Douglass complicates what counts as the conditions of correct reading by
placing himself first inside and then outside the experience of slavery
and suggests that it is precisely a history of changing places that now, in
the *Narrative*, gives him the rhetorical authority to correct the misreadings by the defenders of slavery: "I did not, when a slave, understand the
deep meaning of those rude and apparently incoherent songs. I was my-

---

[9] After having published Garrison's introduction to the *Narrative* the previous week, *The
Liberator* printed the slave songs passage as its first extract from Douglass's story and followed it with this comment: "So much for the songs of the enslaved—so much for their
happy and contented lot" (23 May 1845, p. 82).

self within the circle; so that I neither saw nor heard as those without might see and hear. They told a tale of woe which was then altogether beyond my feeble comprehension."[10]

Only interpreters occupying the subject position of fugitive slave can correctly read the slaves' songs. Thus, the *Narrative* extract that ends Fuller's review turns back upon her opening comment about Douglass's rhetorical effectiveness and corrects that reading of his speaking performances. It is not, as Fuller implies, that Douglass is an authority simply because he speaks directly "from a thorough personal experience"; for Douglass, it is more important that he also speaks at some distance from the experience of the songs he is reading.[11] In other words, his reading of the songs has authority not simply because he was a slave but because he is now an *escaped* slave, and further he has escaped because of what Fuller calls his "life of action or resistance." It is the very act of resisting that most fully authorizes the rhetoric of Douglass's *Narrative*.

And it was the effects of the slave songs that first started Douglass on the path to action and resistance. Though he did not understand the full meaning of the songs while a slave, he did respond to them, and their effects on him had consequences: "The hearing of those wild notes always depressed my spirit, and filled me with ineffable sadness. . . . To those songs I trace my first glimmering conception of the dehumanizing character of slavery" (58). Even if Douglass did not fully understand the songs' "deep meaning," his incomplete reading of those songs had specific rhetorical effects that eventually motivated his later acts of resistance. That development took place at least partly through Douglass's growing awareness of literacy's power. His strategic uses of reading and writing constructed a position of agency through which rhetorical effects had political consequences. Douglass reads and writes himself into an act of rebellion.

The story of that rhetorical process has been told quite effectively by several twentieth-century readers of the *Narrative*.[12] I will simply note

[10] *Narrative of the Life of Frederick Douglass, an American Slave*, ed. Houston A. Baker, Jr. (New York, 1982), p. 57. Subsequent citations of the *Narrative* in the text refer to this edition.
[11] Cf. the similar point made by Albert E. Stone, "Identity and Art in Frederick Douglass's *Narrative*," *CLA Journal* 17 (December 1973): 203. Also see Henry Louis Gates, Jr., "Binary Oppositions in Chapter One of *Narrative of the Life of Frederick Douglass an American Slave Written by Himself*," in *Afro-American Literature: The Reconstruction of Instruction*, ed. Dexter Fisher and Robert B. Stepto (New York, 1979), p. 230; and Sterling Stuckey, "'Ironic Tenacity': Frederick Douglass's Seizure of the Dialectic," in *Frederick Douglass: New Literary and Historical Essays*, ed. Eric J. Sundquist (Cambridge, 1990), pp. 32–38.
[12] For discussions that place Douglass's literacy process within broader histories of literacy, see Dana Nelson Salvino, "The Word in Black and White: Ideologies of Race and Lit-

here that a certain type of reader-response critic would be more interested than most interpreters in the temporal structure of the reader's
experience. That is, this critic would discuss not only how Douglass develops as a reader but also how Douglass's reader develops. How, for example, does the *Narrative*'s rhetoric guide the reader in the sequential
presentation of Douglass's uses of literacy? How does each episode affect
the reading of the next episode? How does the reader make sense of each
along the way?

Let me give just one extended example of how a reader-response critic
might talk about how the *Narrative* structures the reader's experience
through a series of reading episodes leading up to Douglass's achievement of written literacy. After being instructed by the narrator's correction of slave song misinterpretations at the end of chapter 2, the reader
finds in the next chapter's first paragraph an apparently unrelated description of the "large and finely cultivated garden" of Colonel Edward
Lloyd, owner of the home plantation where Douglass lived. "The colonel
had to resort to all kinds of stratagems to keep his slaves out of the garden. The last and most successful one was that of tarring his fence all
around; after which, if a slave was caught with any tar upon his person, it
was deemed sufficient proof that he had either been into the garden, or
had tried to get in. In either case, he was severely whipped by the chief
gardener. This plan worked well; the slaves became as fearful of tar as of
the lash" (59). Here the point is not to correct a misreading, as in the
case of the slave songs, but to show the irrelevance of correcting a misreading. It doesn't matter to the slaveholder whether the tar on the slave's
body was actually caused by the latter's disobedience; the traces of tar
simply come to signify disobedience, whatever the circumstances. The
ploy works because the threat of the lash forces the slaves to acknowledge
the master's general interpretation of tarred bodies, even on a specific
occasion when no act of disobedience occurred. The master's interested
reading gets adopted by the slaves because it serves their interests by
helping them to avoid a whipping.

At least in this situation the absence or presence of tar is a stable enough
sign to read. Not so with the next episode of (mis)reading, which the
reader comes upon in the very next paragraph. Colonel Lloyd's horses
were a prized possession, and the "slightest inattention to these was un-

eracy in Antebellum America," in *Reading in America: Literature and Social History*, ed. Cathy
N. Davidson (Baltimore, 1989), pp. 140–56; and Janet Duitsman Cornelius, *When I Can
Read My Title Clear: Literacy, Slavery, and Religion in the Antebellum South* (Columbia, S.C.,
1991). Also see Henry Louis Gates, Jr., *The Signifying Monkey: A Theory of African-American
Literary Criticism* (New York, 1988), pp. 166–67.

pardonable," resulting in the "severest punishment" for the slaves in charge. But these slaves "never knew when they were safe from punishment. They were frequently whipped when least deserving, and escaped whipping when most deserving it. Every thing depended upon the looks of the horses, and the state of Colonel Lloyd's own mind when his horses were brought to him for use. If a horse did not move fast enough, or hold his head high enough, it was owing to some fault of his keepers" (60). And of course what counts as "fast enough" or "high enough" is what counts as such to Colonel Lloyd. Thus, the slaves are left here with a completely unpredictable act of reading, with the look of the horses dependent on the mind of the master and vice versa.

But if misreadings are correctable in one instance, not correctable but possible to predict in another, and totally unpredictable in a third, it is certainly the position of the reader represented in the text that makes all of the difference: whether slave, master, or escaped slave. This is clearly brought out in the chapter's final reading episode and concluding comments. Walking along a road, a slave from one of the out-farms fails to recognize his master, Colonel Lloyd, misreading him as a stranger. Colonel Lloyd asks him about his treatment, and the slave, ignorant that he is talking to his master, complains. The colonel punishes the slave by selling him, without warning cruelly separating him from his family. Douglass follows this little story with its moral and comments that such incidents partly explain why "slaves, when inquired of as to their condition and the character of their masters, almost universally say they are contented, and that their masters are kind" (62). The reader is not surprised by the consequences of the slave's misreading and has no difficulty supplying the advice behind Douglass's comments: Don't trust the public testimony of *current* slaves.

In transacting the chapter, the reader has seen that in the narrative everything depends on who is doing the reading, from what interested position, within what relationships of power, for what rhetorical purposes, and so forth. More specifically, the question about the reliability of slave testimony has the same answer as the previous chapter's question about slave songs. But here the reader and not the narrator supplies the answer. After engaging chapter 2's rhetorical analysis of reading slave songs and after negotiating chapter 3's sequence of reading episodes, the reader can furnish the hermeneutic guideline: You cannot trust the master or the slave, and therefore it is again, as with the slaves' songs, only the escaped slave, Douglass the author, who speaks from a position of creditable authority. But if the reader contributes this answer, he or she also raises a further question: What are the escaped slave's interests and

purposes in writing narratives like the one being read? The answer to this
question has been read on almost every page of the tale. Like other versions of the genre, Douglass's slave narrative is explicit about its political
interests and rhetorical purposes: to convince readers to support the
abolition of slavery.[13]

The reader talk of the last few paragraphs tells us something about
Douglass's rhetoric of reading in the *Narrative*, but it only begins to address the historicity of that rhetoric. Before pursuing this point further,
I should note that talking about readers reading in texts and about temporal reading experiences are both typical rhetorical strategies practiced
by a kind of seventies reader-response criticism associated with Wolfgang
Iser, Stanley Fish, and Stephen Booth.[14] It is easy to see that this reader
criticism, at least as I have illustrated it here, is in its practice still tied
closely to an ahistorical formalism, which prevents development of a
more historically rigorous and politically connected form of critical work.
Thematizing reading puts the reader in the text and thus enables interpreters to bracket the sociopolitical context of reading.

Such reader talk is still only about the text narrowly defined. But so too
is most talk about the structure of the ideal reader's response. Is there really a significant difference between describing a sequence of textual
episodes and describing the informed reader's reading of those episodes?
The reader vocabulary adds very little to the formalist analysis, except
the term "reader" and some other readerly descriptors. What the reader
vocabulary does do, however, is open up possibilities for different kinds
of reading discussions. One could take the reader focus in a psychological direction (as David Bleich and Norman Holland have done) and talk
about the specific responses of student readers. Or one could take the
reader focus in a semiotic direction (as Jonathan Culler and Umberto
Eco have done) and talk about the codes that constitute the conditions

[13] Though Douglass and other slave narrators were quite explicit about their rhetorical
goals, they often used indirect and subtle strategies in attempting to persuade readers to
identify with their interests and accept their purposes. For discussions of these rhetorical
strategies and additional bibliography, see Lucinda H. MacKethan, "Metaphors of Mastery
in the Slave Narratives"; Keith Byerman, "We Wear the Mask: Deceit as Theme and Style in
Slave Narratives"; and Mary Ellen Doyle, S.C.N., "The Slave Narratives as Rhetorical Art";
all in *The Art of the Slave Narrative: Original Essays in Criticism and Theory*, ed. John Secora and
Darwin T. Turner (Macomb, Ill., 1982), pp. 55–95. Also see Robert B. Stepto, *From Behind
the Veil: A Study of Afro-American Narrative* (Urbana, Ill., 1979), esp. pp. 16–26; William L.
Andrews, *To Tell a Free Story: The First Century of Afro-American Autobiography, 1760–1865*
(Urbana, Ill., 1986), pp. 123–38; and Gregory S. Jay, *America the Scrivener: Deconstruction and
the Subject of Literary History* (Ithaca, 1990), pp. 236–76.

[14] For an institutional history and rhetorical analysis of this form of reader-response
criticism, see my *Rhetorical Power* (Ithaca, 1989), pp. 29–53.

of reading. I would like to pursue a different tack here and suggest that reader-oriented criticism can (indeed has already) become more historical and political in talking about both the reader reading in the text and the past reader of the text.

To begin with the reader in the text, we can look briefly at one of the *Narrative*'s most interesting stories of reading: Douglass's interpretation and response to *The Columbian Orator*, Caleb Bingham's popular anthology of speeches and debates. Critics have used *The Columbian Orator* to interpret Douglass's rhetoric,[15] but I want to look more closely at how the narrator's earlier self reads *The Columbian Orator*. Douglass writes:

> Every opportunity I got, I used to read this book. Among much of other interesting matter, I found in it a dialogue between a master and his slave. The slave was represented as having run away from his master three times. The dialogue represented the conversation which took place between them, when the slave was retaken the third time. In this dialogue, the whole argument in behalf of slavery was brought forward by the master, all of which was disposed of by the slave. The slave was made to say some very smart as well as impressive things in reply to his master— things which had the desired though unexpected effect; for the conversation resulted in the voluntary emancipation of the slave on the part of the master. (*Narrative* 83)

Douglass offers this view of why the slave's persuasion worked: "The moral which I gained from the dialogue was the power of truth over the conscience of even a slaveholder" (84).

On this key point Douglass misreads the dialogue in attributing the slave's rhetorical effectiveness to a successful appeal to the master's conscience. The master wants his slave to admit he has been treated well: "Gratitude! I repeat, gratitude! Have I not endeavoured ever since I possessed you to alleviate your misfortunes by kind treatment; and does that confer no obligation?"[16] But the slave counters every example of his master's generosity with a moral argument against the whole system of slavery itself. The master is not looking for ethical justification, however. He desires a show of gratitude for the practical reason that he doesn't want the

---

[15] See, for example, John W. Blassingame, "Introduction to Series One," in *The Frederick Douglass Papers*, Series One: Speeches, Debates, and Interviews, vol. 1: 1841–46, ed. Blassingame (New Haven, Conn., 1979), pp. xxii–xxiii; and Joseph Fichtelberg, *The Complex Image: Faith and Method in American Autobiography* (Philadelphia, 1989), pp. 120–35.

[16] Caleb Bingham, *The Columbian Orator: Containing a Variety of Original and Selected Pieces; Together with Rules; Calculated to Improve Youth and Others in the Ornamental and Useful Art of Eloquence* (Boston, 1827), p. 241.

slave to run away again, and he clearly feels that an internal motive of gratitude would be more effective than an external threat of punishment.

> *Mast.*   Is it impossible, then, to hold you by any ties but those of constraint and severity?
> *Slave.*   It is impossible to make one, who has felt the value of freedom, acquiesce in being a slave.
> *Mast.*   Suppose I were to restore you to your liberty, would you reckon that a favour?
> *Slave.*   The greatest; for although it would only be undoing a wrong, I know too well how few among mankind are capable of sacrificing interest to justice not to prize the exertion when it is made.
> *Mast.*   I do it, then; be free.
> *Slave.*   Now I am indeed your servant, though not your slave. (*Columbian Orator* 242)

The dialogue ends with the slave returning the master's kindness by advising him about the violent threat posed by the slaves. "You are surrounded with implacable foes, who long for a safe opportunity to revenge upon you and the other planters all the miseries they have endured." He concludes: "Superior force alone can give you security. As soon as that fails, you are at the mercy of the merciless. Such is the social bond between master and slave!"

Whatever else is going on in this dialogue, it is certainly not disinterested altruism that motivates the master to emancipate his slave. Perhaps the slave does appeal to his master's conscience, as Douglass suggests, but it is practical exigency, narrow self-interest, that motivates the master's decision. Douglass has misread the dialogue when he interprets its moral as the "power of truth over the conscience of even a slaveholder."

But Douglass has not misread what is most significant about the debate for him. He reads correctly the slave's complete dedication to resisting his bondage, and he later imitates it. This fact returns us to the whole question of what Fuller calls Douglass's "life of action or resistance." As I have said, that life is significantly constituted by the rhetorical effects of Douglass's reading. In the present case, reading *The Columbian Orator* had very concrete effects on Douglass's condition as a slave. On the positive side, he was empowered by adopting pieces of the book's rhetoric: "The reading of these documents enabled me to utter my thoughts, and to meet the arguments brought forward to sustain slavery." On the negative side, his suffering greatly increased because literacy had given him a view of his "wretched condition, without the remedy." "I would at times feel that learning to read had been a curse rather than a blessing" (*Narrative* 84). These rhetorical effects of reading were eventually to motivate Douglass in trying to find the remedy he required. That remedy, an act of rebellion, develops at least partly through his uses of reading and writing and their rhetorical effects on himself and others.

I say "partly" because Douglass himself represents the initiating moment of rebellion as an act mysterious and inexplicable. Indeed, the *Narrative* resists my attempt to give a rhetorical specificity to the motives for Douglass's initial resistance. He introduces the climactic episode by directly addressing his readers: "You have seen how a man was made a slave; you shall see how a slave was made a man" (107). But when he describes how he physically resisted the slave-breaker Edward Covey, Douglass cannot explain the act of rebellion: "At this moment—from whence came the spirit I don't know—I resolved to fight" (112).[17] Whatever the cause or motive for his resistance, however, Douglass later reads the act as "the turning-point" in his "career as a slave" (113); and by so naming it, he constructs a position of agency, which has been constituted at least partly through his past uses of literacy. Like the slave in *The Columbian Orator*, Douglass would escape from bondage. The battle with Covey, Douglass writes, "rekindled the few expiring embers of freedom, and revived within me a sense of my own manhood. It recalled the departed self-confidence, and inspired me again with a determination to be free" (113).

THE CULTURAL RHETORIC OF 1845

Given Douglass's misreading of the master's motivation in *The Columbian Orator* dialogue and given the incomplete explanation for his own act of rebellion, one might claim that Fuller has misread the *Narrative* in praising Douglass for knowing "how to allow for motives and influences." But such a criticism of Fuller would be misplaced because she praises Doug-

---

[17] The closest Douglass gets to a causal explanation is the magical roots given him by a fellow slave, Sandy Jenkins, but he rejects the claim that his success resulted from the roots' protective powers (119). See Helen Jaskoski, "Power Unequal to Man: The Significance of Conjure in Works by Five Afro-American Authors," *Southern Folklore Quarterly* 38 (June 1974): 106. Later, in his second autobiography, Douglass presents the persuasive case Jenkins made for using the roots: "'My booklearning,' he said, 'had not kept Covey off me [in the past]' (a powerful argument just then)"—*My Bondage and My Freedom* (1855; rpt. New York, 1969), p. 239. For discussion of Douglass's 1855 redescription of his rebellion, see Bernd Ostendorf, "Violence and Freedom: The Covey Episode in Frederick Douglass' Autobiography," in *Myth and Enlightenment in American Literature*, ed. Dieter Meindl and Friedrich W. Horlacher (Erlangen, Germany, 1985), pp. 257–70; and David Leverenz, *Manhood and the American Renaissance* (Ithaca, 1989), pp. 108–34.

lass's knowledge of motives and influences not in relation to his own actions but in relation to the ideological practices of slaveholders. Specifically, Fuller centers her review of the *Narrative* on its treatment of "the subject of Religion," upon which Douglass "speaks with great force, and not more than our own sympathies can respond to." For Fuller, the rhetorical power of the *Narrative* resides especially in Douglass's persuasive critique of "the inconsistencies of Slaveholding professors of religion" (*Tribune* 1).

Reading the cultural rhetoric through which Fuller reviews Douglass and in which she herself speaks on the subject of religion allows me to give a final example of how reader criticism can develop beyond formalism and returns me more explicitly to the task of using rhetoric to practice theory by doing history. Fuller's act of interpreting the *Narrative* can best be understood not through a grand hermeneutic theory (whether formalist or intentionalist, phenomenological or semiotic) but by a rhetorical reception study, a historical interpretation of the cultural debates in which Fuller read Douglass. Here I want to argue not only that every act of reading is a reading rhetorically transacted, but also to emphasize that rhetorical hermeneutics makes every act of reading an act historically read.

I have already begun my historical interpretation of the 1845 cultural conversation by discussing the rhetorical activity in Douglass's *Narrative*, which is, of course, a participant in that conversation. Fuller reads Douglass as intervening in the contemporary debates over proslavery ideology and its relation to organized religion. There are several ways in which Fuller ties her reading to this debate, and in what follows I will explore only some of these rhetorical connections.

Immediately before Fuller turns to Douglass's critique of slave-owning professors of religion, she compares his rhetoric favorably to that of his sponsor, William Lloyd Garrison, whose introduction opens the volume. Fuller laments Garrison's "over emphatic style. His motives and his course have been noble and generous. We look upon him with high respect, but he has indulged in violent invective and denunciation till he has spoiled the temper of his mind. Like a man who has been in the habit of screaming himself hoarse to make the deaf hear, he can no longer pitch his voice on a key agreeable to common ears." Garrison's well-motivated but fanatical rhetoric has, according to Fuller, turned on its user and affected *his* mind rather than his audience's; and rather than getting the deaf to hear slavery's victims, Garrison has made those who might have heard deaf to his own rhetoric. In contrast, Douglass comes across as "very just and temperate" (*Tribune* 1). But it was not simply the style of Garrisonian rhetoric that Fuller rejected; she also had problems with its political arguments for dealing with slaveholders and all those institutionally connected with them.

In 1831 Garrison helped found the New England Anti-Slavery Society and began publication of *The Liberator* in Boston. Garrisonian abolition called for the immediate emancipation of slaves and attacked all forms of compromise with slaveholders, including gradualist antislavery and colonization programs. What particularly distinguished the ideological rhetoric of radical abolition was its heavy investment in moral suasion. From the first, Garrisonian abolitionists focused not on the economic or political arguments against slavery but on a religious critique. When the national American Anti-Slavery Society (AASS) was founded in New York City in 1833, its Declaration of Sentiments, written by Garrison, framed its arguments in an explicitly religious vocabulary combined with the ideological rhetoric of the American Revolution. "The right to enjoy liberty is inalienable. To invade it is to usurp the prerogative of Jehovah." The Declaration goes on to appropriate a biblical trope that appears often in abolitionist rhetoric and figures the economic center of the proslavery argument: "Every American citizen, who detains a human being in involuntary bondage as his property, is, according to Scripture (Ex. xxi, 16), a man-stealer."[18] The use of this trope of property in 1830s abolitionist literature signals a rhetorical continuity with the earlier American debates over slavery, which were most often framed in terms of political economy.

But a break with earlier discussions also marks the radical abolitionist rhetoric of the 1830s. Larry Tise describes the new rhetorical context after the appearance of Garrisonian abolition: "For the first time since the debate on slavery began in the eighteenth century, every writer who favored its perpetuation found it necessary to discuss the manner in which slavery could be viewed as a moral (at least not immoral) institution."[19]

---

[18] "Declaration of Sentiments of the American Anti-Slavery Society," in *The Abolitionists*, ed. Louis Ruchames (New York, 1964), p. 80.

[19] Larry E. Tise, *Proslavery: A History of the Defense of Slavery in America, 1701–1840* (Athens, Ga., 1987), p. 116. Readers of Tise's book will no doubt find it ironic that I am using him to support my argument for a change in rhetorical context when one of his main points is to challenge traditional claims about such changes, in particular the claim that "the positive good argument in defense of slavery" was "unique to the Old South" (98). But while Tise does provide evidence for similarities in the available ideological rhetoric over different periods and in different locations of slavery debates, he also asserts that there were differences in the significance given to, e.g., moral forms of argumentation in the United

Abolitionist rhetoric was ethical in its appeal and specifically religious in its targets. As the AASS declaration put it, "We shall enlist the pulpit and the press in the cause of the suffering and the dumb. We shall aim at a purification of the churches from all participation in the guilt of slavery."[20] The course of this rhetorical effort at moral suasion has been charted by many historians of Garrisonian abolitionism. Suffice it to say here that abolitionist criticism of the Christian clergy became more and more intense as major religious denominations failed to join the call for immediate emancipation of all slaves and for rejection of all support and affiliation with slaveholders. A speech by Wendell Phillips, whose letter follows Garrison's preface and precedes Douglass's narrative, provides an especially useful summary of the radical abolitionist stance toward organized religion in 1845.

In May of that year, the New York *Observer and Evangelist* reported Phillips's rhetorical performance at the annual meeting of the American Anti-Slavery Society: Phillips gave "a speech of some length, but replete with sentiments, which, however repugnant to general opinion, were expressed with a clear and lofty eloquence."[21] The oration focused on the Garrisonian credo that "there must be no union, either in Church or State, with slaveholders." Though Phillips criticized both religious and political institutions, the *Observer and Evangelist* detailed only his attack on the Christian church for its unchristian support of slavery. According to Phillips, abolitionists had for years tried unsuccessfully "to evoke from that Church the voice of Christian remonstrance against the system which

---

States during the 1830s and after. For a rhetorician, such differences in significance are important because they help explain the particular interpretive rhetoric used by a reviewer like Fuller in reading Douglass's *Narrative*. Nevertheless, it is also important for understanding the rhetorical context of Fuller and Douglass to take note of Tise's central thesis. He claims that what makes American proslavery history truly distinctive is not the content of Southern slaveholders' arguments but their origin. Though Southerners developed a proslavery defense, they did so, Tise claims, by adopting the ideological arguments of Northern antiabolitionists, who preceded Southerners in formulating a "proslavery republicanism" in response to the abolitionists in the early 1830s (348). These conservative Northern antiabolitionists remained a significant part of the 1845 audience that read Douglass's abolitionist *Narrative* and Fuller's antislavery review. For general discussion of antebellum readers, see Charles H. Nichols, "Who Read the Slave Narratives?" *Phylon Quarterly* 20 (summer 1959): 149–62; and Nina Baym, *Novels, Readers, and Reviewers: Responses to Fiction in Antebellum America* (Ithaca, 1984).

[20] "Declaration of Sentiments," p. 82.

[21] "American Anti-Slavery Society," New York *Observer and Evangelist*, rpt. *The Liberator*, 16 May 1845, p. 79. All quotations that follow are from this page. In these passages the *Observer and Evangelist* appears to be quoting directly from Phillips's speech though quotation marks are not used.

the spirit of Christ and of humanity both united to condemn." This focus on churches emanated from two factors: the rhetorical effectiveness of ministers—"the people have been clay in the hands of those to whom they looked up as religious teachers"—and the current rhetorical context: "All other influences in this land are but the dust of the balance, compared with that which is exerted by the religious feeling of the country. We have no other source of power to which we can appeal." Thus, Phillips applauds recent controversies within some denominations that led to divisions between Northern and Southern branches: "Two of our great churches are breaking—the Methodist and the Baptist. Thank God!"

Sectional schisms over slavery occurred in the Methodist Episcopal Church in 1844 and in the Baptist Triennial Convention in 1845. In contrast, the Old School Presbyterian General Assembly of 1845 voted overwhelmingly that, though it condemned slavery, it did not believe the Bible required excluding slaveholders from church fellowship.[22] Other churches also confronted the disunion question in 1845, and all such controversies were widely reported in the secular and religious press throughout the country.

Phillips's speech illustrates an assumption shared by both abolitionists and their opponents: the belief in a close interactive relationship between the views of the general citizenry and those of the Christian clergy. Antislavery polemics often targeted public opinion by addressing ministers, who were seen as rhetorically shaping that opinion. In his 1843 pamphlet *The Brotherhood of Thieves*, Stephen Foster justified his abolitionist attack on Christian churches with this analysis of the rhetorical situation: "The will of the people for the time being is the supreme law of the land. . . . Hence the power which controls public opinion does, in fact, give laws to our country, and is, therefore, preëminently responsible for the vices which are sanctioned by those laws. That power in this case, is the priesthood, backed up and supported by the church. They are the manufacturers of our public sentiment; and, consequently, they hold in their hand the key to the great prison-house of Southern despotism."[23] In contrast, some defenders of slavery saw the rhetorical power running in the opposite direction, from a small group of antislavery fanatics to a larger general public, then into Christian congregations.

---

[22] John R. McKivigan, *The War against Proslavery Religion: Abolitionism and the Northern Churches, 1830–1865* (Ithaca, 1984), p. 83.

[23] Stephen S. Foster, *The Brotherhood of Thieves; or, A True Picture of the American Church and Clergy: A Letter to Nathaniel Barney, of Nantucket* (1843; rpt. Concord, N.H., 1884), p. 28.

Reverend William Graham began his 1844 attack on abolitionism:

Public opinion is now regarded as the great instrument of moral and social reform. Its power in a Government like ours cannot be questioned,
but we may doubt whether its use is beneficial to the community. The
public opinion of modern times is the opinion of a few, diffused with
great effort through the multitude; it is manufactured with reference to
a specific result; and in most cases can hardly be distinguished from
highly excited party feeling. This method of reform, with its varied means
of agitation, has been introduced into the Church, and Christians have
felt themselves constrained to employ it, almost to the rending of the
Church.[24]

The abolitionist and the proslavery apologist had rather similar views of
the general populace. Both saw public opinion as rhetorically "manufactured" by small groups of manipulators—either hypocritical clergymen
or fanatical abolitionists. Furthermore, both agreed that they could com-
bat this manipulation and make a case for or against slavery by arguing a
particular reading of Scripture.

Indeed, much of the religious debate over the morality of slavery and
Christian union with slaveholders proceeded through radically divergent
readings of the Christian Bible. Fuller's review of Douglass enters directly
into this multifaceted and highly contested "Bible politics" of interpretation. When she praises Douglass for his attack on the "inconsistencies of
Slaveholding professors of religion," she places herself with the forces of
Northern antislavery. But when she claims not to be "disposed to detest,
or refuse communion with" slaveholders, she just as clearly declares herself not to be a Garrisonian abolitionist. In reviewing the *Narrative*, Fuller
stands as an antislavery advocate between radical abolitionists and proslavery ideologues.[25] And from that position she joins in the "Bible politics" herself when she quotes Isaiah 1 : 13, "Bring no more vain oblations,"

[24] William Graham, *The Contrast; or, The Bible and Abolitionism: An Exegetical Argument*
(Cincinnati, 1844), p. 3.
[25] Earlier in the year, Fuller had praised the "noble" and "calm" tone of Richard Hil-
dreth's antislavery novel *The Slave: or, Memoirs of Archy Moore,* 5th ed. (Boston, 1845), concluding her review, "Such productions have results upon the world, such as fierce invective
and mechanical arrangements for the expression of opinion never can" (*New-York Daily
Tribune,* 4 February 1845, p. 1). Also see Fuller, *Woman in the Nineteenth Century* (New York,
1845). For a more general discussion of Fuller's views, see Francis E. Kearns, "Margaret
Fuller and the Abolition Movement," *Journal of the History of Ideas* 25 (January–March 1964):
120–27; and on antislavery feminism, see Jean Fagan Yellin, *Women & Sisters: The Antislavery Feminists in American Culture* (New Haven, Conn., 1989).

against proslavery Christians and when she alludes to the Gospel parable of the mustard seed in declaring, "We had a right to expect a fuller growth [in the kingdom of God] than can be believed to exist, when we read such a book as this of Douglass" (*Tribune* 1).

But Fuller's entry into the religious debate over slavery includes another aspect of the controversy, an aspect we might call the Bible politics of *literacy*: she condemns those clergy who "to-day command Slaves to obey a Gospel which they will not allow them to read, and call themselves Christians amid the curses of their fellow men." Fuller is referring to the Southern policy of restricting slaves to oral instruction in religion. Taught that Scripture required obedience to their masters, most slaves were unable to read the Bible for themselves. In response to slave insurrections and abolitionist literature, Southern states passed laws making it a crime to teach slaves to read and write, and even in states without such laws, local custom usually discouraged any fostering of slave literacy. It was argued that, as North Carolina law put it, "the teaching of slaves to read and write has a tendency to excite dissatisfaction in their minds, and to produce insurrection and rebellion."[26] In Douglass's case, this argument turned out to be correct. Hugh Auld forbade his wife to teach Douglass to read, claiming that "there would be no keeping him. It would forever unfit him to be a slave. He would at once become unmanageable, and of no value to his master. As to himself, it could do him no good, but a great deal of harm. It would make him discontented and unhappy" (*Narrative* 78). All of these predictions come true as Douglass overhears Auld's warning to his wife and realizes that "the white man's power to enslave the black man" resides in keeping the slave illiterate. He therefore resolves to learn to read on his own. "From that moment, I understood the pathway from slavery to freedom" (78).

Douglass does not mention in the *Narrative* a detail he later notes in a speech given before the Belfast Anti-Slavery Society. As a token of remembrance, the Society presented Douglass with an "elegantly bound" and "beautifully gilt" Bible. In his speech he makes use of the Bible to attack slavery but also employs it as a pretext for the following story:

[26] *Laws of North Carolina, 1830–31*, chap. 6, p. 11; rpt. in Earle H. West, ed., *The Black American and Education* (Columbus, Ohio, 1972), p. 21. On Southern laws and policies against teaching slaves to read, see C. G. Woodson, *The Education of the Negro Prior to 1861* (2d ed. 1919; rpt. New York, 1968), chap. 7; and Thomas D. Morris, *Southern Slavery and the Law, 1619–1860* (Chapel Hill, N.C., 1996), pp. 347–48. The situation in Douglass's state is discussed by Jeffrey R. Brackett, *The Negro in Maryland: A Study of the Institution of Slavery* (Baltimore, 1889), p. 197; and Dickson J. Preston, *Young Frederick Douglass: The Maryland Years* (Baltimore, 1980), pp. 93–94, 115–16.

> I remember the first time I ever heard the Bible read, and I tell you the
> truth when I tell you, that from that time I trace my first desire to learn
> to read. I was over seven years old . . . I had crawled under the centre
> table and had fallen asleep, when my mistress commenced to read the
> Bible aloud, so loud that she waked me—she waked me to sleep no
> more! I have found, since I learned to read, that the chapter which she
> then read was the 1st chapter of Job. I remember my sympathy for the
> good old man; and my great anxiety to know more about him led me to
> ask my mistress . . . to teach me to read. She commenced, and would
> have, but for the opposition of her husband, taught me to read. She
> ceased to instruct me, but my desire to read continued, and, instead of
> decreasing, increased.[27]

Thus, Douglass attributes to the Bible the origin of his own desire for literacy, which enabled him to understand *The Columbian Orator*, fulfill the
worst fears of his Southern masters, and eventually rebel against his condition as a slave.

Though Douglass does not include in his *Narrative* this story of biblical
influence, he does provide other examples of the Bible politics of literacy: he describes the suppression of a Sabbath school for slaves being
taught to read the New Testament (98), and he condemns the man "who
proclaims it a religious duty to read the Bible" but "denies me the right
of learning to read the name of the God who made me" (154). In her review, Fuller picks up on these powerful complaints against the "professors of religion."

This last phrase refers in Fuller's and Douglass's texts to those defenders of slavery who profess Christianity as they misread Scripture to justify
slaveholding practices. Douglass describes the "nigger-breaker" Covey as
"a professor of religion—a pious soul—a member and a class-leader in
the Methodist Church" (100). Covey's employer and Douglass's second
master, Captain Thomas Auld, "found religious sanction for his [own]
cruelty" and justified whipping a lame young woman by citing the scriptural passage, "He that knoweth his master's will, and doeth it not, shall
be beaten with many stripes" (98–99).

This paraphrase of Luke 12:47 appears as an especially ironic misreading when compared with most traditional interpretations. The passage forms part of Jesus' own reading of the parable about a householder
surprised by a thief. Peter asks Jesus about the intended audience for the

---

[27] "The Bible Opposes Oppression, Fraud, and Wrong: An Address Delivered in Belfast,
Ireland, on 6 January 1846," *The Frederick Douglass Papers*, 1:127. Another version of the incident appears in *My Bondage and My Freedom*, p. 145.

story—the disciples or everybody? Jesus replies that the parable is directed at the "faithful and wise steward, whom his lord" has made "ruler over his household," that is, at the disciples who have been given responsibility for the kingdom of God. The person referred to in Luke 12:47 is this servant, the steward in charge of the household, whose disobedience should be punished with "many stripes."[28] Auld ignores Jesus' reading which focuses on the responsibility of church leaders, and instead puts himself in God's place so that the passage is turned on the disobedience of *his* slaves rather than on his own responsibility as God's steward.[29]

But a Bible politics of interpretation was employed not just by individual slaveholders to defend slave management techniques nor simply by abolitionist reformers in moral appeals to the consciences of the Christian churches. The debate over "Bible politics" was indeed a popular lay debate over slavery practices; however, it was also a specifically professional controversy among theologians and philosophers arguing over the morality of slavery. Douglass might have been right (in the Fuller review extract) when he argued that hearing slave songs more effectively revealed the "horrible character of slavery, than the reading of whole volumes of philosophy" (*Narrative* 57); but it was the reading and debate over such writings by certified experts in ethics that often focused the slavery controversy in the 1840s.

One example of professional Bible politics from 1844–45 received wide newspaper coverage during the reception of Douglass's *Narrative*. In a letter to the editor of the Boston *Christian Reflector*, Reverend Richard Fuller of Beaufort, South Carolina, made the usual proslavery arguments that "the Old Testament did sanction slavery" and that "in the Gospels and Epistles, the institution is to say the least tolerated."[30] In the course of his argument, Fuller quotes the charge that slavery is a "moral evil" from *The Elements of Moral Science*, a text frequently used in moral philosophy courses in antebellum colleges.[31] The author of that book, Francis

---

[28] George Buttrick et al., eds., *The Interpreter's Bible* (New York and Nashville, 1952), vol. 8, p. 234.

[29] Auld's misreading of the passage to justify whipping the woman becomes even more appallingly and directly ironic when one notes Jesus' warning that if the servant left in charge begins "to beat the menservants and maidens . . . the lord of that servant will come" when not expected and "cut him in sunder" (Luke 12:45–46).

[30] "Letter from the Rev. Richard Fuller, on the Subject of Slavery," *Christian Reflector*, rpt. Boston *Christian Watchman*, 6 December 1844, p. 196.

[31] Originally published in 1835, *The Elements of Moral Science* by Francis Wayland went through several editions. An 1859 reprint of the 1837 fourth edition claims 73,000 copies in print (Boston, 1859).

Wayland, president of Brown University and a fellow Baptist minister, responded to Fuller's defense of slavery in a series of letters to the *Christian Reflector*. In the first he agrees with Fuller "that the tone of the Abolitionists at the North has been . . . 'fierce, bitter and abusive.'"[32] Having established his antiabolitionist credentials, he goes on, at very great length, to demonstrate how Fuller has misread or misapplied various biblical references to slavery. Wayland clarifies what he meant by "moral evil" and, of course, quotes the Bible to establish his own overriding principle for condemning slavery: slavery is a "transgression of the law of our Creator, *Thou shall love thy neighbor as thyself.*"[33] Not surprisingly, when Fuller's and Wayland's letters were published as a book in May 1845, the review in Garrison's *Liberator* suggested that both were misreading the Bible. The reviewer especially criticizes Wayland and complains that "compromise is the peculiar danger of the Anti-Slavery cause." Abolitionists must never "recognize slaveholders as Christian brethren" and should reject all invitations to do so by answering with the words of Nehemiah, the Old Testament patriarch: "I am doing a great work, so that I cannot come down; why should the work cease, whilst I leave it, and come down to you?"[34]

Bible politics and its interpretive controversies took many forms throughout the 1840s. Professional and popular discussions intersected, as different contestants occupied a wide spectrum of ideological positions: Southern slaveholders, proslavery clergy, Northern antiabolitionist conservatives, Christian (non-Garrisonian) abolitionists, radical Garrisonians, and others. Margaret Fuller explicitly joins these debates as she reads the Bible politics of Douglass's *Narrative* and declares her own non-Garrisonian antislavery views.

One of the most interesting aspects of that reading is Fuller's comment on the "blindness" of proslavery ideology. She compliments Douglass for his just and reliable treatment of even those slaveholders who injured

[32] Francis Wayland, "To the Rev. Richard Fuller, D.D.," *Christian Reflector*, rpt. *Christian Watchman*, 6 December 1844, p. 196.
[33] "Dr. Wayland to Dr. Fuller: Letter IV," *Christian Reflector*, rpt. *Christian Watchman*, 20 December 1844, p. 204.
[34] C. K. W., "Drs. Wayland and Fuller," *The Liberator*, 16 May 1845, p. 79. This review of Wayland and Fuller's *Domestic Slavery, considered as a Scriptural Institution* appears on the same page in *The Liberator* as the news report of Wendell Phillips's speech at the AASS meeting discussed above. That report also includes a summary of Douglass's speech at the same meeting. A week earlier *The Liberator* had published Garrison's preface to Douglass's *Narrative* (9 May 1845, p. 75), and a week later (23 May 1845, p. 82) began a series of *Narrative* extracts, comments, and review reprints, including on 20 June (p. 97) a reprinting of Fuller's *Daily Tribune* review (without the concluding extract).

him most. "He knows how to allow for motives and influences." She implies that those "motives and influences" account for the "blindness" of
slavery's defenders to the "inconsistencies" of their proslavery ideology.
"Their blindness is but one form of that prevalent fallacy which substi-
tutes a creed for a faith, a ritual for a life" (*Tribune* 1). At times Douglass
seems to agree with this ideological reading of slaveholders, for example,
when he charges even Covey less with hypocrisy than with self-deception
(*Narrative* 104).[35] Later, in responding to a Southerner's attack on the
credibility of his narrative, Douglass develops further his ideological
critique of slavery as a self-validating system of belief: "Slavery has its
own standard of morality, humanity, justice, and Christianity. Tried by
that standard, it is a system of the greatest kindness to the slave—sanctioned by the purest morality—in perfect agreement with justice—and,
of course, not inconsistent with Christianity."[36]

No better illustration of Douglass's and Fuller's point about ideological
blindness can be found than the following passage from A. C. C. Thompson, the critic of the *Narrative* to whose earlier letter Douglass had responded. Thompson writes:

> But tell me, is the Southerner to be deprecated because he owns a slave,
> more than the Northern Abolitionist, who, in defiance of all law and
> honor, steals a slave from his lawful owner, and will then manufacture
> an incredible story without the least shadow of truth, to defame the
> character of slaveholders? If such is your opinion, you have studied
> some code of morality that I have never seen.[37]

No long philosophical argument could make Douglass's point more
clearly than these two sentences from his opponent. Thompson apparently cannot even *see* the code of morality that reveals his own slave code
ethics as false or even questionable. But, as Douglass argues further, when
slavery is "tried by any other" system, "it is doomed to condemnation."[38]

[35] But cf. Douglass's assertion that "the religion of the south is a mere covering for the
most horrid crimes" (117) and his condemnation of the South's "corrupt, slaveholding,
woman-whipping, cradle-plundering, partial and hypocritical Christianity" (153).

[36] "Letter from Frederick Douglass: Reply to Mr. A. C. C. Thompson," *The Liberator*,
27 February 1846, p. 35. Thompson's attack on the *Narrative*, "To the Public: Falsehood Refuted," had been reprinted from the *Delaware Republican* in *The Liberator*, 12 December 1845,
p. 197.

[37] A. C. C. Thompson, "Narrative of Frederick Douglass," *Albany Patriot*, rpt. *The Liberator*, 20 February 1846, p. 29. Earlier Thompson wrote, "I do not wish to be understood as
advocating slavery, for I am convinced that it is a great evil—but not sinful under ordinary
circumstances."

[38] "Letter from Frederick Douglass," *The Liberator*, 27 February 1846, p. 35.

And indeed from those other positions slavery *must* be condemned, as Fuller puts it, even if we grant that those supporting the evil of slavery may have at one time had "good intentions" and are now deserving of our "deepest pity." That fact "is no reason why the truth should not be uttered, trumpet-tongued, about the thing" (*Tribune* 1).

Both Fuller and Douglass here contribute to what might be called a rhetorical view of ideology: interpretive arguments are produced and read within positions constituted by specific ideologies of particular historical communities. If *rhetoric* is defined as the political effectivity of trope, argument, and narrative in culture, one might ask how such a notion relates to that even more problematic term, *ideology*. Elsewhere I have treated *ideologies* as sets of beliefs and practices furthering sociopolitical interests in certain periods and locations; these ideological networks define positions within cultural conversations where they appear as strategic arguments and rhetorical figures.[39] Thus, we might say: Rhetoric is potentially ideology in the making; and ideologies are at least partly forms of rhetoric. As rhetoric, ideology's tropes (ways of figuring the real), arguments (persuasive means for analyzing and changing the world), and narratives (storied embodiments of tropes and arguments representing past and future) are interwoven together in a self-identified or recognizable ensemble (of desires, beliefs, and practices) that is interpreted as serving interests of specific political agents.[40] Some rhetorics are not so identified, and some aspects of ideology are not, in the first instance, rhetorical—though all rhetoric can become ideological and all ideology can be rhetoricized.[41]

From this rhetorical perspective, the practices of slavery can be seen as constructing subjects—both masters and slaves—within an ideology of proslavery religion.[42] In his later rereading of his own rebellion, Douglass

---

[39] Mailloux, *Rhetorical Power*, p. 60.

[40] Cf. Paul Hirst, *On Law and Ideology* (Atlantic Highlands, N.J., 1979), p. 54: "We use the word 'ideological' to refer to a non-unitary complex of social practices and systems of representations which have political significances and consequences. . . . Hence 'ideological' analysis involves the calculation of the political consequences of social relations and representations. This analysis, however, cannot be one 'outside' of politics; what the calculation of effect *is* depends upon one's political position."

[41] Cf. Althusser on the material existence of ideology and his (initially) nonrhetorical and rhetorical examples of different "modalities of materiality": actions such as walking to church, kneeling down, gazing heavenward, and producing "an external verbal discourse or an 'internal' verbal discourse (consciousness)." Louis Althusser, "Ideology and Ideological State Apparatuses," in his *Lenin and Philosophy and Other Essays*, trans. Ben Brewster (New York, 1971), p. 169.

[42] See Althusser, "Ideology," esp. pp. 170–76; and Robert Wess, "Ideology as Rhetoric," chap. 1 of his *Kenneth Burke: Rhetoric, Subjectivity, Postmodernism* (Cambridge, 1996).

makes explicit how the Bible politics of the slaveholder's ideological rhetoric positions slaves as well as masters. In *My Bondage and My Freedom*, where Douglass retells the story of his fight with Covey, not only does he give himself more agency in choosing to fight, he also identifies his acceptance of proslavery "religious views" as a reason he had not resisted sooner.[43] Both slave and slaveholder are subjects constructed by the cultural rhetoric of proslavery ideology, an ideology consisting significantly of an interested reading of "the African Race" and of the Christian Bible. Douglass's and Fuller's readings of the Bible are no less interested, but obviously their interests differ radically from those of slavery's defenders. It is in direct and pointed opposition to the latter that Fuller reads Douglass's *Narrative*, and her review constitutes a rhetorical act within the 1845 debate over biblical interpretation, antislavery politics, and proslavery ideology.

Fuller's reading of Douglass can now be heard as transacting business with the *Narrative* as a participant and topic within the cultural conversation over Bible politics. In reviewing Douglass, Fuller is responding to the current debates over Christianity and slavery; in responding to these debates, she is reading Douglass. Fuller's rhetorical exchanges with the debates and with the *Narrative* cannot be separated, and neither can be isolated from the historically specific, politically charged configuration of cultural rhetoric I have analyzed in this chapter. One can talk as a formalist about the rhetoric of the text; but that text is rhetorically constituted by its location and activity within an intertextual space of cultural rhetoric, which includes the subject positions of its author, Frederick Douglass, and its reader, Margaret Fuller. And one can talk as a reader-oriented critic about a specific reader reading; but that transaction, in-

---

[43] Douglass, *My Bondage and My Freedom*, p. 241. Douglass does not, however, escape religious ideology when, by rebelling, he fully rejects the proslavery version. Rather the ideological subject of resistance is constructed as a Christian abolitionist (and later as a specifically Garrisonian lecture agent for the Massachusetts Anti-Slavery Society). In contrast to Douglass's own emphasis on the liberatory powers of literacy, Houston Baker points out the "intriguing restrictions" of the slave's literacy process, which result from the wholesale adoption of a "white, Christian, abolitionist framework"—Houston A. Baker, Jr., *The Journey Back: Issues in Black Literature and Criticism* (Chicago, 1980), pp. 36–37. (For further discussion in the Foucauldian terms of an archaeology of knowledge, see Baker, *Blues, Ideology, and Afro-American Literature: A Vernacular Theory* [Chicago, 1984], chap. 1; but also cf. Baker, *Modernism and the Harlem Renaissance* [Chicago, 1987], pp. 102–3.) The story of Douglass's later break with Garrison is told in many places. See, for example, Douglass, *My Bondage and My Freedom*, pp. 395–98; Benjamin Quarles, "The Breach between Douglass and Garrison," *Journal of Negro History* 23 (April 1938): 144–54; Tyrone Tillery, "The Inevitability of the Douglass-Garrison Conflict," *Phylon* 37 (June 1976): 137–49; and John R. McKivigan, "The Frederick Douglass–Gerrit Smith Friendship and Political Abolitionism in the 1850s," in Sundquist, *Frederick Douglass*, pp. 205–32.

cluding the agency of the reader and the theme of reading in the text, is constituted by its location and activity within the cultural rhetoric of 1845. Does Fuller misread Douglass? Not within the story I have told about the cultural rhetoric of Bible politics. But my reading is, of course, only as strong as the case I have made. And this rhetorical act of reading will itself be historically read and rhetorically transacted.

5

GOOD AND BAD PERSUASIONS:
CRITICS READING BUNYAN

There was some books too, piled up perfectly exact, on each corner of the table. One was a big family Bible, full of pictures. One was "Pilgrim's Progress," about a man that left his family it didn't say why. I read considerable in it now and then. The statements was interesting, but tough.
—Mark Twain, *Adventures of Huckleberry Finn*

Reader, I have told my Dream to thee;
See if thou canst Interpret it to me;
Or to thy self, or Neighbour: but take heed
Of mis-interpreting: for that, instead
Of doing good, will but thy self abuse:
By mis-interpreting evil insues.

—John Bunyan, *The Pilgrim's Progress*

*P*ersuasion refers to both a rhetorical process and a result of that process. To be persuaded is to take on a new persuasion. This double meaning plays a pivotal role throughout Bunyan's *Pilgrim's Progress*, long one of the most widely read and rhetorically effective texts in the English-speaking world. The second epigraph above suggests one turn Bunyan gives this topic: To interpret correctly, the reader must be of the right persuasion, which requires being properly persuaded by the Word, which must first be interpreted correctly. This rhetorical hermeneutic circle circumscribes many of this chapter's preoccupations.

Bunyan's allegory served as a special object of interpretive attention for early reader-response criticism. In the following pages, I examine the relation between rhetoric and hermeneutics in this criticism as well as in Bunyan's text. After doing a rhetorical reading of *The Pilgrim's Progress*, I compare two classic reader-response interpretations of that text to bring out in more detail the rhetorical aspects of reader-oriented criticism. Then I juxtapose these three readings of *The Pilgrim's Progress* to a reception history of the book, a history I relate to rhetorical hermeneutics and, in the next chapter, to a broader cultural rhetoric study.

READING RHETORIC IN *THE PILGRIM'S PROGRESS*

In "Dialogue and Debate in *The Pilgrim's Progress*," David Seed makes a persuasive case for Bunyan's rhetorical skill in representing verbal exchanges and describes in detail how dialogue "becomes a means of dramatizing self-examination as well as presenting confrontations with hostile agencies."[1] However, though Seed does usefully examine the dialogic mode of the allegory, he only begins to demonstrate the centrality of rhetorical persuasion to the success of Bunyan's ideological performance. To understand that performance more fully, we need to focus on how Bunyan guides his readers to his interpretation of biblical truth by presenting a series of good and evil persuasions both within and among his characters. These staged arguments in turn mirror the successful persuasion Bunyan hopes to achieve with his reading audience.

To accomplish these rhetorical effects, in his allegory and with his readers, Bunyan depends upon a biblical theory of persuasion worked out exhaustively among his Puritan and sectarian contemporaries in England and its New England colonies.[2] In this theory, persuasion takes place in three interrelated rhetorical exchanges: among the psychological faculties within each person, between the Bible and individual readers, and between ministers and their congregations. When successful, these internal and external acts of persuasion are ultimately grounded in the rhetorical power of God, speaking through the words of the Bible and often using the words of his preachers as a means for conversion. "Though it is God only can draw & perswade," wrote Jonathan Mitchell in 1677, "yet he does it by his Word."[3] Or as one allegorical Minister of the Word puts it to Mansoul in Bunyan's *Holy War*: God "by us reasons

[1] David Seed, "Dialogue and Debate in *The Pilgrim's Progress*," in *The Pilgrim's Progress: Critical and Historical Views*, ed. Vincent Newey (Liverpool, 1980), p. 73.

[2] Many historians and critics have carefully summarized the details of this theory. See, for example, Perry Miller, *The New England Mind: The Seventeenth Century* (Cambridge, Mass., 1939); Eugene E. White, *Puritan Rhetoric: The Issue of Emotion in Religion* (Carbondale, Ill., 1972); and E. Brooks Holifield, *Era of Persuasion: American Thought and Culture, 1521–1680* (Boston, 1989).

[3] Jonathan Mitchell, *A Discourse of the Glory to which God hath called believers by Jesus Christ* (London, 1677; 2d ed. Boston, 1721), p. 170.

with you, in a way of intreaty and sweet perswasions, that you would subject your selves to him."[4] Because of the covenant he has chosen to make,
God "deales with man answerable to the nature of a man, not with blowes,
but with reasonings and disputes," a manner of interaction Bunyan represents again and again throughout *The Pilgrim's Progress.*[5]

In "The Author's Apology for His Book," Bunyan begins with a spirited
defense of his allegorical strategies. The "Apology" attempts to justify its
rhetorical aims—a defense of the fiction's style and mode—and its own
rhetorical strategies in mounting that defense. That is, the "Apology"
uses a figurative style and a dialogic mode to defend the main text's use
of these same rhetorical techniques. But the "Apology" is both more and
less than the text it defends, more because it self-consciously foregrounds
the problem of rhetoric in its own arguments and biblical allusions and
less because it does so at the service of a more extensive and consistent
use of metaphor and dialogue in the main allegory it introduces.

Bunyan asks, "May I not write in such a stile as this? / In such a method
too, and yet not miss / Mine end, thy good? why may it not be done?"[6]
The method—allegory—and the style—metaphoric—are immediately
defended in a figurative argument, in which Bunyan reverses traditional
tropes of light to suggest that the "Dark Clouds" of indirection may sometimes bring forth the "Waters" of life or enlightenment while the "bright"
clouds of direct, literal language "bring none" (2). Later, Bunyan transforms such figurative replies to his critics' objections into a dialogue between those critics and himself. His textualized accuser, a "Man of God,"
objects:

> Well, yet I am not fully *satisfied,*
> That this your Book will stand, when soundly try'd.
> *Why, what's the matter?* It is dark, *what tho?*
> But it is feigned, *what of that I tro?*
> *Some men by feigning words as dark as mine,*
> *Make truth to spangle, and its rayes to shine.*
> But they want solidness: *Speak man thy mind:*
> They drown'd the weak; Metaphors make us blind. (3)

---

[4] John Bunyan, *The Holy War made by Shaddai upon Diabolus. For the Regaining of the Me-
tropolis of the World. Or, the Losing and Taking Again of the Town of Mansoul,* ed. Roger Sharrock and James F. Forrest (1682; Oxford, 1980), p. 45.
[5] Thomas Hooker, *The Saints Guide* (London, 1645), p. 10.
[6] John Bunyan, *The Pilgrim's Progress from this World to That which is to Come,* ed. James
Blanton Wharey and Roger Sharrock (1678; Oxford, 1960), p. 2. Further references to this
edition are given in the text.

Here Bunyan's critic objects to the fictional status of *The Pilgrim's Progress*, its "feigning words," which lack the required solidity. Furthermore, the critic picks up the earlier water and light metaphors and argues that the effects of the figures are literally too much: the "Waters" from the "Dark Clouds" of indirect language will drown the reader's understanding, not nourish it; and whatever "rayes" of enlightenment shine through, the metaphors will "blind" readers, not make them see.

But Bunyan responds to these objections by authorizing his fiction's allegorical mode and figurative style through an appeal to Holy Scripture, asking, "was not Gods Laws, / His Gospel-laws in older time held forth / By Types, Shadows and Metaphors?" (4). Bunyan's citation of biblical rhetoric ("Dark Figures, Allegories") to defend his own culminates in a reference back to his critic's opening objection to the soundness of his words:

> *Sound words I know* Timothy *is to use,*
> *And old Wives Fables he is to refuse,*
> *But yet grave* Paul *him no where doth forbid*
> *The use of Parables; in which lay hid*
> *That Gold, those Pearls, and precious stones that were*
> *Worth digging for; and that with greatest care.* (5)

Bunyan here provides an important key to the text that follows: the allegorical fiction must be read, interpretive digging will be necessary to find the valued meaning, and part of that meaning will be the proper stance taken toward the sound and unsound words, that is, toward God's truthful words and the "perverse disputings of men of corrupt minds . . . destitute of the truth" (1 Tim. 6:5). It is this conflict between God's true Word and men's perverse rhetoric that is the repeated topic of the staged debates throughout *The Pilgrim's Progress*.

Indeed, the allegory of *Pilgrim's Progress* proceeds, for the most part, "Dialogue-wise" (6). In these allegorical dialogues, Bunyan cautions his readers against the dangers of rhetoric, the power of misguided persuasion, and the wrong types of rhetors and audiences. Here we might note James Kinneavy's recent claim concerning the origin of Christian faith in Greek rhetoric. Kinneavy argues that *pistis*, used by the ancient Greeks to refer to rhetorical persuasion, became the basis for the early Christian use of *pistis* to designate their novel concept of faith. Kinneavy provides detailed semantic, historical, and analytical arguments to make his case for how a word with such negative associations—sophistry, mere opinion, transient belief—could become the central element in a new religion despite its subordinate relation to Greek philosophy's privileged notions of absolute knowledge, universal truth, and permanent reality, upon which that religion builds. I will return later to these negative associations, but for now I want to repeat Kinneavy's point about the double meaning of *pistis* and its English equivalent. *Pistis* refers to both the process of persuading and the resultant belief, and similarly "'persuasion' refers to two related but different things: the process that brings about an eventual result and the result itself. 'Persuasion' is a process (persuading) and the product (being persuaded)."[7] Bunyan works with both senses of "persuasion" throughout his dialogic allegory about Christian faith.

When Bunyan's Dreamer first sees Christian he is reading the Bible and painfully recognizing his own sinfulness. He declares to his family that their city will be destroyed unless they all find a way to be delivered. His relations think his head has a "frenzy distemper" and hope sleep will "settle his brains"; but later when he continues the same talk, they become "hardened" and simply ridicule him. Thus, Christian's first rhetorical acts are unsuccessful, his audience unpersuaded, and he must set out alone to answer the question, "What shall I do to be saved?" (9).

At this point Evangelist appears. This spiritual advisor directs Christian onto the road of salvation, giving him a parchment with the warning, "Fly from the wrath to come." Bunyan's marginal note interprets this whole passage as a reminder that salvation is through interpreting God's written message: "Christ and the way to him cannot be found without the Word" (10). This Word must be read, accepted, and proclaimed, but successful attempts at preaching, spiritual persuasion, depend on the right kind of audience, and certainly not those typified by the two figures met in Christian's next encounter: Obstinate and Pliable. Christian asks these neighbors why they have pursued him, and they respond, "To perswade you to go back with us." Christian refuses and instead entreats them: "go along with me." Obstinate inquires about what Christian seeks, and he answers with the biblical promise of eternal inheritance, imploring his audience to "Read it so, if you will, in my Book" (11). Obstinate rejects Christian's book and moves to return home, but Pliable is inclined to join Christian. As Obstinate and Christian "*pull for* Pliable's *Soul*," Christian again appeals to the Bible, asking Pliable, "If you believe not me, read here in this Book" (12). This rhetorical appeal to interpreting the Bible will be repeated again and again in the allegorical arguments to follow: it turns out to be interpretation all the way down and rhetoric all around,

---

[7] James L. Kinneavy, *Greek Rhetorical Origins of Christian Faith: An Inquiry* (New York, 1987), p. 22; also see p. 33.

not in Bunyan's explicit theology (which declares a God-given bottom line) but in his ideological performance. Bunyan attempts to control the reading of this performance through his marginal glosses and verse summaries, which are simultaneously interpretations of his allegory and arguments for his religious ideology.

In this exchange Christian seems to have won the struggle of words as Pliable agrees to join him and Obstinate leaves the scene. Christian rejoices, "I am glad you are perswaded to go along with me" (12), but this rhetorical victory is short-lived. When the fellow travelers get mired in the Slough of Despond and Christian's companion changes his mind and returns home, Bunyan's marginal note brings out the lesson: "It is not enough to be Pliable" (14). Neither a too obstinate nor a too pliable audience is the Christian rhetor's ideal.

After being aided by Help to escape the Slough of Despond, Christian next meets Mr. Worldly-Wiseman, the exact antithesis of the spiritual advisor Evangelist. Not only does this citizen of Carnal-Policy condemn Evangelist's good counsel to Christian, he also condemns the book grounding Evangelist's message; or more exactly, as Bunyan's gloss puts it, "Worldly-Wiseman *does not like that Men should be Serious in reading the Bible*" (18). There are much easier ways of relieving the burden of sin. Alas, Christian falls victim to this tempting rhetoric, "*[s]nared by Mr.* Worldly-Wisemans *Word.*" Deciding that his "wisest course" was to follow his new counselor's advice, Christian "turned out of his way to go to Mr. *Legality's* house for help" but is soon paralyzed under a high Hill (Mount Sinai) and cannot move (19–20).

Again Evangelist comes to the rescue. In response to his question about why he was "so quickly turned aside" from the true path, Christian explains: "a Gentleman . . . perswaded me, that I might in the *Village* before me, find a man that could take off my burden," and talking "much to me" the gentleman "got me at last to yield; so I came hither." Using "the words of God," Evangelist warns Christian: "See that ye refuse not him that speaketh" and reminds his pupil that "the just shall live by faith" (Heb. 10:38). He accuses Christian of rejecting "the counsel of the most high," of being "deluded" by a man favoring "only the Doctrine of this World" (20–22). "Believe me," Evangelist continues, "there is nothing in all this noise, that thou hast heard of this sottish man, but a design to beguile thee of thy Salvation, by turning thee from the way in which I had set thee." Once again convinced by Evangelist, Christian calls himself "a thousand fools for hearkening to" the counsel of Mr. Worldly-Wiseman and declares himself "greatly ashamed to think that this Gentlemans arguments, flowing only from the flesh, should have that prevalency with him as to cause him to forsake the right way" (23–24).

Back on the right path, Christian reaches the gate pointed out by Evangelist. When asked by the gate-keeper, Good-Will, whether his neighbors followed him to "perswade" him to return, Christian tells the story of Obstinate and Pliable, but now realizes the parallel between the latter and himself:

> Truly, said *Christian*, I have said the truth of *Pliable*, and if I should also say all the truth of my self, it will appear there is no betterment 'twixt him and my self. 'Tis true, he went back to his own house, but I also turned aside to go in the way of death, being perswaded thereto by the carnal arguments of one Mr. *Worldly Wiseman*. (26)

The rhetorical power of "carnal arguments" later becomes one of the crucial topics during Christian's instruction in the Interpreter's house. Explaining the tableau of Patience and Passion, the Interpreter warns that "since things present, and our fleshly appetite, *are such near Neighbours one to another*; and again, because things to come, and carnal sense, are such strangers one to another: therefore it is, that the first of these so suddenly fall into *amity*, and that *distance* is so continued between the second" (32). In being so readily persuaded by Mr. Worldly-Wiseman's carnal arguments, Christian had demonstrated the truth of the Interpreter's lesson.

After visiting the house of the Interpreter and having all the emblems read to him, Christian comes to the place of Christ's Cross, where he is relieved of his burden of sin. Christian soon tries again to convince others to join him on the path. "I will help you off with your Irons," he says to the three men asleep with "Fetters upon their heels." But once again he fails. Simple sees no danger and doesn't believe; Sloth might be capable of seeing but is too lazy to embrace belief actively; and Presumption is too self-satisfied in his own knowledge to either believe or act differently. This audience just goes back to sleep, for as Bunyan's gloss puts it, "There is no perswasion will do, if God openeth not the eyes" (39).

Still later, in dialogue with Charity, Christian notes the difference between the example one sets and the arguments one makes: "I know also that a man by his conversation, may soon overthrow what by argument or perswasion he doth labour to fasten upon others for their good" (51). Action here is represented by verbal activity—conversation—indicating that Bunyan is not making a simple distinction between states of the soul manifest in bodily acts and uses of words manifest in mental persuasion.

Rather, the distinction is between God's words enacted by the saints and arguments either opposed to or disconnected from those words. This distinction is more fully exemplified and complicated in the later dialogue with Talkative.

After Christian resists Apollyon's flattering attempt "*to diswade* Christian *from persisting in his way*" (57) and then listens to Faithful's story of being tempted by Wanton's "flattering tongue" (68), both pilgrims meet up with Talkative, a neighbor who talks the talk but believeth not. As Christian puts it, "Religion hath no place in his heart, or house, or conversation; all he hath lieth in his *tongue*, and his Religion is to make a noise *therewith*." Faithful is in danger of being beguiled by Talkative's tongue, until Christian explains how he "*talketh* of Prayer, of Repentance, of Faith, and of the New-birth: but he knows but only to *talk* of them" (78). To Faithful the lesson is clear: "I see that Saying and Doing are two things, and hereafter I shall better observe this distinction" (79).

Christian seems to confirm this lesson, declaring that men will be judged by their answers to the question "Were you *Doers*, or *Talkers* only?" But the "only" here also complicates the distinction between "doers" and "talkers." First, Christian quotes Paul's condemnation of "those great Talkers too, *sounding Brass, and Tinckling Cymbals* [1 Cor. 13:1]" and then explains this scriptural passage with still another: "*Things without life, giving sound* [1 Cor. 14:7]. Things without life, that is, without the true Faith and Grace of the Gospel; and consequently, things that shall never be placed in the Kingdom of Heaven among those that are the Children of life: Though their *sound* by their *talk*, be as if it were the *Tongue*, or voice of an Angel" (80). But the point of the passage from 1 Corinthians and the implication of Bunyan's exegesis is that both talking *and* doing are empty without the proper state of grace. All are at fault, talkers and doers alike, if they "have not charity" in their hearts (1 Cor. 13:1). As Bunyan goes on to illustrate, words and deeds must be accompanied by true faith, the right persuasion.

Christian makes this point to Faithful by encouraging him to engage Talkative on the topic of "the power of Religion" and to ask whether it is "set up in his Heart, House, or Conversation" (81). This Faithful does, and the ensuing dialogue demonstrates the importance of a correspondence among soul, body, and mind—among a state of grace (heart), place of doing (house), and act of talking (conversation). That is, words must correspond to both inward state and outward act. The distinction between talking words and performing acts is further blurred when Faithful presents the true signs of grace:

a life of holiness; heart-holiness, family-holiness (if he hath a Family) and by
Conversation-holiness in the world: which in the general teacheth him, inwardly
to abhor his sin, and himself for that in secret, to suppress it in his Family, and
to promote holiness in the World; not by talk only, as an Hypocrite or Talkative
person may do: but by a practical Subjection in Faith, and Love, to the power of
the word. (83)

Ultimately, then, Talkative is condemned not because he uses words but
because his religion stands "only in word" (85) and not in *the* Word.
Words are on both sides of the distinction between talking and doing.
And it is precisely the importance of words in the Word that forms the
basis of Bunyan's written allegory.

This lengthy dialogue with Talkative takes place near the middle of *The
Pilgrim's Progress*, but the text's obsession with words, verbal exchange,
persuasion—in short, rhetoric—continues throughout the second half
of the allegory. The narrative concludes not with Christian's arrival at the
Celestial City but with Ignorance being carried off to Hell, Ignorance
whose earlier dialogue with Christian demonstrated his failure to follow
Christian's advice to "pass the same Judgement upon our selves which the
Word passes" (146). That is precisely what Ignorance is ignorant of: He
is unaware that reading the Bible or even reading oneself is not enough;
one must "allow" oneself to be read by God's Word. And his sin is revealed, appropriately enough, when he attempts to answer Christian's
question: "But why, or by what, art thou perswaded that thou hast left all
for God and Heaven?" Ignorance answers: "My heart tells me so." Noting
that the heart may be deceitful in its persuasion, Christian remonstrates
with Ignorance: "Except the word of God beareth witness in this matter,
other Testimony is of no value" (145). And what is the scriptural testimony? "The imagination of mans heart is evil from his Youth" (Genesis
8:20), quotes Christian. It is this testimony as interpreted by Christian
that Ignorance cannot accept: "I will never believe that my heart is thus
bad" (146). By the interpretive lights of Christian (and Bunyan), Ignorance remains ignorant and is finally condemned because he is of the
wrong persuasion. He is one of those who "presumptuously continue to
flatter themselves in the way of their own hearts" (150).[8]

[8] For further discussion, see James Large, *Evenings with John Bunyan; or, The Dream Interpreted* (London, 1861), p. 287; James F. Forrest, "Bunyan's Ignorance and the Flatterer: A
Study in the Literary Art of Damnation," *Studies in Philology* 60 (January 1963): 12–22; and
Richard F. Hardin, "Bunyan, Mr. Ignorance, and the Quakers," *Studies in Philology* 69 (October 1972): 496–508.

Before leaving the topos of rhetoric in Bunyan's text, let me make passing comment on a figure that seems to be the exact representation of perverse rhetoric: the Flatterer. He makes only a brief appearance in the narrative, and ironically we are given very few of his flattering words, yet his rhetorical presence is felt everywhere throughout *The Pilgrim's Progress*. As Christian and his second companion, Hopeful, are deciding which way to proceed, "a man black of flesh, but covered with a very light Robe" comes and tells them to follow him to the Celestial City. Easily convinced, they follow but soon find themselves entangled in a net. "*The white robe fell off the black mans back*: then they saw where they were." Christian exclaims: "Did not the Shepherds bid us beware of the flatterers? As is the saying of the Wise man, so we have found it this day: *A man that flattereth his Neighbour, spreadeth a Net for his feet* [Prov. 29:5]." The pilgrims are saved by a Shining One, who identifies the "*Flatterer*, a false Apostle, that hath transformed himself into an Angel of Light." Christian and Hopeful escape, admitting they had been warned to "beware of the *Flatterer*" but they "did not imagine . . . that this fine-spoken man had been he" (133–34).

So much for the "fine-spoken" rhetoric of the staged dialogues. I turn now to the rhetorical effects of those dialogues on the reader by comparing two classic reader-response interpretations of Bunyan's narrative.

READER-RESPONSE CRITICISM AS RHETORICAL STUDY

The previous section demonstrates how *The Pilgrim's Progress* thematizes several rhetorical issues: the proper use of metaphor in fiction, the power of good and bad persuasion, the danger of empty talk, and the hermeneutics of the Word. Such a reading is rhetorical precisely because it dwells on these topics. There are, however, more expansive ways to go rhetorical, which I can illustrate by discussing Bunyan's book in terms of reader-response criticism and reception study. We will look first at two early interpretive efforts by Wolfgang Iser and Stanley Fish. Both critics appended theoretical arguments to their ground-breaking books of practical criticism, Iser's *The Implied Reader* and Fish's *Self-Consuming Artifacts*, but it was the many examples of critical practice that made the strongest case for their new versions of reader talk. Comparing their interpretations of *The Pilgrim's Progress* will illustrate the similarities and differences between these two influential reader critics, provide some examples of their critical rhetoric, and suggest a basis for relating reader-response criticism to reception history and rhetorical hermeneutics.

Iser subtitles his chapter on Bunyan's book "The Doctrine of Predestination and the Shaping of the Novel," and this literary-historical question plays a prominent role in his interpretation of *The Pilgrim's Progress*.
Puritan ideology required from each person a scrupulous internal examination to discover signs of salvation or damnation. As Iser puts it,
"only through self-observation was it possible to attain any degree of as-
surance" about one's own spiritual destiny.[9] In *The Pilgrim's Progress*, Bunyan demonstrates that this "self-awareness requires experience," which is
"what Christian gains in his confrontation with the world" (28). However, experiential self-examination is not easy, "because each experience
can only call forth subjective and, therefore, unreliable reactions." The
solution, according to Iser, is that Bunyan's pilgrim must go through
more and more experiences to develop certainty about his preordained
future. Thus, "in *Pilgrim's Progress* the theological withholding of certitude stimulates human self-assertion, the development of which fore-
shadows the pattern of the eighteenth-century novel" (24). Or as Iser explains, since self-examination requires individual experience, Bunyan
emphasizes "human situations" and "individuality increasingly becomes
an end in itself," so that "Christian's story is one of an increasing self-
awareness, and in this respect it is indisputably a novel, or at least a novel
in-the-making" (28).

The reader-response aspect of Iser's interpretation appears when he
relates his literary-historical arguments to claims about Bunyan's implied
reader: "The members of Calvinist sects discovered themselves in Christian—not only in their weak humanity but also through the promise that
by self-examination they could overcome their weakness and so attain an
increasing degree of certitude" (23). In other words, *The Pilgrim's Progress*
was a fictional conduct book for its seventeenth-century Puritan readers.
The monologues "were of particular interest . . . for Christian's search for
reassurance offered [readers] a guideline as to how they should examine
themselves" (19), and the dialogues were "another edifying element of
the book, for here the Puritan reader is shown how to overcome the
doubts and temptations which the prose dialogue enabled him to experience virtually as his own" (11). Thus, up to a point the reader's experience paralleled that of the hero as they both progressed toward greater
and greater certainty about their individual destinies. In this way, *The Pilgrim's Progress* responded effectively to the prior psychological and spiritual needs of its Puritan readership.

---

[9] Wolfgang Iser, *The Implied Reader: Patterns of Communication in Prose Fiction from Bunyan
to Beckett* (Baltimore, 1974), p. 27; further citations are given in the text.

But Iser argues further that the identification of reader and character is never complete. Bunyan continually offers contrasting perspectives—of dream narrator to Christian, of human characters to functional characters, of prose dialogue to verse summary—so that Puritan readers, by putting these perspectives together, finally have a more encompassing knowledge than Christian's and thus attain an experience in narrative reading that he never achieves in his narrated life. Puritan readers may not be absolutely certain about their own salvation—such certainty is impossible in this life—but reading *The Pilgrim's Progress* has given them more knowledge about the process of self-examination and the certainty of its effectiveness. In various ways reading Bunyan's book filled a "psychic gap that had been created by the doctrine of predestination" (18). Christian must discover the meaning of his own destiny for himself, as the Puritan readers combine the story's different perspectives to discover its meaning for themselves. "The fictionally presented certainty of fulfillment of the yearnings shared by all Puritans was a vital feature of the process of edification, because it offered the imaginary achievement of what was excluded by the doctrine of predestination" (26).

The gap-filling described by Iser works in two directions: the reader fills gaps between perspectives in the text, and reading the text fills gaps in the reader's psychological and spiritual fulfillment. It is precisely the latter compensating function that defines for Iser the most important characteristic of reading literature:

> Obviously, the fictional humanizing of theological rigorism must have fulfilled an elementary historical need, since the Calvinists' strict distinctions between truth and fiction were allowed to fade into the background. And from this historical observation, we might draw a conclusion that will apply to all forms of fiction, from *Pilgrim's Progress* right through to the experimental works of today: namely, that literature counterbalances the deficiencies produced by prevailing philosophies. (28)

So it is not simply that Iser's Puritan reader takes the narrative representation of Christian's conduct as exemplary; rather by combining perspectives, the reader constructs a position not explicitly stated in the text nor readily available in the nonfictional discourses of seventeenth-century Puritanism. For Iser, then, the rhetorical power of *The Pilgrim's Progress* is that it not only represents Christian's experience but also furnishes a Christian experience for its readers. In this way, *The Pilgrim's Progress* offered satisfaction to its seventeenth-century Puritan readers, whose preexisting needs were met through the compensating function of literature.

It is a very different reading process that Stanley Fish describes in his interpretation of *The Pilgrim's Progress*. For Iser, Bunyan presents a progression toward certitude for both his character and his reader, but for Fish *The Pilgrim's Progress* is "antiprogressive, both as a narrative and as a reading experience."[10] For Iser, the allegory finally makes good on the promise of its title and thus the experience it offers is "self-fulfilling"; while for Fish, the text "consistently disappoints the expectations generated by the title" (229) and the resulting experience makes the text "self-consuming." In fact, Fish argues, *"The Pilgrim's Progress* is the ultimate self-consuming artifact, for the insights it yields are inseparable from the demonstration of the inadequacy of its own forms, which are also the forms of the reader's understanding" (264).

Fish's description of the reading experience differs from Iser's at almost every point. Not only do Fish and Iser disagree over whether a progression takes place for the character and the reader, but they also attribute diametrically opposite values to self-assertion. For Iser, the representation of self-assertion becomes a defining characteristic of the book's novelistic qualities, and the reader's recognition of Christian's growing self-awareness becomes the lesson of a text that is labeled, consequently, a "novel in-the-making." But for Fish, it is precisely at "moments of apparent self-assertion that Christian's dependence [on God] is most clearly and forcefully revealed; so that if we do think in terms of a progress, it is never felt to be the pilgrim's" (233). Every act of deluded self-assertion becomes part of the nonprogressive cycle of Christian's failures, his continual errors in judgment, his repeated displays of weakness, and his perpetual forgetfulness about his total dependence on God's grace. This antiprogressive pattern is paralleled in the reader's experience: "For the reader as well as for the pilgrim, to believe in the metaphor of the journey and in the *pilgrim's* progress, is to believe in himself, to prefer the operations of his discursive intellect to the revealed word of God. (*I* am the way.) It is Bunyan's method alternately to encourage and then disallow this prideful self-reliance by encouraging and then disallowing the interpretative pretensions of his prose" (237).

I can contrast the interpretations of Fish and Iser in another way, borrowing a distinction posited by Fish, a distinction organizing his whole book but which his later work makes problematic: the opposition between

[10] Stanley E. Fish, *Self-Consuming Artifacts: The Experience of Seventeenth-Century Literature* (Berkeley, Calif., 1972), p. 229; further references appear in the text.

"rhetorical" and "dialectical" presentations. Fish's explanation of this opposition is worth quoting in full:

> A presentation is rhetorical if it satisfies the needs of its readers. The
> word "satisfies" is meant literally here; for it is characteristic of a rhetor-
> ical form to mirror and present for approval the opinions its readers al-
> ready hold. It follows then that the experience of such a form will be
> flattering, for it tells the reader that what he has always thought about
> the world is true and that the *ways* of his thinking are sufficient. . . . A
> dialectical presentation, on the other hand, is disturbing, for it requires
> of its readers a searching and rigorous scrutiny of everything they be-
> lieve in and live by. It is didactic in a special sense; it does not preach the
> truth, but asks that its readers discover the truth for themselves, and this
> discovery is often made at the expense not only of a reader's opinions
> and values, but of his self-esteem. If the experience of a rhetorical form
> is flattering, the experience of a dialectical form is humiliating. (1–2)

Given this distinction between "dialectical" and "rhetorical," we can
recharacterize the interpretations of Fish and Iser in this way: Fish argues
that *The Pilgrim's Progress* is a dialectical text providing a humiliating but
beneficial experience for its readers who are changed by being disap-
pointed in the course of reading; while Iser argues that Bunyan's is a
rhetorical text providing a satisfying experience for readers whose needs
are successfully met as they become self-aware as a result of reading.

One could easily argue that both reading experiences are rhetorical—
in the sense of being effects of texts on audiences—and thus Fish's and
Iser's reader-response approaches are similar in their shared rhetorical
orientations. From this perspective, Fish's terms "rhetorical" and "dialectical" simply name two versions of the rhetorical, and indeed Fish and
Iser in their early work are both engaged in related forms of rhetorical
criticism with a reader vocabulary.[11] But more important for my concerns
here is the notion of rhetoric Fish uses to make his original distinction.
On the very first page of *Self-Consuming Artifacts*, Fish declares that he is
using "rhetorical" precisely "in the sense defined and attacked by Plato
in the *Gorgias*." For Plato's Socrates, as we have seen, rhetoric is a form of
flattery, which misleadingly imitates the true arts of the body and soul.[12]
Just as cookery is the false imitation of bodily medicine, so too is rhetoric
the mere simulacrum of ideal justice.

[11] See my *Rhetorical Power* (Ithaca, 1989), chap. 2.
[12] See Plato, *Gorgias* 463–65 and the use of this passage in my Preface, above.

Fish uses this figurative ratio as tropological grounding for his discussion of Plato's *Phaedrus*, the first self-consuming artifact he considers. In a table contrasting the qualities of the "Bad Lover–Rhetorician" to those of the "Good Lover–Dialectician," Fish characterizes the former as "flatterers who provide a pleasant and comfortable experience, an ego-satisfying experience" and the latter as "physicians whose ministrations are often painful because they force their charges to face unpleasant truths about themselves and counsel abandonment of the values they have always lived with" (18). Flattering rhetoricians are fake physicians supplying audiences with self-satisfying experiences; while true dialecticians minister to the soul with disturbing but beneficial self-consuming artifacts. Flattering rhetoricians deal in bad persuasion and mere opinion; philosophical dialecticians deal in good instruction and true knowledge.

There are two points I want to make about these Platonic notions and Fish's use of them in his early work. First, in *Self-Consuming Artifacts*, Fish accepts, at least as a working distinction, the negative view of rhetoric presented in Plato's *Gorgias* (and only partially retracted in his *Phaedrus*) and rhetoric's opposition to a privileged activity called dialectic.[13] To accept this opposition is to follow a long tradition that unquestioningly adopts Plato's invention of the distinction between rhetoric and philosophy in his coining of the term *rhētorikē*. Thomas Cole and Edward Schiappa have made a strong case that prior to Plato in the older Greek Sophists the concerns of rhetoric and philosophy were treated together under the study of *logos*. In the *Gorgias*, the term *rhētorikē* appears for the first time, and Plato's coining of this new term was a crucial moment in the separation of two aspects of the same study—of *logos*—into two competing enterprises—rhetoric and philosophy.[14]

In Fish's later neopragmatism, it is exactly this separation that he questions and ultimately rejects as a theoretical position. But Fish also acknowledges the force of the distinction in its historical manifestations, and this is my second point. Though Fish now agrees with Richard Rorty that the separation of good philosophy from bad rhetoric is a misleading

---

[13] See also Stanley E. Fish, *Surprised by Sin: The Reader in Paradise Lost*, 2d ed. (Berkeley, Calif., 1971), pp. 6–7, 49–50. However, even Fish's early employment of antirhetorical Platonism was not as uncomplicated and straightforward as I am suggesting here. See, for example, the reading of the *Cratylus* he uses to explain Milton's suspicion of seventeenth-century attempts to find the perfect language in *Surprised by Sin*, chap. 3.

[14] Thomas Cole, *The Origins of Rhetoric in Ancient Greece* (Baltimore, 1991); and Edward Schiappa, *Protagoras and Logos: A Study in Greek Philosophy and Rhetoric* (Columbia, S.C., 1991). For discussion of this thesis, see Ian Worthington, ed., *Persuasion: Greek Rhetoric in Action* (London, 1994); also see Carol Poster, "Being and Becoming: Rhetorical Ontology in Early Greek Thought," *Philosophy and Rhetoric* 29, no. 1 (1996): 1–14.

invention of philosophical foundationalism starting with Plato, he also recognizes that Western intellectual history has continually restaged the conflict between these oppositions, whether they are called relativism and absolutism, appearance and reality, opinion and knowledge, sophistry and Platonism, or rhetoric and philosophy.[15]

Foundationalism versus antifoundationalism is another way of characterizing this conflicted history. Foundationalism, as described by Fish, refers to "any attempt to ground inquiry and communication in something more firm and stable than mere belief or unexamined practice." In contrast, antifoundationalism rejects the effort "to identify that ground and then so to order our activities that they become anchored to it and are thereby rendered objective and principled." Antifoundationalists give up on this project to find "a 'method,' a recipe with premeasured ingredients which when ordered and combined according to absolutely explicit instructions . . . will *produce*, all by itself, the correct result."[16] A rhetorical hermeneutics goes antifoundational when it moves traditional interpretive theory away from proposing universal accounts of interpretation in general and toward doing mininarratives of historically situated acts of rhetorically using texts. Such reception studies focus less on the interaction of reader and text and more on the relations among historical interpreters arguing over and otherwise using texts within specific cultural conversations at particular historical moments.

Now, a rhetorical hermeneutics would attempt to account for Fish's and Iser's acts of interpreting *The Pilgrim's Progress* by providing a detailed rhetorical analysis of those acts within their respective historical contexts. For example, to present such descriptions, we would first need to outline the theoretical details of Iser's phenomenology of reading and Fish's affective stylistics.[17] We could then place these theoretical assumptions within the different literary-historical arguments each was making, Iser for the gap-filling increasingly required by the developing genre of the novel and Fish for the contrasting discourse traditions of self-fulfilling versus self-consuming artifacts. Then we would need to place the two critic-theorists within a reception history of academic interpre-

[15] See, especially, Stanley Fish, "Rhetoric," in his *Doing What Comes Naturally: Change, Rhetoric, and the Practice of Theory in Literary and Legal Studies* (Durham, N.C., 1989), pp. 471–502; Richard Rorty, *Philosophy and the Mirror of Nature* (Princeton, 1979), pp. 156–57; and Chap. 2, above.

[16] Fish, *Doing What Comes Naturally*, pp. 342–43. For further discussion, see Chap. 3, n. 6, above.

[17] See my *Interpretive Conventions: The Reader in the Study of American Fiction* (Ithaca, 1982), chaps. 1 and 2; and Robert C. Holub, *Reception Theory: A Critical Introduction* (London, 1984).

tations of Bunyan and his texts, examining with and for whom Fish and Iser argue, placing both critics within their contrasting national contexts of English studies, German and Anglo-American.

And this would not be all. Such a delimited description of their differing rhetorical contexts would "explain" their differing interpretive arguments about *The Pilgrim's Progress* in the sense of providing a fuller, but certainly not exhaustive, account of why they argued the way they did. But instead of providing the details of this rhetorical hermeneutic account of Iser's and Fish's differences, I want to emphasize the way they are the same, how their reader-response criticism contrasts with a more historically situated reception analysis, and then use this reception study to elaborate further the theoretical side of rhetorical hermeneutics.

RECEPTION HISTORY AND READER TALK

In *Reading "Piers Plowman" and "The Pilgrim's Progress"*, Barbara A. Johnson presents a reception history of two texts that allow her to trace the development of certain religious and secular interpretive conventions. What she calls the "Protestant reader" is a set of interconnected assumptions and strategies for reading and using books:

> For the Protestant reader, texts are instruments rather than objects, and they are viewed in salvational rather than recreational terms. Inspiration comes from God, and specifically the Holy Spirit, rather than other works in a literary tradition. Finally, the stature of authors depends not on personal "genius" . . . but on their function as God's servants.[18]

In contrast, a "lettered reader . . . processes texts in terms of generic categories, searches for a 'prototype,' and speculates about what the author had read" (162). Such readers "are often highly educated and well read" and "typically approach texts as imaginative productions and as art" (253, n. 2). Their way of reading treats literature as "a distinct classification with its own taxonomy, separable from all others" and assumes "that books beget other books" and "that a writer's appropriation and manipulation of a literary tradition is of paramount interest" (162).[19]

---

[18] Barbara A. Johnson, *Reading "Piers Plowman" and "The Pilgrim's Progress": Reception and the Protestant Reader* (Carbondale, Ill., 1992), p. 26.

[19] Johnson is careful to explain that she is describing a continuum of historical ways of reading. She notes that "the dividing line in terms of Protestant or lettered responses to texts is one of emphasis rather than division until the late seventeenth century" (*Reading*

Johnson's reception history of *The Pilgrim's Progress* frames itself as a combination of *rezeptionsästhetik* and *l'histoire du livre*.[20] She explicitly uses Jauss's notion of horizons of expectations to describe the beliefs of historical audiences, and she supplements her method by arguing that "the history of reading can be traced in the history of books" (21). This self-consciously historical approach to readers reading can be contrasted to much reader-response criticism, and in passing Johnson implicitly opposes her reading of Bunyan's book to Fish's interpretation with its "unusual, ahistorical view of the reader's role" (285, n. 87).

Curiously, Johnson does not mention Iser's readerly interpretation of *The Pilgrim's Progress*. But her brief remarks on Iser's phenomenology of reading are suggestive and worth further comment. Instead of linking Iser's practical criticism with Fish's, as I have always done, Johnson associates it with Jauss's project.[21]

Reception theorists, most notably Wolfgang Iser and Hans Robert Jauss of the Konstanz school, place more emphasis on the text in their investigations of the interactions between work and audience. For example, Iser posits an "implied reader" that can be assembled from the structures of the text itself by focusing on the "gaps, blanks, and indeterminacies" that provoke varied responses. But it is Jauss, in his quest to bridge the gap between historical and aesthetic approaches to the writing of literary history, who supplies the best model for understanding the text's role in the production of meaning and how that role evolves over time. (14)

There are two distinctions at work in Johnson's comments on Fish's and Iser's reader-response criticism. The first, and less useful, is the reader/

"Piers Plowman" and "The Pilgrim's Progress," p. 3) and that she is "not arguing that these two poles of readership are mutually exclusive or monolithic" (26).

[20] At p. 256, n. 38, Johnson (*Reading "Piers Plowman" and "The Pilgrim's Progress"*) specifically compares her method to the similar combination of reception theory and book history found in Cathy N. Davidson, *Revolution and the Word: The Rise of the Novel in America* (New York, 1986). On the history of books, especially in relation to histories of reading, see Davidson, ed., *Reading in America: Literature and Social History* (Baltimore, 1989); and Michele Moylan and Lane Stiles, eds., *Reading Books: Essays on the Material Text and Literature in America* (Amherst, 1996).

[21] As have many other historians of recent critical theory: see Brook Thomas, "Reading Wolfgang Iser or Responding to a Theory of Response," *Comparative Literature Studies* 19 (spring 1982): 54–66; and Robert Holub, "Reception Theory: School of Constance," in *The Cambridge History of Literary Criticism*, vol. 8, ed. Raman Selden (Cambridge, 1995), pp. 319–46.

text opposition. Johnson uses the opposition to distinguish between the more text-oriented approaches of Iser and Jauss and the more reader-oriented theories of Jonathan Culler (reading conventions) and later Fish (interpretive communities). The theoretical distinction Johnson makes here is not only misguided, as I have elsewhere tried to show, it is unnecessary.[22] It is misguided because foundationalist theories of autonomous readers interacting with independent texts continue a bankrupt philosophical tradition of assuming a subject/object split, a tradition in which 1970s reader-response theory participated. Not only have some reader theorists abandoned this tradition, but some (Fish in his neopragmatism) have attempted to explain how the text/reader distinction has worked historically: how "text" and "reader" are mutually dependent and come into view simultaneously within particular interpretive communities.

All this is to say that the distinction between text- and reader-oriented approaches among theories of reading hardly seems worth making, unless of course there is a desire to distinguish between comparative talk of readers and texts within interpretive vocabularies. But on this point, there is very little to choose between Iser's and Fish's interpretive rhetorics. Iser and Fish both talk a great deal about texts in their practical criticism. Indeed, they share a common rhetorical focus that emphasizes the effects of texts on readers. At the level of theory and of practice, then, the reader/text distinction does no useful work in contrasting these two cases of readerly interpretation.[23]

The second opposition posited by Johnson—between historical and ahistorical inquiries—does mark an important distinction among reader-oriented critics, but not quite in the way she supposes. It could easily be argued that Iser's interpretation of reading *The Pilgrim's Progress* is just as "ahistorical" as Johnson claims Fish's is. Thus, her silence on this fact is a bit puzzling. But the real issue here is what counts as "historical." On this point, I have been as guilty as others in making a too easy distinction between recent historical approaches and a 1970s reader-response

[22] See my *Rhetorical Power*, chap. 1; and "The Turns of Reader-Response Criticism," in *Conversations: Contemporary Critical Theory and the Teaching of Literature*, ed. Charles Moran and Elizabeth Penfield (Urbana, Ill., 1990), pp. 38–54.
[23] To clarify further: the seventies theory and practice of Fish's affective stylistics and Iser's phenomenological criticism differ insignificantly in their talk of readers and texts. It was only later when Fish made his move toward neopragmatism that he called into question at the metacritical level a certain foundationalist distinction between reader and text. Only at that point did important theoretical differences emerge between Fish and Iser: see their 1980–81 *Diacritics* exchange; and my *Interpretive Conventions*, chap. 2.

criticism characterized as ahistorical. Actually, some early reader criticism, including that of Fish and Iser, was very historical but historical in a way different from, say, reception study and the New Historicism. For example, it is quite historical to talk about how a text's rhetoric fits into or contradicts the beliefs of specific historical audiences even if this talk is based exclusively on reading the audience's beliefs off the text being interpreted. That is, when Iser and Fish read *The Pilgrim's Progress* and find it assuming a certain view of predestination or spiritual progress and then posit this view in the late seventeenth-century reader, they are being historical. Indeed, this is what the supposedly more historical Jauss has often done in establishing a contemporary audience's horizon of expectations, and it is exactly what Johnson does in interpreting various rhetorical strategies in Bunyan's "Apology." In all these cases, the reader-oriented critic rhetorically reads the literary texts as evidence for sets of beliefs that the text is either reinforcing or upsetting in its readers.

But the historical/ahistorical distinction does usefully mark a difference in *how* one interprets historically: what kinds of textual evidence are used, what aspects of past contexts are foregrounded, what types of connections are made, and so on. Much traditional reader-response criticism interprets texts closely to reveal the potential ways they might affect readers. To interpret historical texts for their rhetorical effects is to do a kind of historical work. Furthermore, Fish and Iser give hints of an expanded historical project when they occasionally draw attention to the details of the historical context in which their object texts are produced, for example, noting the assumptions of an intended reader or the appeals to a historical repertoire.

The difference, then, between earlier reader criticism and that of current reception study is not between doing historical interpretation and not doing it. The distinction is between doing history one way and doing it another.[24] Jauss promotes and Johnson practices a form of reception study that goes well beyond reading literary texts and citing a few surrounding documents in order to establish a contemporary audience's beliefs. Johnson demonstrates how a focus on the history of reception means reading textual interpretations as closely as the texts they interpret. I want to push this difference further by making reception history into rhetorical hermeneutics, focusing not only on the rhetoric of literary texts but on the rhetoric of their historical interpretations and the diachronic and synchronic dimensions of the cultural conversations in

---

[24] See Fish's critique of historicist claims to a unique historicity in Stanley Fish, *Professional Correctness: Literary Studies and Political Change* (Oxford, 1995), pp. 128–29.

which those interpretations participate.[25] To advocate such a project does not leave the work of Fish and Iser behind but rather builds on it and reuses those aspects contributing to reception studies.

In the previous chapter, I illustrated some reader-oriented talk about Douglass's *Narrative* and rhetorically examined Fuller's 1845 review to demonstrate how that interpretation was simultaneously a reading of Douglass and an intervention in the "Bible politics" of debates over slavery and abolition. That reception history could be extended to include some nineteenth-century readings of *The Pilgrim's Progress*, readings presented in various genres such as sermons and lectures, commentary in new editions, and even rewritings and imitations of Bunyan's popular text.[26] For instance, the anonymous *Pilgrim's Progress in the Last Days* (1843) describes an updated Christian encountering a fugitive slave seeking protection from the "cruel giant" Slavery, who "hunteth me with hounds" and "who hath devoured millions and millions of my nation." Opposed by Conformity and Expediency, a character named Christian Abolition calls not only for sheltering the fugitive but for overthrowing the castle of Slavery, who "hath for ages made captive of the helpless, and fattened on the bodies and souls of men, women and children."[27]

The old giant's ideological brother, Pro-Slavery, acts as his foremost defender, with powerful minions and an "almost impregnable castle" of his own. But Pro-Slavery has other, more subtle weapons at his disposal, for "he was privately betrothed to a daughter of Mr. Expediency called False-Charity, who with her tongue did utter much love, but her heart went after her covetousnes." Supporting the giant's party and condemning those who pitied his captives, "she could quote scripture as readily as him who

---

[25] To restate my earlier claims: These reception histories participate, as historical practice, in the heterogeneous movement known as cultural studies. But such participation forms only one side of the coin in rhetorical hermeneutics, for this reception analysis is also historical practice standing in for hermeneutic theory. That is, rhetorical hermeneutics argues against foundationalist accounts of interpretation in general by putting forward specific studies of historical acts of reading in particular. Thus, a reception study within rhetorical hermeneutics functions simultaneously as an instance of antifoundationalism, replacing general hermeneutic theorizing, and as an example of cultural rhetoric study, presenting historical accounts of individual interpretive acts within specific cultural conversations. In still other words, this reception study practices hermeneutic theory by doing rhetorical history.

[26] "Until the Civil War, *The Pilgrim's Progress* continued a lively best-seller, reaching the height of its popularity in the 1840's"—David E. Smith, *John Bunyan in America* (Bloomington, Ind., 1966), p. 16.

[27] Anonymous, *Pilgrim's Progress in the Last Days* (New England, 1843), pp. 52–53; further references are given in the text.

beset the Prince in the wilderness" (56–57). Indeed, during Christian's
initial encounters with the abolitionists and proslavery advocates, both
sides heatedly engage in 1840s Bible politics as they prepare for battle.

Later in the adapted narrative, Christian counsels Peace Man who plans
preaching to a now divided House Beautiful: "We are to forgive, as Christ
also forgave us. That's the persuasive—we have no heart to forgive till
forgiven ourselves. By the experienced sweets of pardon obtained, the
Holy Ghost prevailingly persuadeth to peace; nay, binds us to it" (132).
The exact nature of this persuasion continued as a topic in nineteenth-
century receptions of Bunyan's text, both in its connection with pro- and
antislavery polemics and in relation to rhetorically influenced conver-
sions more generally. In the 1849 *Pilgrim's Progress in the Nineteenth Century*,
the orthodox Presbyterian William Weeks has his hero, Thoughtful, complain about what might be called the rhetorical theory of grace underlying views of "moral suasion" among "new-measure" preachers. Mr. Bold,
for instance, suggests that "the sinner changes his heart through the
influence of motives alone, as presented by the word, the preacher, and
the Spirit." This view Thoughtful condemns as an Arminian doctrine
"that the nature of moral agency is such that God cannot change the
heart by an act of power, but can only use persuasion; and all the persuasion he can use may be resisted. This scheme makes it depend upon
man's sovereign will, and not upon God's sovereign will, whether the sinner shall be saved or not."

In contrast, Thoughtful praises another preacher's more traditional
Calvinist views of conversion: "Dr. Eloquent does not believe the change
is produced by physical power, nor by moral power, as these terms are usually understood; nor without the instrumentality of divine truth. Physical
power usually denotes the application of matter to matter, as when a mill
is moved by water or by steam. Moral power denotes the use of motives
to persuade. Men are not converted by either of these, but by the new-
creating power of the Holy Spirit."[28] From such technical theology and

[28] William R. Weeks, *The Pilgrim's Progress in the Nineteenth Century* (New York, 1849),
pp. 410–14. The author of *Pilgrim's Progress in the Last Days* appends to his text a reference
to another rewriting of Bunyan's text, Hawthorne's "The Celestial Rail-road," published in
the same year and containing a very different representation of the rhetorical effect of contemporary sermons and lectures. The narrator in Hawthorne's travesty comments on the
Rev. Dr. Wind-of-Doctrine, Rev. Shallow-Deep, Rev. Mr. Bewilderment, and their fellows in
a modernized Vanity Fair: "The labors of these eminent divines are aided by those of innu-
merable lecturers, who diffuse such a various profundity, in all subjects of human or celestial science, that any man may acquire an omnigenous erudition, without the trouble
of even learning to read." Nathaniel Hawthorne, "The Celestial Rail-road" (1843), in
Hawthorne: Tales and Sketches, ed. Roy Harvey Pearce (New York, 1982), p. 818.

homiletic treatises to popular conversion narratives and partisan debates over manufacturing public opinion, concern for reader/listener agency continued to be tied to conceptualizations of how cultural persuasion did its work.

The 1840s reception of *The Pilgrim's Progress* not only contributed to religious discussions of adult persuasion; it also supplied a prized example for arguments about the beneficial effects of good reading on children. In his 1844 *Lectures on the Pilgrim's Progress*, George Cheever wrote, "We speak from experience, and from what we have heard others describe of its effect upon their minds in early youth, when we suggest the importance of children early reading the Pilgrim's Progress. . . . It becomes a series of holy pictures engraven on the soul in its early, simple, childlike state." Cheever encourages parents to "write God's name upon your children's minds; and in order to do this, you must use the graving tools, which God himself has given you, the diamond pen of the Word of God."[29]

Cheever notes that *The Pilgrim's Progress* "never seems so beautiful, so fascinating a book, to those who read it first in later life as to those who, having read it in childhood, when its power over the imagination is unbounded, read it afterwards with a grave perception and understanding of its meaning" (274). No better example of this phenomenon of reception through rereading can be found than in the experiences documented by Bronson Alcott. In an 1839 journal entry, this transcendental philosopher and experimental educator wrote that "the *Pilgrim's Progress* is a work of pure genius. Reading this evening a passage from it, my early childhood was revived in my memory with a freshness and reality that no ordinary mind could have caused."[30] Years later, Alcott recommended that Bunyan's book "should be on the desk of every teacher, and in every home throughout Christendom. It never tires; it cannot be read too frequently; it is never finished, and the thousandth perusal is as new and as charming as the first." He went on to explain that *The Pilgrim's Progress* was "the first classic" next to the New Testament "that opened upon my eyes, and took captive all that was best in me; I read it again and again through all my childhood and youth; and have read it to thousands of children dur-

---

[29] George B. Cheever, *Lectures on the Pilgrim's Progress, and on the Life and Times of John Bunyan*, 3d ed. (New York, 1845), pp. 273–75. Cheever was Hawthorne's classmate at Bowdoin, a professor with Weeks at Andover, and an ardent abolitionist. His lectures, originally published in 1844, were perhaps the most popular American commentaries on Bunyan's book (Smith, *Bunyan in America*, p. 126, n. 26).

[30] Entry for 8 January 1839, *The Journals of Bronson Alcott*, ed. Odell Shepard (Boston, 1938), p. 111.

ing the last thirty years, in schools private and public, in Sunday schools and families, where I have chanced to be."[31]

Alcott's writings thus vividly illustrate Cheever's rhetorical point about children reading *The Pilgrim's Progress*. But they do more. In her reception history of Bunyan's allegory, Johnson adds a third type of reader to her taxonomy when she turns to the nineteenth century. These "ordinary readers" used the book "as a secular rather than a religious model for their lives."[32] Alcott seems to be one of these "secular readers" whose response to *The Pilgrim's Progress* shaped the rhetorical construction of his developing subjectivity: "This book is one of the few that gave me to myself. It is associated with reality. It unites me with childhood, and seems to chronicle my Identity. . . . That book was incorporated into the very substance of my youthful being. I thought and spoke through it. It was my most efficient teacher."[33] Here Alcott's description of his reading experience troubles a distinction between response and use that Johnson relies upon to contrast two categories of readership: "Whereas the book had acted upon Protestant readers, secular readers [presumably like Alcott] act upon the book, appropriating its structures to organize their own experience, whatever that experience may be."[34] To the contrary, Alcott's account suggests that reading as such is constituted by the various usages a text receives (as religious inspiration, as doctrinal resource, as aesthetic object, as identity paradigm), usages emerging while a reception unfolds for specific reading subjects within specific interpretive conventions (which might be characterized generally as Protestant, lettered, secular, or whatever).[35]

---

[31] A. Bronson Alcott, *Superintendent's Report of the Concord Schools to the School Committee, for the Year 1860–61*, p. 15; rpt. Alcott, *Essays on Education (1830–1862)*, ed. Walter Harding (Gainesville, Fla., 1960), p. 163.

[32] Johnson, *Reading "Piers Plowman" and "The Pilgrim's Progress,"* pp. 215–17.

[33] *Journals of Bronson Alcott*, p. 111. Also see A. Bronson Alcott, *New Connecticut: An Autobiographical Poem* (1881; rpt. Philadelphia, 1970), pp. 49–50, 143–44.

[34] Johnson, *Reading "Piers Plowman" and "The Pilgrim's Progress,"* p. 244.

[35] Actually, Alcott's pedagogical theory of reading books puts more emphasis on the individual using than on the communal strategies employed in the using: "Next to thinking for themselves, the best service any teacher can render his scholars is to show them how to use books. There are better or worse ways of studying, and a child should be helped to possess himself of the contents of a book in manners most consonant to his tastes and aptitudes. No two persons read after the same fashion, nor can books be studied alike by different persons" (Alcott, *Superintendent's Report*, p. 158). On the theoretical point about the misleading distinction between response and use, see Richard Rorty's comment on Eco's related "distinction between *interpreting* texts and *using* texts": "This, of course, is a distinction we pragmatists do not wish to make. On our view, all anybody ever does with anything is use it." Rorty, "The Pragmatist's Progress," in Umberto Eco with Rorty, Jonathan Culler,

Alcott's assistant at his Concord school enthusiastically praised his transactional view of teaching literacy: "It is a common remark, that the age of much reading is not an age of creative power. Yet why should it not be? Would the human mind cease its own appropriate action, if fed with proper food, in the proper way? . . . Mr. Alcott thinks that every book read, should be an event to a child; and all his plans of teaching, keep steadily in mind the object of making books live, breathe, and speak."[36] Writing specifically of *The Pilgrim's Progress*, Alcott himself treats his favorite book as "proper food" for the children he taught, recounting in his journal how he shows "them at each reading, what promises of pleasures they have in reserve in the leaves yet unread" and then exclaiming, "Ah! could the parents come as unreservedly to the tasting from the Springs, and taste deeply as these little ducks, and as gaily."[37] As we will see in the next chapter, Alcott's own children (or at least his daughter's famous creations) perfectly exemplified this ideal reception of *The Pilgrim's Progress*.

---

and Christine Brooke-Rose, *Interpretation and Overinterpretation*, ed. Stefan Collini (Cambridge, 1992), p. 93.

[36] [Elizabeth Palmer Peabody], *Record of a School: Exemplifying the General Principles of Spiritual Culture*, 2d ed. (1836; rpt. New York, 1969), p. 17.

[37] Alcott's journal entry for 18 January 1861, quoted in Dorothy McCuskey, *Bronson Alcott, Teacher* (1940; rpt. New York, 1969), p. 150.

CHAPTER 6

THE USE AND ABUSE OF FICTION:
READERS EATING BOOKS

Reade not to contradict, nor to belieue, but to waigh and consider. Some bookes are to bee tasted, others to bee swallowed, and some few to bee chewed and digested.

—Francis Bacon, "Of Studies" (1597)

Do not read as a glutton eats. Digest your books, turn them into nourishment, make them a part of your life that lives always.

—Annie H. Ryder, *Go Right On, Girls! Develop Your Bodies, Your Minds, Your Characters* (1891)

The first American review of *Huckleberry Finn* began, "'Good wine needs no bush;' and a book by Mark Twain needs no beating around the bush. One takes it as children do sweetmeats, with trusting confidence."[1] In December 1884, the month before this review appeared, the Philadelphia *Bulletin* published a letter from a Texas correspondent. It began: "I am a young woman, twenty-one years old, and am called bright and intelligent. I fear I have seriously impaired my mind by novel reading. Do you think I can restore it to a sound and vigorous condition by eschewing novels and reading only solid works?" The editor responded to this letter first by commenting that the writer "proves herself a less hopeless case than most of her sisters in the east, who are not only saturated with the dilute sentimentality of fiction, but who also are completely satisfied with their condition." He then went on to advise these "young ladies who feed their brains with novels, and their palates with confectionery": Avoid "silly or pernicious trash"; shun "the monstrous

---

[1] Review of *Huckleberry Finn*, Detroit *Free Press*, 10 January 1885, p. 8.

volume of wishy-washy, sensational, or at best neutral fiction which the reading public demands."[2]

As an example of cultural rhetoric study, this chapter teases out the sociopolitical implications of the tropes used here to describe novel reading in the United States during the last half of the nineteenth century. I sketch out how American cultural rhetoric presented and orchestrated the effects of reading fiction for various members of its audience, how it enabled and constrained the interpretation and use of fiction during one historical period. This rhetorical construction and management of reading took place in various cultural sites, including the home, the school, and the reformatory. Taking up Louisa May Alcott's *Little Women* at the outset, I argue that the use of fiction involved, among other things, the circulation and transformation of particular tropes and arguments through various narratives of "evil reading," "juvenile delinquency," and "social disorder." This cultural talk about reading fiction was focused by an interpretive rhetoric of self-transformation and inner discipline, a late nineteenth-century American version of what Foucault called in his last works "technologies of the self."[3]

Typical of this talk is the materiality, or better, the physicality of the tropes used to figure the reader's activities: reading as eating, critical reading as an exercise in mental discipline, and evaluative reading as "moral gymnastics," in Twain's vivid phrase.[4] Such tropes and their accompanying arguments assumed the close cultural connection among moral order, mental development, and bodily exercise. These rhetorical interconnections not only conditioned the reception of a new kind of children's literature after the Civil War but also enabled reforms in the cultural management of delinquency and perhaps even the institutionalization of literary study in the university.

To start with, then, let me suggest two ways of interpreting the physicality of these tropes for reading. One way is to interpret the comparisons figuratively, as the nineteenth century sometimes did: reading as eating or exercise symbolized the widely held social belief in the actual positive or negative effects of reading on the nineteenth-century reader, especially the vulnerable child, the malleable adolescent, and the potential

---

[2] "Young Women and Novels," Philadelphia *Bulletin*, rpt. in Austin *Daily Statesman*, 28 December 1884, p. 2.

[3] Michel Foucault, *The Care of the Self*, trans. Robert Hurley (New York, 1986); and *Technologies of the Self: A Seminar with Michel Foucault*, ed. Luther H. Martin, Huck Gutman, and Patrick H. Hutton (Amherst, Mass., 1988).

[4] Samuel Clemens to Pamela Moffett, 15 April 1885, in *Mark Twain: Business Man*, ed. Samuel Charles Webster (Boston, 1946), p. 317.

criminal. But there is another way to read these tropes: interpreting the metaphors literally, again as the nineteenth century sometimes did. Literalizing these physical tropes means to institute practices that make reading itself part of the specific disciplinary targeting of the body. The rhetorical logic goes something like this: In the figurative meaning, reading is *like* eating (or study is *like* bodily exercise) in that both affect the individual though in very different ways—one mental, the other physical. Then in the literalization of the trope, reading and eating are viewed as aspects of the same activity, the materially effectual ingestion of nourishment (for mind and body), and the regulation of reading and eating becomes part of the same material disciplining of individual subjects.

Because this distinction between figurative and literal interpretation is somewhat slippery in theory and always historically contingent in actual practice, I will present several concrete examples of its functioning. The initial one introduces the first cultural sphere in which I want to locate the use of reading fiction: the social theorizing about child rearing and juvenile delinquency.

THE RHETORIC OF AFFECTIONATE DISCIPLINE

By the early nineteenth century, Enlightenment beliefs about childhood exerted strong and steady pressure on the ideology of parenting throughout middle-class American society. An influential Lockean pedagogy advocated a balance between parental love and filial obedience, an emphasis that altered authoritarian child rearing practices and established a new preoccupation with affectionate discipline.[5] The Lockean view of successful childhood fostered a reconception of its opposite, juvenile delinquency. Beginning in the mid-1820s, new institutions emerged to deal with the problem of young law-breakers, separating them from adult criminals and prescribing different forms of discipline and punishment.

---

[5] Cf. Steven L. Schlossman, *Love and the American Delinquent: The Theory and Practice of 'Progressive' Juvenile Justice, 1825–1920* (Chicago, 1977), p. 50: "As in earlier periods, the ultimate aim of child rearing was to cultivate obedience and instill an unwavering moral sense. But now the motivational techniques were to be different: the stress was on persuasion, kindness, empathy—what I term affectional discipline—rather than on breaking a child's will through force." Also see the detailed analysis of advice manuals on child rearing in Bernard Wishy, *The Child and the Republic: The Dawn of American Child Nurture* (Philadelphia, 1968), chaps. 1–8; and Richard H. Brodhead's discussion of "disciplinary intimacy" in "Sparing the Rod: Discipline and Fiction in Antebellum America," *Representations* 21 (winter 1988): 67–96. For my own analysis of this nineteenth-century context of discipline, censorship, and "The Bad Boy Boom," see *Rhetorical Power* (Ithaca, 1989), chap. 4.

In 1825 the Society for the Reformation of Juvenile Delinquents was organized, and it soon established the New York House of Refuge, the first of several such institutions founded before the Civil War.[6]

These houses of refuge built for handling juvenile delinquents were, in a sense, only miniature adult prisons. Though the managers of these institutions sometimes compared them to public schools, they also affirmed, as one historian has put it, that a refuge "was a 'juvenile penitentiary,' a prison scaled down to children's size and abilities. Of necessity, its officers were caretakers forced to regard inmates as potentially dangerous criminals with vicious habits requiring thorough eradication."[7] Built as large custodial institutions, refuges employed corrective practices that often appeared designed to punish rather than to reform. But in the 1850s an anti-institutional rhetoric began influencing the theory and practice of delinquent management as preventative agencies and reform schools started replacing some houses of refuge.

One such preventative agency was the New York Children's Aid Society, founded by Charles Loring Brace in 1853. Brace had studied at Yale in the 1840s, where he was inspired by the lectures of Horace Bushnell, author of the highly influential book *Views of Christian Nurture* (1847). Bushnell emphasized the role of parents in using their sensitivity and feelings to shape their children's characters and to extend God's grace to the individual boy or girl. He used organic metaphors to describe the process of child rearing, calling the parent "God's gardener," and he rhetorically reversed the institutional emphasis in dealing with juvenile delinquents by referring to the family as "God's reformatory."[8]

Brace literalized Bushnell's tropes by advocating that delinquents not be institutionalized in houses of refuge but be "placed out" in farm families whose influence would cultivate morality in the urban children who had gone astray. As he wrote in his 1872 book, *The Dangerous Classes of New York, and Twenty Years' Work among Them*, "The founders of the Children's Aid Society early saw that the best of all Asylums for the outcast child, is the *farmer's home*. . . . [T]he cultivators of the soil are in America our most solid and intelligent class."[9] In Brace's rhetoric, farmers of the land became the best framers of the children.

[6] See Robert S. Pickett, *House of Refuge: Origins of Juvenile Reform in New York State, 1815–1857* (Syracuse, 1969); Robert M. Mennel, *Thorns and Thistles: Juvenile Delinquents in the United States, 1825–1940* (Hanover, N.H., 1973), chap. 1; and Schlossman, *Love and the American Delinquent*, chaps. 2–3.

[7] Schlossman, *Love and the American Delinquent*, p. 28.

[8] Bushnell, *Views of Christian Nurture*, quoted in Mennel, *Thorns and Thistles*, p. 36.

[9] Charles Loring Brace, *The Dangerous Classes of New York, and Twenty Years' Work among Them* (New York, 1872), p. 225.

The anti-institutional placing-out movement, with its ideological rhetoric of the family, had its institutional counterpart in the introduction of the "cottage plan" into state reformatories. Also called the "family system," this approach to rehabilitation differed radically from the old custodial model of the adult prisons and juvenile houses of refuge. Rather than one large building for incarceration, the cottage plan called for several smaller buildings, each with its own family or group of inmates.[10] This new architectural organization of delinquents was coupled with a new style of management following from the rhetoric of affectionate discipline already at work in theories of child rearing.

The first family plan in America was introduced into the first state reformatory for female delinquents, the Massachusetts State Industrial School for Girls in Lancaster. The trustees wrote in their first annual report in 1856 that the reformatory

> is to be a *home*. Each house is to be a *family*, under the sole direction and control of the matron, who is to be the *mother* of the family. The government and discipline are strictly parental. It is the design . . . to educate, to teach [the girls] industry, self-reliance, morality and religion, and prepare them to go forth qualified to become useful and respectable members of society. All this is to be done, without stone walls, bars or bolts, but by the more sure and effective restraining power—*the cords of love.*[11]

Even where the architecture remained custodial and the prison policy more authoritarian, the rhetoric of affectionate discipline—the cords of love—made headway at least in the case of antebellum prisons for women. For example, the first woman's prison in the United States was the Mt. Pleasant Female Prison at Ossining, New York, where beginning in 1844 the chief matron, Eliza Farnham, experimented with reform practices that emphasized education and sympathy rather than punishment. The techniques she introduced prefigured the post–Civil War reformatory movement and the gentler management techniques in dealing with juvenile delinquency. Among the practices Farnham initiated was the use of fiction for reformatory effect. In 1846 she added novels

[10] Mennel, *Thorns and Thistles*, pp. 35–42, 52–56.

[11] Trustees, Massachusetts State Industrial School for Girls, *First Annual Report*, p. 6, quoted in Schlossman, *Love and the American Delinquent*, pp. 40–41. Also see Barbara M. Brenzel, *Daughters of the State: A Social Portrait of the First Reform School for Girls in North America, 1856–1905* (Cambridge, Mass., 1983), chap. 4.

such as *Oliver Twist* to the prison library against the wishes of the Sing Sing chaplain, who viewed all novel reading as irreligious.[12]

After the Civil War, Zebulon Brockway led the movement to replace the large, impersonal custodial institutions like the New York House of Refuge with reformatories specializing in more individualized technologies of discipline. As superintendent of the Detroit House of Correction he developed the educational practices that aimed to reform young male criminals, adolescent and young adult. He visited the Lancaster, Massachusetts, Industrial School for Girls and was deeply impressed by its family system, its gentler disciplinary techniques, and its domestic training. Then in 1868 he helped establish the Detroit House of Shelter, affiliated with his House of Correction but restricted to female prisoners, including "wayward girls."[13] The institution's inspectors described the shelter's aims: "It is intended to receive here as into a home, women who . . . seem willing to accept a reform of life. It is intended that they should be received here into a family life, where they shall receive intellectual, moral, domestic, and industrial training, under the influence, example, and sympathy of refined and virtuous women."[14] Describing one of the rituals that made up an important part of her reformatory routine, Emma Hall, the second matron, wrote in her annual report:

> The most interesting feature of the house, and I am prone to say the most useful, is the Thursday evening exercise and entertainment. On this evening the whole family dress in their neatest and best attire. All assemble in our parlor . . . and enjoy themselves in conversation and needlework, awaiting the friend who week by week on Thursday evening, never failing, comes . . . to read aloud an hour entertaining stories and poetry carefully selected and explained.

The ritual of reading to the inmates was repeated in a more formal setting on Sundays when Brockway as superintendent would himself visit the shelter and, in Hall's words, read "to the assembled family from suitably selected literature."[15]

[12] Estelle B. Freedman, *Their Sisters' Keepers: Women's Prison Reform in America, 1830–1930* (Ann Arbor, Mich., 1981), p. 48; and Nicole Hahn Rafter, *Partial Justice: Women in State Prisons, 1800–1935* (Boston, 1985), p. 18.

[13] Rafter, *Partial Justice*, p. 26.

[14] Detroit House of Correction *Annual Report* (1868), p. 7; quoted in Rafter, *Partial Justice*, p. 26.

[15] Hall's 1872 report quoted in Zebulon Reed Brockway, *Fifty Years of Public Service: An Autobiography* (New York, 1912), pp. 410–11.

Of course, these same rituals using literature for reformatory effect were repeated in other cultural sites outside reform school walls. Similar scenes are represented many times in a piece of fiction published in the same year as the founding of the Detroit House of Shelter. In Louisa May Alcott's *Little Women*, the intended girl audience could read how the March daughters gathered each evening, talking and sewing together, often listening to their mother read from some suitable fiction or tell them some uplifting story. During a scene very much like that described by Hall, one of the March daughters exclaims: "Tell another story, mother; one with a moral to it . . . I like to think about them afterwards, if they are real, and not too preachy."[16]

"Real and not too preachy" is an apt description of how Alcott's contemporary audience evaluated *Little Women* itself. The conservative Presbyterian periodical *Hours at Home* called the book a "capital story for girls" and later declared, "It will delight and improve the class to whom it is especially addressed." In a notice of the sequel, a reviewer for the *Commonwealth* wrote that *Little Women* "was one of the most successful ventures to delineate juvenile womanhood ever attempted." The sequel "continues the delight—it is the same fascinating tale, extended without weakening, loading the palate without sickishness."[17] As many literary historians have noted, Alcott's realistic characters represented a new departure from the idealized good girls and good boys in the dominant modes of didactic children's fiction.

Little Women, published in October 1868, tells the story of the family life of the four March daughters. Amy, Beth, Jo, and Meg range in age from twelve to sixteen, all at that stage of development the later nineteenth century came to call the period of adolescence. The popularity of this domestic novel among its youthful readers called forth a sequel almost immediately, and *Little Women, Part Second* appeared in April 1869, picking up the narrative three years later and telling the story of the courtship and marriage of the daughters. The first volume emphasizes the perseverance of stable principle and the reading and imitation of books, while the second emphasizes growth into early adulthood and the production of books and children. In the first, reading books is a synecdo-

[16] Louisa M. Alcott, *Little Women or, Meg, Jo, Beth and Amy* (Boston, 1868), p. 69; further citations are given in the text.

[17] *Hours at Home* 8 (November 1868): 100, and *Hours at Home* 9 (June 1869): 196, both quoted in Richard L. Darling, *The Rise of Children's Book Reviewing in America, 1865–1881* (New York, 1968), p. 242; and *Commonwealth* 7 (24 April 1869): 1, rpt. in *Critical Essays on Louisa May Alcott*, ed. Madeleine B. Stern (Boston, 1984), p. 82.

che for adolescents gaining inner stability and self-discipline, while in the second, writing books is a metonymy for change and growth into maturity.

In trying to decipher what effects reading *Little Women* had on some of its 1868 readers and to what uses they put the fiction, we might turn again to the contemporary reviews. A writer in *Arthur's Home Magazine* summarized both the plot and its "not too preachy" moral: "The father is in the army, and it is to please him that his daughters make an effort of a year to correct certain faults in their dispositions. In this they are quite successful, and the father comes home, after many sad war scenes, to find his little ones greatly improved in many respects, a comfort and joy to both their parents."[18] At least for this reviewer, Alcott comes closest to declaring her message when she has the mother read aloud a letter from the father, who, too old to be drafted, had volunteered as a chaplain during the Civil War. Referring to his four daughters, the father writes to his wife: "I know . . . they will be loving children to you, will do their duty faithfully, fight their bosom enemies bravely, and conquer themselves so beautifully, that when I come back to them I may be fonder and prouder than ever of my little women" (18).

This letter from an absent father both symbolizes and literally names the disciplinary strategy that is so much a part of this novel's rhetorical unfolding. First, in its consequent influence despite its author's absence, the letter symbolizes the patriarchal power, offstage though it might be, that continues to control the action of the story and the life of the family. Second, and more important, the letter explains how this power works, naming the strategy of familial love that fosters inner self-discipline.

It is this latter thematization that I wish to explore here in some detail. As we have seen, by the 1850s theories of child rearing, educational practices, and institutional policies for dealing with juvenile delinquency had all been influenced by a rhetoric of affectionate discipline, which emphasized sympathy over severity, internal motivation over external control, shaping character through love rather than breaking will by punishment. By the late sixties, a cultural rhetoric circulated that used images of the "family home" to represent this constellation of techniques for gentle management.

Throughout *Little Women*, the comforting, supportive home with its atmosphere of familial love remains a constant presence, a background

---

[18] *Arthur's Home Magazine* 32 (December 1868): 375.

against which all the individual problems are worked out. The Marches are a "happy family" (321) despite their lack of money. A dissatisfied daughter comes to realize that "home *is* a nice place, though it isn't splendid" (142). The mother warns her daughter about yearning after "splendid houses, which are not homes, because love is wanting" (146). And when the first daughter is about to leave the home, her sister exclaims: "I just wish I could marry Meg myself, and keep her safe in the family" (295).

But familial love is not represented as an end in itself. Remember the absent father's letter: he predicts and thus requests that his "loving children . . . do their duty faithfully." The mother takes special care to teach her daughters, by example and precept, the lesson of duty toward others. After letting them off their household chores for a week, she remarks on "what happens when every one thinks only of herself. Don't you feel that it is pleasanter to help one another, to have daily duties which make leisure sweet when it comes, and to bear or forbear, that home may be comfortable and lovely to us all?" (172). With the house in a shambles from neglect of their duties, the daughters learn their lesson.

However, even understanding one's duty is not the most important lesson to be learned. Again the father's letter: his "loving children" must "fight their bosom enemies bravely, and conquer themselves so beautifully that when [he] comes home to them [he] may be fonder and prouder than ever of [his] little women." Being a little woman means gaining self-control—not by obeying external laws but through achieving inner discipline. Being a little woman means constituting oneself as a certain kind of subject, employing a particular technology of the self.

And how is this self-discipline to be achieved? For Jo March, the author's alter ego, this self-mastery must take place by fighting her "bosom enemy" within: In an early chapter, the narrator comments that "Jo had the least self-control" for "anger . . . her bosom enemy was always ready to flame up and defeat her; and it took years of patient effort to subdue it" (111). This patient effort demanded a self-surveillance that had to be constant: her mother, who had the same inner conflict, advised Jo to "keep watch over your 'bosom enemy'" (121). Jo's self-discipline was to earn her, in the narrator's words, "the sweetness of self-denial and self-control" (122).

It is precisely here that the use of literature is employed just as strategically as it had been in girls' reformatories. Alcott uses Bunyan's *Pilgrim's Progress* to organize her narrative, inspire her characters, and figure their growth in self-discipline. Alcott's preface adapts a passage from *Pilgrim's*

Progress to express the wish that her own book would make her readers "pilgrims better, by far, than thee or me." It is Bunyan's book that Mrs. March cites to encourage her daughters on the path to reformation: referring to a children's game modeled on *Pilgrim's Progress* that they used to play, she says, "Now, my little pilgrims, suppose you begin again, not in play, but in earnest, and see how far on you can get before father comes home" (20). Meg comments that in "trying to be good . . . the story may help us," while Jo finds that reading her personal challenge as parallel to Christian's "lent a little romance to the very dull task of doing her duty" (20–21). For the rest of the novel, *Pilgrim's Progress* not only supplements the Bible as a "guide-book" (21) for the girls, but it also functions as an explicit gloss on their inner struggles. For example, the chapter describing Jo's battle with anger, her bosom enemy, is entitled "Jo Meets Apollyon." Other chapters have such titles as "Beth Finds the Palace Beautiful," "Meg Goes to Vanity Fair," and "Amy's Valley of Humiliation."

Thus, the reader of *Little Women* can use *Pilgrim's Progress* to interpret the girls' inner lives while they use it as a guide to self-discipline, for writing the selves they wish to be. Jo tells her friend Laurie to change his life, to "turn over a new leaf and begin again," but he responds: "I keep turning over new leaves, and spoiling them, as I used to spoil my copy-books" (314). Such new beginnings are many times more frequent for the daughters than for their young male friend. Their resolutions to try harder directly follow from their repeated examinations of conscience and their frequent confessions of failure to their mother. And this secularization of Christian self-disciplining through confession is aided by the reading of books like *Pilgrim's Progress*. Indeed, reading *as* self-reform takes place while the daughters read *about* self-reform. Consuming books like *Pilgrim's Progress* helps the girls refigure the disorderly process of growing up as an orderly progression of moral development.

But such books are not all the daughters read. "Meg found her sister eating apples and crying over the 'Heir of Redcliffe.' This was Jo's favorite refuge; and here she loved to retire with half a dozen russets and a nice book" (42). Reading and eating are joined together in various ways throughout the story. At one point, Jo offers to read to Laurie and then brings food instead (74–75). While reading aloud to her aunt, Jo would nod off over a book she disliked and give "such a gape" that her aunt would ask what she "meant by opening [her] mouth wide enough to take the whole book in at once." "I wish I could and be done with it" was her reply (65). And then there was Scrabble, Jo's pet rat, "who, being likewise of a literary turn, was fond of making a circulating library of such books as were left in his way, by eating the leaves" (217). And, of course, Jo herself is called a "bookworm" (8) constantly feeding on romances and novels of her liking.[19]

The use of fiction for female self-discipline and pleasure can be briefly contrasted to that found in a boy's book first published in the same year, 1869, as *Little Women, Part Second*. Here we will not only see the differences in how gender is rhetorically constructed in two popular children's novels but also the similarities in how reading fiction disciplines as it engenders action. Like Alcott's classic, Thomas Bailey Aldrich's *The Story of a Bad Boy* was viewed by contemporaries as a new departure in children's fiction.[20] In this semiautobiographical novel, Aldrich attempts a more realistic representation of boyhood, distinguishing his "bad boy" from "those faultless young gentlemen" usually represented in didactic Sunday School fiction.[21] Aldrich tells the story of a boy's pranks and adventures as he is growing up in small-town America, and his series of sketches begins the tradition of bad-boy books that Mark Twain's *Tom Sawyer* and *Huckleberry Finn* culminate. But it is not my purpose here to compare Aldrich's book to Twain's, a job ably done by recent Twain critics, but to use the book selectively to highlight the rhetorical strategies of *Little Women*.[22]

Tom Bailey, the author's alter ego, is, like Jo March, also described as a "bookworm" (45), but his appetite is more limited and his taste in books quite different from the romances Jo reads for entertainment or the books, like *Pilgrim's Progress*, she studies and tries to imitate. Of his first reading of the *Arabian Nights* and particularly *Robinson Crusoe*, the adult narrator says: "The thrill that ran into my fingers' ends then has not run out yet. Many a time did I steal up to this nest of a room, and, taking the dog's-eared volume from its shelf, glide off into an enchanted realm, where there were no lessons to get and no boys to smash my kite" (45).

---

[19] For an account emphasizing the pleasures of reading in Alcott's life and fiction, see Jesse S. Crisler, "Alcott's Reading in *Little Women*: Shaping the Autobiographical Self," *Resources for American Literary Study* 20, no. 1 (1994): 27–36.

[20] See, for example, William Dean Howells, review of Thomas Bailey Aldrich, *The Story of a Bad Boy, Atlantic Monthly* 25 (January 1870): 124.

[21] Thomas Bailey Aldrich, *The Story of a Bad Boy* (Boston, 1870), p. 8; further citations are given in the text.

[22] On Aldrich, Twain, and bad-boy fiction, see especially Albert E. Stone, Jr., *The Innocent Eye: Childhood in Mark Twain's Imagination* (1961; rpt. Hamden, Conn., 1970), pp. 58–90; and Alan Gribben, "'I Did Wish Tom Sawyer Was There': Boy-Book Elements in *Tom Sawyer* and *Huckleberry Finn*," in *One Hundred Years of Huckleberry Finn: The Boy, His Book, and American Culture*, ed. Robert Sattelmeyer and J. Donald Crowley (Columbia, S.C., 1985), pp. 149–70.

The young Tom later finds a trunk full of other "novels and romances" which he "fed upon like a bookworm" (45).

What Tom learns in his books differs a bit from what the March girls learn in theirs. From Thomas Hughes's British boys' book, *Tom Brown's School Days at Rugby*, the American Tom takes the lesson: "Learn to box . . . there's no exercise in the world so good for the temper, and for the muscles of the back and legs" (111–12). And the only duty that seems to concern Tom is the duty to be loyal to his secret gang and to have as many adventures and pull off as many pranks as possible with them. Besides standing by each other, the members of his secret society, the Rivermouth Centipedes, "had no purpose, unless it was to accomplish as a body the same amount of mischief which we were sure to do as individuals. To mystify the staid and slow-going Rivermouthians was our frequent pleasure" (103).

Like his more famous namesake, Tom Sawyer, Bailey has his fancy inflamed by the adventure books he reads. Moreover, he comments on how "hints and flavors of the sea . . . feed the imagination and fill the brain of every healthy boy with dreams of adventure" (147) and notes that "all the male members of [his] family . . . exhibited in early youth a decided talent for running away. It was an hereditary talent. It ran in the blood to run away" (236). Reading and imitating adventure books was as much a part of Tom Bailey's self-fashioning as those reading activities described earlier were a part of Jo March's self-disciplining. The different gender roles constructed by such narratives may be obvious, but it is only Alcott's more perceptive novel that explicitly marks these differences. She ironically foregrounds them throughout her narrative by having Jo constantly allude to her preference for the opportunities available to boys but not to girls. To her best male friend, she laments: "If I was a boy we'd run away together, and have a capital time; but as I'm a miserable girl, I must be proper, and stop at home" (309).

Alcott's book is a female bildungsroman, with the adolescent girls molding their characters "as carefully as [Amy] moulds her little clay figures" (324), a simile used by Mrs. March to describe the growth of one of her daughters.[23] In contrast, Aldrich's story is finally only a series of sketches, more like a picaresque, taking his younger self through a series of adventures with no change in his character. But what is less apparent is the underlying similarities in the effects of the fictions, both as represented

---

[23] See Eve Kornfeld and Susan Jackson, "The Female Bildungsroman in Nineteenth-Century America: Parameters of a Vision," *Journal of American Culture* 10 (winter 1987): 69–75.

and performed. As represented in the two books, fiction affects internal motivation through imitation and reading fiction has actual physical effects, whether in Jo's crying over *Wide, Wide World* or in Tom's thrilled fingertips in reading *Robinson Crusoe*. And as rhetorical performances themselves, both Alcott's and Aldrich's books, described as realistic by their readers, become useful as models for "appropriate" adolescent behavior. I have dwelt on the technologies of the self, the example of self-discipline offered by *Little Women*, but *The Story of a Bad Boy* also made for safe reading, at least according to the new view of middle-class youth then developing that conceptualized adolescent delinquency as merely a temporary stage soon to be outgrown.[24] Or as the town watchman puts it in Aldrich's story: "Boys is boys" (77).

Finally, as others have pointed out, Tom Bailey, like Tom Sawyer after him, is one of the good bad boys, entertaining to his young male readership and nonthreatening to his adult audience.[25] Even if there are few of the examinations of conscience and self-disciplining rituals that we find abundantly in *Little Women*, the adventurous spirit supposedly fostered by *The Story of a Bad Boy* certainly has its limits, as Tom refuses to disobey his guardian on more serious matters and, in one of the few self-examinations in the book, we see a boy motivated less by anxiety over a beating than embarrassment inspired by affectionate discipline: "It was n't the fear of any physical punishment that might be inflicted; it was a sense of my own folly that was creeping over me; . . . I had examined my conduct from every stand-point, and there was no view I could take of myself in which I did not look like a very foolish person indeed" (249). Thus, Aldrich himself is most accurate when he concludes: "So ends the Story of a Bad Boy—but not such a very bad boy, as I told you to begin with" (261).

"Nourishing Food" versus "Insidious Poison"

At the end of *Little Women, Part Second,* Jo March marries Professor Bhaer and exchanges a "wilderness of books" for a "wilderness of boys," as she and her husband establish a home for male orphans.[26] It took Alcott seven years of interrupted writing to complete the fourth and final vol-

---

[24] See G. Stanley Hall, *Adolescence: Its Psychology and Its Relation to Physiology, Anthropology, Sociology, Sex, Crime, Religion, and Education* (New York, 1904).

[25] See Leslie Fiedler, "Good Good Girl and Good Bad Boy," *New Leader* 41 (14 April 1958): 22–25.

[26] The first quoted phrase is from the initial volume of *Little Women*, p. 60, and the second is from Alcott, *Little Women or Meg, Jo, Beth and Amy. Part Second* (Boston, 1869), p. 347.

ume of the *Little Women* series, an 1886 book called *Jo's Boys, and How They Turned Out: A Sequel to "Little Men."* During that period, she was invited to local reformatories attempting to use fiction as one of many strategies for instilling self-discipline in adolescent and older inmates. In June 1879 Alcott and her father spoke to four hundred young men at the Concord State Reformatory. She told a story from her earlier Civil War nursing experiences, and later described her success in affecting her listeners. First in her journal, using one of the tropes we've come to recognize, she wrote that by "watching the faces of some young men" near her, she could see that they "drank in every word," and she became so interested in watching these faces that she forgot herself and "talked away 'like a mother.'"[27] Alcott represented this maternal disciplining through fiction in her own domestic novels for adolescents, and her journals further demonstrated the confidence she shared with her community in the reformatory effectiveness of literary reading and listening.

A year after Alcott's storytelling at the Concord State Reformatory, a young ex-inmate paid her a visit. She wrote in her journal that he "came to thank me for the good my little story did him since it kept him straight & reminded him that it is never too late to mend." She concluded the entry, "Glad to have said a word to help the poor boy."[28] Another time Alcott represented the self-disciplining that can follow from hearing the right kind of story was when she reused this incident in one of the central chapters of *Jo's Boys*.

Dan, a neglected boy taken into the Bhaer home at Plumfield in *Little Men*, had become a young man by the time of *Jo's Boys*, still with "wayward impulses, strong passions, and the lawless nature born in him."[29] During a return visit, he confesses to Jo that his "devilish temper" is more than he can manage, and Jo, who had a similar "bosom enemy" in *Little Women*, responds sympathetically and counsels her ex-ward to "guard your demon well, and don't let a moment's fury ruin all your life. . . . Take some books and read; that's an immense help; and books are always good company if you have the right sort" (127–28). She gives him the Bible but also some German tales, which she uses to allegorize his search for "peace and self-control" (130).

Jo's counsel fails, however, for when Dan leaves Plumfield on his trek west he ends up killing a man in self-defense and is thrown into prison.

---

[27] *The Journals of Louisa May Alcott*, ed. Joel Myerson, Daniel Shealy, and Madeleine B. Stern (Boston, 1989), p. 215.

[28] "December [1880]," in *Journals of Louisa May Alcott*, p. 229.

[29] Louisa M. Alcott, *Jo's Boys, and How They Turned Out. A Sequel to "Little Men"* (Boston, 1886), p. 80; further citations are given in the text.

The prison warden was "a rough man who had won the ill-will of all by unnecessary harshness" (213), and Dan, in humiliation and despair, soon resolves to attempt an escape. But before he can bring off his plan, the prisoners are visited during chapel by a "middle-aged woman in black, with a sympathetic face, eyes full of compassion" (216). She tells them a story and gives as its moral the hope that all was not lost if they would be patient, penitent, and submissive and learn to rule themselves. Like the ex-prisoner who visited Alcott, Dan is changed by the story he hears and resolves to wait out his sentence and "like the wiser man in the story, submit, bear the just punishment, [and] try to be the better for it" (218).

Alcott also visited another reformatory while writing *Jo's Boys*. At the Women's Prison at Sherbourne, she read a story to the inmates and took time to talk with the resident physician about the health of the female prisoners.[30] Perhaps such a juxtaposition of activities suggests a connection made between moral and physical reform in the prison's gentler methods of affectionate discipline, which Alcott's journal describes as working "wonders by patience, love, common sense & . . . the belief in salvation for all."[31] Certainly the connection of the physical with the intellectual and moral development of juvenile inmates was made more directly at some institutions, such as Brockway's Elmira State Reformatory in New York.

Having moved from the Detroit House of Correction to become superintendent at the Elmira facility, Brockway was the foremost authority on the reformatory techniques of managing older delinquents and first-time offenders. As superintendent, he introduced literature courses into the Elmira curriculum during 1884. Besides classic British drama and poetry, the curriculum included reading fiction by Goldsmith and Irving, Hawthorne and Howells, and even Hughes's *Tom Brown's School Days*. The school secretary noted that literature was studied "over and over and minds heretofore innocent of culture became saturated with the drinkable gold of the classics."[32] But the reformative effect intended by reading such books went beyond simply using good literature to teach love of culture and desirable morality. The results of the first examination for the course showed signs "of mental confusion, of indifference, of in-

---

[30] Martha Saxton, *Louisa May: A Modern Biography of Louisa May Alcott* (New York, 1978), p. 390.

[31] "October [1879]," in *Journals of Louisa May Alcott*, p. 217.

[32] F. Thornton Macaulay, "Report of the Secretary of Schools," *Annual Report of the Board of Managers of the New York State Reformatory at Elmira, for the Year Ending September 30, 1885* (Elmira, N.Y., 1885), p. 30.

effectual groping after an author's very palpable meaning, signs which revealed a likely material for mental discipline of the most valuable kind." Thus the school secretary concluded, "The only means of removing these difficulties seemed to lie in repeated doses of the same medicine."[33]

In 1886 Brockway proposed an experimental "Class in Physical Culture." The instructor, Hamilton D. Wey, reported that the object was to discover whether "physical culture as comprised in frequent baths, and massage, and daily calisthenics under the care of a competent instructor, would . . . result in at least a partial awakening and stimulation of dormant mental power." The first class had some success, according to Wey, though the students' "advancement in school work was not steadily onward, but rather intermittently progressive. . . . For a time they would learn with comparative ease and appear to assimilate their mental food, when suddenly and without apparent cause . . . their minds would cease to work" and their "mental awakening" would stop for as long as several days.[34]

Wey later remarked that the foundation of his course was the "recognition of physical training as a factor in mental and moral growth," and he criticized earlier pedagogical theories for ignoring the laws of physiology and overlooking "the physical basis of brain work."[35] Institutional practices and scientific assumptions like Wey's constituted a significant part of the rhetorical context in which the physicality of reading metaphors became literalized in advice manuals and education guides of the 1870s and 1880s. Chapter 17 of *Jo's Boys* refers to several of these books, including an 1874 collection of essays edited by Anna Brackett, *The Education of American Girls*.[36] In a section of her essay called "Physical Education, or, the Culture of the Body," Brackett comments on the extreme difficulty in separating the "physical" from the "moral side of education" in considering the effects of a girl's active imagination (62).

She then notes the availability of the "most dissipating, weakening, and insidious books that can possibly be imagined" and complains about "the immense demand which there is for these average novels." Brackett asks, "How stem this tide of insidious poison that is sapping the strength of body and mind? How, but by educating [girls'] taste till they shall not de-

[33] Macaulay, "Report of the Secretary," pp. 28–29.

[34] H. D. Wey, M.D., "Report of the Experimental or Class in Physical Culture," *Annual Report of the Board of Managers of the New York State Reformatory at Elmira, for the Year Ending September 30, 1886* (Elmira, 1887), pp. 59, 66–67.

[35] H. D. Wey, "A Plea for Physical Training of Youthful Criminals," *Proceedings of the Annual Congress of the National Prison Association of the United States, Held at Boston, July 14–19, 1888* (Chicago, 1888), pp. 185–87.

[36] Anna C. Brackett, *The Education of American Girls* (New York, 1874); further citations are given in the text.

sire such trash." Such "trashy books" must be kept out of the house; when they are "not actually exciting and immoral in tone and sentiment, they are so vapid, . . . so devoid of any healthy vigor and life, that they are simply dissipating to the power of thought, and hence weakening to the will." Brackett does not condemn all novels, only "poisonous and weakening literature." She concludes: "As we are grateful to our parents for the care and simple regimen which preserved our physical health for us, we thank them also for the care which kept out of our way the mental food which they knew to be injurious, and for which they themselves had been too well educated to have any taste" (64–66). In a later section, "Mental Education, or, the Culture of the Intellect," Brackett advocates "plenty of good reading" for girls (77) but also includes this advice: "Exercise . . . must, in mind as well as body, be regular, and increase steadily in its demand. . . . Our first work must be to give such judicious exercise that the mind shall acquire a habit of exercise and an appetite for it, and not to spoil at the outset the mental digestion" (75).

Brackett's more figurative use of the reading metaphor is echoed later in the collection. Edna D. Cheney (soon to become Alcott's first biographer) employs the trope against arguments that young women are physically incapable of strenuous intellectual activity. In "A Mother's Thought" she rejects the claim that "an idle brain insures a healthy body" and argues that "the brain, as the ruling organ of the body, requires a healthy, rich development; and this can only be secured by regular exercise and training, fully using but not overstraining its powers" (135). She adds later: "We must remember that the brain craves thought, as the stomach does food; and where it is not properly supplied it will feed on garbage. Where a Latin, geometry, or history lesson would be a healthy tonic, or nourishing food, the trashy, exciting story, the gossiping book of travels, the sentimental poem, or, still worse, the coarse humor or thin-vailed vice of the low romance, fills up the hour—and is at best but tea or slops, if not as dangerous as opium or whisky" (137).

Indeed, throughout Brackett's collection, this rhetoric of reading serves a dual purpose: it continues to figure the physical effects of reading fiction while it gets adapted to new arguments recognizing women's abilities and advocating their rights in higher education. Brackett gives the latter argument its final form when in her concluding essay she proposes the only jury she thinks capable of evaluating the sources of women's mental and physical health: Only when we have all the cases and statistics before us, she writes, "shall we be in a condition to attempt a rational solution of the question, what it is that makes our American girls sick. . . . But . . . we venture to claim that this is a woman's question—that the women themselves are the only persons capable of dealing with it" (388).

Alcott writes this empowering rhetoric into *Jo's Boys* when she gives a different turn to her gustatory metaphors for reading. In "Among the Maids," Jo advises one of her female college students concerned about what the doctors called her "inherited delicacy of constitution": "Don't worry, my dear; that active brain of yours was starving for good food. . . . It is all nonsense about girls not being able to study as well as boys. . . . [W]e will prove that wise head-work is a better cure for that sort of delicacy than tonics, and novels on the sofa, where far too many of our girls go to wreck nowadays. They burn the candle at both ends; and when they break down they blame the books, not the balls." Thus, a nourishing book not only satisfies a girl's intellectual hunger but also prevents the weakening effects of novel reading and replaces other unhealthy activities as well. Following Jo's advice, any girl might develop a "lively brain . . . in good working order" and enjoy "the daily gymnastics she gave it" (288–89).

In the 1870s and 1880s, college professors justified the academic study of modern languages and literatures by similarly arguing that a philological approach to this subject matter offered as much exercise in "mental discipline" as the same study of the Greek and Latin classics.[37] Some argued, in fact, that courses in the modern languages offered more benefits in mental training than those offered by the classical curriculum. As one professor put it: "The sense of discrimination in regard to the meaning and force of words is sharpened. The literary taste is developed by contact with" the best of modern literature. "And above all, the reasoning, judging, and combining faculties are in constant exercise."[38] But it was not only advocates of the new university who used physical tropes for reading and study. Even the defenders of the old college did so: Noah Porter, president of Yale, put the negative spin on the metaphors for reading novels: "The spell-bound reader soon discovers . . . that this appetite, like that for confectionary and other sweets is the soonest cloyed, and that if pampered too long it enfeebles the appetite for all other food. The reader of novels only, especially if he reads many, becomes very soon an intellectual voluptuary, with feeble judgment, a vague memory, and an incessant craving for some new excitement. . . . It now and then happens that a youth of seventeen becomes almost an intellectual idiot or an ef-

[37] See Gerald Graff, *Professing Literature: An Institutional History* (Chicago, 1987), chap. 4; and Michael Warner, "Professionalization and the Rewards of Literature, 1875–1900," *Criticism* 27 (winter 1985): 1–28.

[38] F. V. N. Painter, "A Modern Classical Course," *Transactions of the Modern Language Association of America* 1 (1884–85): 116.

feminate weakling by living exclusively upon the enfeebling swash or the poisoned stimulants that are sold so readily under the title of tales and novels."[39]

This final quote illustrates the complex way in which assumptions about gender traverse the cultural rhetoric of reading in the late nineteenth century. Here the debilitating effects of novels are themselves figured as feminine: not only are female book readers susceptible to injury but male novel readers are in danger of being feminized. In any case, by the 1880s, the physical tropes for mental activity were constantly employed within the gendered assumptions about the dangers and benefits of reading books.[40] Cultural arbiters of taste worried most about boys who might become criminals through imbibing too many sensational adventure tales or crime stories and about girls who either weakened their minds by consuming sentimental romances or overtaxed their brains with too much strenuous mental exercise in the study of books.

In several cultural sites, feeding on fiction was carefully monitored so the use of books would not be abused. Many agreed with the editor I quoted at the beginning of this chapter, who advised his female correspondent: "Patrons of fiction—the large majority of whom are women—waste their time and fritter away their intellectual force upon [worthless] productions. . . . Let them not think that they do themselves no harm by accustoming their brain to insipid food. Like the rest of the moral, intellectual and physical man, if the mind is not exercised it deteriorates, the deterioration becoming more and more apparent after each failure to supply proper aliment."[41] Thus, the condescending editor figuratively

[39] Noah Porter, *Books and Reading: or, What Books Shall I Read and How Shall I Read Them*, 4th ed. (New York, 1877), pp. 231–32; quoted in Catherine Sheldrick Ross, "Metaphors of Reading," *Journal of Library History* 22 (spring 1987): 149. In this extremely useful article, Ross demonstrates how the trope of reading as eating influenced the policies of librarians as they followed the lead of other groups and began professionalizing their activities in the 1870s and 1880s. She writes, "The real content of a book, its ideas or information, is thought of as a *thing* that can be swallowed. The relationship between the librarian who knows which books are healthful and the passive reader who is wheedled into swallowing resembles that existing between a doctor and a patient. As Charles A. Cutter put it [in an 1881 *Library Journal* editorial], the librarian has a new role that is not just a 'book-watchman' but a 'mental doctor for his town'" (p. 157).

[40] For more on American attitudes toward female fiction reading in other periods, see Cathy N. Davidson, *Revolution and the Word: The Rise of the Novel in America* (New York, 1986); and Janice A. Radway, *Reading the Romance: Women, Patriarchy, and Popular Literature* (Chapel Hill, N.C., 1984). Also relevant to this chapter's rhetorical preoccupations is Radway's "Reading Is Not Eating: Mass-Produced Literature and the Theoretical, Methodological, and Political Consequences of a Metaphor," *Book Research Quarterly* 2 (fall 1986): 7–29.

[41] "Young Women and Novels," p. 2.

shakes his head in despair over the poor, hopeless women readers "who feed their brains with novels and their palates with confectionary."

Metaphors of reading as eating are not, of course, unique to nineteenth-century U.S. culture. Indeed, such tropes follow in a long tradition of figuring the effects of rhetoric in both oral and written forms. Sometimes these tropes were negatively deployed with disparaging associations, as in Plato's attack on sophistic rhetoric as analogous to the false art of cooking. This specific antirhetorical rhetoric lived on into the nineteenth century with the wide distribution of European texts reproducing and commenting on Plato's *Gorgias*. For instance, English translations of Fénelon's influential *Dialogues on Eloquence* summarized Plato's attack on the Sophists—"a set of spurious philosophers, who abuse reason; and, having no sense of public good, aim only at promoting their own selfish ends"—and reproduced *Gorgias's* arguments in detail along with Fénelon's own metaphorical elaborations: Socrates "observes, that those orators, who, in order to cure men, should have given them bitter physic, and, with authority, have inculcated the most disagreeable truths; have on the contrary done for the mind, what cooks do for the body; their rhetoric is only an art of dressing up delicacies to gratify the corrupted taste of the people."[42]

But sometimes rhetoricians adopted the tropes of food more positively in their theorizing. In the most influential rhetoric text circulating in the early nineteenth century, Hugh Blair commented explicitly on the figurative origin of the name for his central topic, "taste," that "faculty which is always appealed to, in disquisitions concerning the merit of discourse in writing." Taste is "more nearly allied to a feeling of sense, than to a process of the understanding; and accordingly from an external sense it has borrowed its name; that sense by which we receive and distinguish the pleasures of food, having, in several languages, given rise to the word taste, in the metaphorical meaning under which we now consider it."[43]

[42] M. de Fénelon, "Dialogues concerning Eloquence in General" [1722 trans. William Stevenson], rpt. in *The Young Preacher's Manual, or a Collection of Treatises on Preaching*, ed. Ebeneezer Porter (Boston, 1819), pp. 66–67. On other U.S. reprintings of Stevenson's translation from 1810 through 1845, see Wilbur Samuel Howell, introduction to *Fénelon's Dialogues on Eloquence*, trans. and ed. Howell (Princeton, 1951), pp. 50–51.

[43] Hugh Blair, "Lecture II: Taste," in his *Lectures on Rhetoric and Belles Lettres*, 2 vols. (London, 1783); rpt. in *The Rhetoric of Blair, Campbell, and Whately*, ed. James L. Golden and Edward P. J. Corbett (Carbondale, Ill., 1990), p. 37. On the influence of Blair's *Lectures* and its widespread adoption as a college textbook in the U.S., see Nan Johnson, *Nineteenth-Century Rhetoric in North America* (Carbondale, Ill., 1991).

Popular composition texts published early in the nineteenth century deployed similar physical tropes to direct practice in writing. John Walker advocated a "happy medium" in literacy exertion: "The mind should advance in strength by the same insensible degrees as the body. Too strong exercise in either will prevent the growth of both, just as the want of proper exercise in either will infallibly hinder their arriving at the greatest degree of strength they are capable of."[44] And much later in the century, rhetoric anthologies presented their models as "intellectual food for all the varying tastes and desires of a reading people."[45]

With such rhetorical traditions in place, I certainly cannot claim that either metaphors of reading as eating or beliefs about the dangers of misusing fiction are unique to late nineteenth-century America. I do claim, however, that these tropes and arguments interacted and functioned differently than they had in the past because they informed and enabled new social practices and new institutions using literature for various purposes, practices and institutions that I have been describing throughout this chapter. It is this detailed description of troping and arguing within discourses and institutions that I offer here as an extended example of cultural rhetoric study.

[44] John Walker, *The Teacher's Assistant in English Composition; or Easy Rules for Writing Themes and Composing Exercises on Subjects Proper for the Improvement of Youth of Both Sexes at School* (Carlisle, Pa., 1808), p. 5. In one model theme, "Evil communication corrupts good manners," Walker provides still another example of the typical figure for bad rhetoric, using it as a paradigm for paragraphs of "similitude": "As a young unvitiated appetite generally dislikes high-seasoned dishes and poignant sauces, but at last becomes fond of them; so a virtuous mind, which at first is disgusted with vice, by too much familiarity becomes enamoured with it" (p. 34).

[45] Phineas Garrett, preface to *The Speakers Garland and Literary Bouquet*, vol. 2 (Philadelphia, 1874); quoted in Nan Johnson, "The Popularization of Nineteenth-Century Rhetoric: Elocution and the Private Learner," in *Oratorical Culture in Nineteenth-Century America: Transformations in the Theory and Practice of Rhetoric*, ed. Gregory Clark and S. Michael Halloran (Carbondale, Ill., 1993), p. 149.

PART THREE

RHETORICAL STUDIES
AND THE CULTURE WARS

RHETORIC RETURNS TO SYRACUSE: THE RECEPTION OF CURRICULAR REFORM

> After the expulsion of tyrants, when after a long interval restitution of private property was sought by legal means, Corax and Tisias the Sicilians, with the acuteness and controversial habit of their people, first put together some theoretical precepts [of rhetoric].
>
> —Cicero, *Brutus*

> After the death of Hiero, when a republic was established in Syracuse, Corax by his rhetorical art was able to sway the new assembly and direct the democratic state. This art he formulated in rules and undertook to teach for a fee.
>
> —D. A. G. Hinks, *Classical Quarterly* (1940)

In these final chapters, I want to consider some possible institutional consequences of adopting cultural rhetoric studies as a model for humanistic scholarship and teaching. I begin rather unpromisingly by telling the tale of my failure to convince one English department to use "rhetoric" as an organizing term for curricular reform. This reception study is then followed by another focusing on the reforms actually made in that department and their reception within local and national contexts of the so-called Culture Wars.

Let me set the rhetorical stage with two citations from the history of curricular reform at Syracuse University.

The first statement comes from the cultural right. In winter 1986 I visited Syracuse as a candidate for chair of the English department. During that visit I asked for an open faculty-student forum so that I could hear negative as well as positive views of my (at that point) rather vague proposals for curricular change. I remember giving a little campaign spiel in which I said something like "I hope to lead us into a discussion in which together we rethink the relations among the various parts of traditional English departments." At the end, I asked my audience for responses and called on the first raised hand I saw. This future colleague stood up and declared, "It took fascist tactics to bring someone with your Althusserian ideology here as candidate for chairman," and then sat down. This declaration was a one-sentence prefiguring of the rhetorical politics to follow when I accepted the offer to join the Syracuse faculty as department chair, a faculty that did in fact reconceptualize English studies in its new major three years later, though not according to my particular plan. The reformed major is now called "English and Textual Studies" (ETS).

The second statement comes almost a decade after the first. It too is brief and was written by another Syracuse colleague but one who might be seen as representing an extreme cultural left position: "The analytic banality and political complicity of . . . [rhetorical] analysis can best be seen in the narratives that Steven Mailloux is producing about the institutional changes at Syracuse: social change, in his analyses, is the effect of 'persuasion' not the contradictions of forces of production and social relations of production—trope not class—is the dynamics of history."[1]

These two statements name the rhetorical parameters of verbal persuasion and ideological coercion that reappear as motifs throughout the narrative to follow. Within the temporal frame of these two declarations, 1986 through 1995, I situate the Syracuse ETS major and its reception as part of the ongoing debates over the future of the academic humanities. To carry off this rhetorical analysis, I resort to some shorthand: for example, I have already used two such terms, "cultural right" and "cultural left." I want to acknowledge from the start that this shorthand terminology is not innocent; it is, in fact, an important part of what I call the *rhetorical politics of naming* that plays such a constitutive role in curricular and other contemporary debates. By "cultural right and left," I simply mean two opposed stances within current educational and disciplinary controversies. One topic within these debates is whether and how to change the structures and practices of humanities schools and their departments. In my rhetorical shorthand, "cultural right" names those who tend to resist major changes within the academic humanities; and "cultural left" refers to those who promote significant changes. Of course, what counts as "significant" or, for that matter, what counts as "change" is often itself a point of contention, as we will see in the case of Syracuse.

---

[1] Mas'ud Zavarzadeh, "'The Stupidity That Consumption Is Just as Productive as Production' (Marx, *Theories of Surplus-Value*): In the Shopping Mall of the Post-al Left," *Alternative Orange* 4 (fall/winter 1994–95): 12, n. 5.

I should also note in passing that these designations do not coincide exactly with the terms referring to the right and left in national party politics, though there is often important, at the least symbolic, overlap. The two critical statements from my ex-colleagues at Syracuse with which I began are comments from people who were both on the political left, indeed at the moment of enunciation they both labeled themselves Marxists, albeit of very different stripes. The first in 1986 was a pre-Althusserian unreconstructed Marxist; while the second continues to be an Althusserian postmodern Marxist.[2] Ah, the politics of naming.

Indeed, these names I'm giving to agents of change and their opponents, and the more technical characterizations I'm using for particular positions on both sides, are further examples of the rhetorical politics to which I continually return. For the moment, let me say again that I constantly oversimplify—for example, there are certainly more than two positions within the Culture Wars—but I try to oversimplify in a complicated way. I want to claim that stereotyping and caricaturing are rhetorical strategies defining the curricular and more general educational debates. They apparently can't be avoided but perhaps they can be understood rhetorically in more useful ways.

THE MAGIC TRIANGLE

I served as chair of Syracuse University's forty-member English department from August 1986 through July 1989. During my first semester, I proposed to use rhetorical study as a framework for bringing together the distinct segments of the department: creative writing, traditional literary history and criticism, linguistics, English as a second language, critical theory, composition, and cultural studies. There were radical disagreements within and among these different groups of faculty. My proposals concerning rhetoric were not intended to resolve these differences but to explain and organize them in a new and productive way.

Even my initial proposals, however, did not get off on the right rhetorical foot. At the first department meeting in fall 1986, before E. D. Hirsch

[2] Certain interpretations and misinterpretations of Althusserianism played a peculiarly prominent role in some episodes of the Syracuse debates. See, for example, Judith Weissman, "Masters of the Universe: Deconstruction and the Yuppies," and Donald Morton and Mas'ud Zavarzadeh, "The Nostalgia for Law and Order and the Policing of Knowledge: The Politics of Contemporary Literary Theory," *Syracuse Scholar: An Interdisciplinary Journal of Ideas Published by Syracuse University*, supplementary issue (spring 1987). For a recent assessment of Althusser's more general influence, see E. Ann Kaplan and Michael Sprinker, eds., *The Althusserian Legacy* (London, 1993).

had actually published a famous book by the same name, I proposed to use "cultural literacy" as the term organizing our curricular reform efforts. This terminological proposal met with an immediate and decisive negative response. It soon became clear that Hirsch had already achieved possession of this term in the series of articles published before the book and its sequels appeared.[3] There was simply too much undesirable intellectual and political baggage accompanying any effort to appropriate the term "cultural literacy" as a label for a new curricular structure. I quickly learned my first lesson in the rhetorical politics of naming and switched terms. "Rhetoric" and later "cultural rhetoric" became the new organizing terms that I promoted to conceptualize our effort at curricular reform.

Understanding "rhetoric" as the effects of texts, of their production and reception, I came to define "cultural rhetoric" as the study of the political effectivity of trope and argument in culture.[4] But it was not my primary goal to persuade my colleagues to accept any particular definition. Rather, I urged them to work with the vocabulary of rhetoric, to rethink their own theories and practices in its terms, to propose their own definitions. That is, I presented "rhetoric" as a framework for reinterpreting our disciplinary activities.

I was, of course, coming late to the history of rhetorical conflict in SU's English department. Two recent events in that history turned out to be particularly significant for the outcome of my curriculum proposals centered on rhetoric. The first event was the institutional separation of the composition program from the English department. The semester before my arrival, a decision had been made to transform freshman English into a new college-based, university-wide Writing Program, which eventually became budgetarily and administratively independent from the Department of English. The new director, Louise Wetherbee Phelps, hired at the same time I was, reported directly to the dean of Arts and Sciences, and the Writing Program eventually became a separate curricular unit with the old freshman writing courses receiving a "WRT" rather than an "ENG" designation. Writing Program faculty were given joint appointments (technically 60 percent Writing Program, 40 percent English

---

[3] See E. D. Hirsch, Jr., "Cultural Literacy," *American Scholar* 52 (spring 1983): 159–69; Hirsch, "Reading, Writing, and Cultural Literacy," in *Composition & Literature: Bridging the Gap*, ed. Winifred Bryan Horner (Chicago, 1983), pp. 141–47; and Hirsch, *Cultural Literacy: What Every American Needs to Know* (Boston, 1987).

[4] This definition of cultural rhetoric was not the first one presented to the department but rather the end result of a series of responses to requests that I clarify my theoretical terms.

department) but had their offices in a different building from the rest of the English faculty. These institutional rearrangements evolved over several semesters, but early on I failed to realize how significantly my plans would be affected by such changes in the material circumstances of the curricular debate.

The second important event prior to my arrival was the establishment of a specific rhetorical practice within the department. Long before I appeared on the scene, my new colleagues, primarily those interested in poststructuralist theory, had developed the practice of writing memos to argue for curricular change. I had never seen anything like it. After I accepted the offer to become chair, three different people sent me packets of past memos, a testimony to the archive that had already been created and a concrete foreshadowing of what was to come. These memos were remarkable examples of polemical critique, theoretically sophisticated and intellectually challenging.

During my first semester, fall 1986, I proposed replacing the traditional coverage model for organizing the undergraduate English major. Instead of conceptualizing our object of study in terms of literary historical periods, I suggested we rethink our shared enterprise in terms of a new set of categories. My first detailed proposal was that we begin working with "rhetoric," "theory," and "culture" as our primary terms and that such a trio of categories could be spatially represented by a triangle:

At a department meeting early on, I tried to foster discussion of this model by roughly glossing its terms, equating culture with history, rhetoric with politics, and theory with philosophy. This triangular proposal and its simplistic interpretive glosses were then taken up in various memos by department faculty.

Some of the theorists attempted to work with my suggested terms while others rejected the proposals completely. Of the former, Stephen Melville provided the most important addition: filling the middle of the triangle with the term "reading." Though he accepted the triangle as "a very useful way to think about the department," he disagreed with the preliminary glosses I had given it. Instead, he proposed an alternative interpretation of its terms: "'Culture' picks out the specificity of any linguistic act—that it is performed in a particular language and in a particular world and history. 'Theory' points toward the explicitly communicative dimensions of any such act, that such an act means to convey a meaning. 'Rhetoric'—perhaps the most difficult term in the current constitution of the department—points to the fact that anything said is said in a certain way that exerts effects both upon its receiver and upon the message itself (effects traditionally recognized as persuasive and tropological)."[5] Melville's comment about the "most difficult term" in our debates turned out, at least for my own rhetorical plans, to be especially prescient. But for the eventual outcome of our departmental discussions, it was his proposal for filling the center of the triangle that became most important: there he placed "our common object—linguistic practices in general, the reading of texts in particular" (3).

One of the most powerful critiques of my triangular proposal came from the department's political left, the position with which I most often identified. Jean Howard and Felicity Nussbaum, two materialist feminists, wrote of "the Mailloux triangle as modified by various hands" that "a possible danger of this schematization is that it will enable us to rename what we do without changing anything. If rhetoric = writing, culture = period courses, and theory = theory, then we are effectively held right where we are."[6] While granting the "widely accepted view that we want to be a department of reading and writing (though these terms are also contested),"

[5] Stephen Melville, "Toward a Re-Imagining of Our Object," memo [October 1986], pp. 1–2. For Melville's deconstructive take on rhetoric, see his *Philosophy Beside Itself: On Deconstruction and Modernism*, Theory and History of Literature, 27 (Minneapolis, 1986). Also see his entertaining and insightful Syracuse account, "Memoir: In Celebration of Academic and Athletic Excellence," *Surfaces* 6 (1996); *http://pum12.PUM.UMontreal.CA/revues/surfaces/vol6/melville.html.*

[6] Jean Howard and Felicity Nussbaum, memo [October 1986], p. 1. For more on materialist feminism during the eighties, see Judith Newton and Deborah Rosenfelt, "Introduction: Toward a Materialist-Feminist Criticism," in *Feminist Criticism and Social Change: Sex, Class, and Race in Literature and Culture*, ed. Newton and Rosenfelt (New York, 1985), pp. xv–xxxix; Felicity A. Nussbaum, *The Autobiographical Subject: Gender and Ideology in Eighteenth-Century England* (Baltimore, 1989), esp. pp. 131–38 and works cited in n. 14, p. 245; and Valerie Wayne, ed., *The Matter of Difference: Materialist Feminist Criticism of Shakespeare* (Ithaca, 1991), which reprints Jean Howard's "Scripts and/versus Playhouses: Ideological Production and the Renaissance Public Stage," from *Renaissance Drama* 20 (1989): 31–49. Also see Jean E. Howard, *The Stage and Social Struggle in Early Modern England* (New York, 1994), and Rosemary Hennessey, *Materialist Feminism and the Politics of Discourse* (New York, 1993).

Howard and Nussbaum argued for "a department of Text Critique which focuses precisely on the role of textual production and reception in the circulation of ideology and the construction of particular modes of subjectivity, and which aims to produce students who actively occupy positions from which to critique and intervene in the discourses by which the real is established and power relations secured" (2). This memo also suggested one way the department was being remapped, a fact that became increasingly important as the curricular discussions continued: "For us, the greatest value of the discussion of the rhetoric-culture-theory triangle to date has been to reveal that any reading of the department based on a binary opposition between theory and non-theory is at best reductive. There are differences of more importance" (1). Indeed there were, as we will shortly see.

Not all the objections to the curricular triangle took the form of serious critique. There were also responses in a quite different rhetorical vein. One such memo began:

To: Members of the English department, soon to be given a more Advanced Name

From: the She-Ra, Princess of Power Space

Retrogradation has once again hegemonically privileged itself in antinominiacal contestatory opposition to the non-essentialized astral projections of the Divine Will. Triangles printed on flat pieces of paper? Prima facie outmoded, kids. What we need is a Departmental Plan revolving first around an irregular, open, eleven-sided polygon. These sides will be labelled:

Recrudescence.

Effervescence.

Irridescence.

Pneumonoultramicroscopicsylicovolcaniconiosis OR antidisestablishmentarianism

Neo-hegelian theosophy

Metampsychosis

Quarks

Quirks

The Royal Road to Geometry

The Royal Nonesuch

Telekinesis

Continuing in this parodic mode, the memo concluded triumphantly: "Excelsior! Today the department, tomorrow the solar system!"

In response to both serious and humorous criticisms, I attempted once more to clarify my position by addressing my own memo to "the Chairman's argument."[7] Taking up the triangle as modified by Melville:

I claimed that "the Chairman" had failed "to exploit the heuristic power of the term 'rhetoric' as strategically, as imaginatively as he might have" and proposed rewriting the triangle still again:

I went on to argue that each side of the triangle named a potential set of courses—on textuality, culture, and theory—and that these categories of courses could be understood in relation to various definitions of rhetoric.

What did my proposal imply about relevant definitions of rhetoric? This question could be answered by taking each side of the triangle as a domain for defining "rhetoric." From the perspective of textuality, rhetoric is simply "tropes and arguments in texts." (This mundane definition borrows from two long rhetorical traditions—rhetoric as figurative language and rhetoric as persuasion—two traditions currently represented, for example, by deconstruction and reader-response criticism, respectively.) From the perspective of culture, rhetoric is the "materiality of cultural politics in discourse." (This definition needs more justification, which would begin with a Foucauldian thesis that relations of power/knowledge permeate rhetorical practices and a Burkean thesis that rhe-

---

[7] Mailloux, memo (10 November 1986), p. 1.

torical practices—the employment of tropes and arguments—constitute cultural discourse.) And from the perspective of theory, rhetoric is
the emphasis on local practices and historical beliefs in contrast to philosophy's concern over general foundations and universal Truth. (This
definition participates in the rhetorical line from the Greek Sophists and
Isocrates through Chaim Perelman and contemporary neopragmatists.)

Textuality, culture, and theory do more, however, than simply function
as perspectives for defining (and arguing over) rhetoric. Rhetoric itself
also provides a frame for defining and arguing over textuality, culture,
and theory. "Rhetoric is a subject matter *and* a mode of inquiry" (2). A
major organized around rhetoric would emphasize the dialectical relation between what would become three categories of courses and the
rhetorical framework.

The discussions of "the magic triangle" continued throughout the first
semester, though my own interpretive glosses became more and more
marginal, that is, rhetorically unsuccessful. Why this was so will be the
topic of the third section. But before continuing with the department
narrative, let me briefly mention another actor in the rhetorical drama.
At the end of the first semester, I sent to the dean of Arts and Sciences a
collection of the department's memos, attempting, I suppose, to give him
some sense of what I believed to be an interesting curricular debate going on in the English department. The dean, a philosopher by trade,
handed me this and only this response:

"Do you swear to tell the truth, the whole truth, and nothing but
the truth, and not in some sneaky relativistic way?"

I was tempted to interpret the dean's response as (among other things) a repetition of that age-old conflict between philosophy and rhetoric, more exactly a replay of Plato versus the Sophists, with the philosopher viewing the Sophists as relativists partly because of their preoccupation with rhetoric. This take on the dean's response made it unintentionally ironic, of course, since the supposedly relativistic theorists in the English department were in the process of rejecting rhetoric as the central component of the new curriculum.

ENGLISH AND TEXTUAL STUDIES AND ITS PERIPHERY

Many other topics were covered in the memo exchanges—arguments about classroom pedagogy, statements by the Student Marxist Collective, debates over creative writing, and much, much more. I am thus leaving out an enormous chunk of what I sometimes call the return of rhetoric to Syracuse. In any case, by the end of my first year, that return had become somewhat sidetracked, at least from my perspective. True, the new Writing Program had successfully replaced freshman English courses with freshman and sophomore writing studios, which were putting rhetoric and composition on a stronger theoretical base and giving instruction in writing an unprecedented visibility at Syracuse. But this return of rhetoric was happening outside the English department.[8]

My failure in arguing for rhetoric was most evident at the end of the first year when a new triad of terms was adopted to organize the major. Though the form of the triangle had been preserved, its sides were now labeled "history," "theory," and "politics," and we moved into the 1987–88 school year focusing on "textual studies," not "cultural rhetoric," as the organizing term for the continuing discussion of the new major.

While the flurry of memos slowed in the second year, one interesting exchange relevant to rhetoric's return did take place. In the fall, two de-

[8] On the Syracuse Writing Program, see Louise Wetherbee Phelps, "Developmental Challenges, Developmental Tensions: A Heuristic for Curricular Thinking," in *Developing Discourse Practices in Adolescence and Adulthood*, ed. Richard Beach and Susan Hynds (Norwood, N.J., 1990), pp. 386–414; her "The Institutional Logic of Writing Programs: Catalyst, Laboratory, and Pattern for Change," in *Politics of Writing Instruction: Postsecondary*, ed. Richard Bullock and John Trimbur (Upper Montclair, N.J., 1991), pp. 155–70; her "Practical Wisdom and the Geography of Knowledge in Composition," *College English* 53 (December 1991): 863–85; Margaret Himley, *Shared Territory* (New York, 1991), pp. 47–88; James T. Zebroski, *Thinking through Theory* (Upper Montclair, N.J., 1994), pp. 119–45, 251–71; and his "The Syracuse Writing Program and Cultural Studies: A Personal View of the Politics of Development," in *Cultural Studies in the English Classroom*, ed. James A. Berlin and Michael J. Vivion (Portsmouth, N.H., 1992), pp. 87–94.

partment members, Mas'ud Zavarzadeh and Donald Morton, who had been active in the previous year's "memo wars," published in the socialist newspaper *In These Times* a critique of the not-yet-passed SU curriculum as part of a larger attack on reformist curricular changes taking place at universities such as Carnegie Mellon and Duke. In "War of the Words: The Battle of (and for) English," these postmodern Marxists claimed that at Syracuse "the 'new' English curriculum reintroduces a politically oppressive form of eclectic pluralism by simply providing three levels of study: the political, the historical and the theoretical. Once again (as in the traditional curriculum), the notion is that a liberal education should produce a well-rounded individual. What better way to do so than to expose students to many modes of knowing?"[9] In contrast, they argued, a truly radical pedagogy attempts to empower the student, making him or her into "a critical subject who knows that knowledge is a social product with political consequences and is therefore willing to 'intervene' in the way knowledge is produced not only in the classroom, but in all other sites of culture" (19).

My memo in reply to Zavarzadeh and Morton quoted from a document being written by the department's Theory Group: "A new curriculum in textual studies will be organized not by coverage of a literary or critical canon but by a focus on the problematics of reading and writing texts. Such a curriculum attempts to distinguish between a traditional pluralism, in which there are many separate viewpoints and each exists without locating itself in relation to opposing viewpoints, and a plurality of interested yet interlocking positions, in which each position acknowledges its allied or contestatory relation to other positions." The Theory Group argued further that the "pedagogical goal of such a curriculum is to make students aware of how knowledge is produced and how reading takes place and thus make them capable of playing an active and critical role in their society, enabling them to intervene in the dominant discourses of their culture."[10] I asked Morton and Zavarzadeh: Are the pedagogical goals stated here really all that different from those advocated in "War of the Words"?

There was, however, at least one important difference between the two statements, a difference in what might be called the "logic" of these pedagogies, which I tried to articulate in this way:

---

[9] Mas'ud Zavarzadeh and Donald Morton, "War of the Words: The Battle of (and for) English," *In These Times* 11, no. 41 (October 28–November 3, 1987): 18.

[10] Mailloux, memo (11 November 1987), pp. 1–2, quoting from a circulating document that eventually in revised form became "Not a Good Idea" (see note 27 below).

My only problem with [your pedagogical] statement is the "therefore." I still don't understand why you think it logically follows that once you get students to see how the Real is not naturally given but socially constructed, once you get them to recognize how their interpretations of texts result from their "situatedness in a complex network of gender, class, and race relations" ("War," p. 19), how it necessarily follows that they will "therefore" intervene in the rhetorical/ideological process they now understand and intervene in such a way that changes their class's patterns of political oppression. Maybe they will, maybe they won't. This is not an argument against your project, just a less assured prediction of its success.[11]

In a peculiar way, Morton and Zavarzadeh's notion of pedagogy depended on a view of persuasion that elsewhere they rejected as mystifying ideological manipulation, as we will see later in this chapter.

Still, all these questions were certainly worth raising about the developing curricular proposals in textual studies. However, what came next in "War of the Words" struck less at the department's future major than at my rhetorical version of it, a version that by fall 1987 was no longer a viable candidate for adoption as an overarching framework. Zavarzadeh and Morton claimed that "Syracuse's 'new' curriculum is similar to many other 'new' curricula in that it is part of a concerted political effort by conservatives to contain change by recycling traditional educational ideas and practices by up-dating 'literary studies' as the study of 'rhetoric.' By reviving the concept of 'rhetoric' that is basically 'formalist': its main concern is with 'how' discourses are produced and received without any concern with 'why' they are there to begin with" (18). Such a rhetorical framework, they went on to argue, ends up treating all discourses as equally worthy of study, and this flattening-out process actually trivializes the radical potential of contemporary critical theory.

In my reply I found it noteworthy that in a previously published essay the authors had equated rhetorical reading with a caricature of deconstruction. In "The Nostalgia for Law and Order and the Policing of Knowledge: The Politics of Contemporary Literary Theory," Zavarzadeh gave rhetoric over entirely to a form of de Manean deconstruction that he then characterized as a(nti)political formalism.[12] Indeed, "Nostalgia" dis-

---

[11] Mailloux, memo (11 November 1987), p. 5. For another response to "War of the Words" from faculty at Carnegie Mellon University, see David Shumway and Paul Smith, "Off Our Backs!" *In These Times* 12, no. 3 (18–24 November 1987): 15.

[12] Zavarzadeh and Morton, "Nostalgia for Law and Order," p. 59. (An opening footnote states that this section of the essay was written by Zavarzadeh.) This article has been revised and incorporated into Zavarzadeh and Morton, *Theory, (Post)Modernity, Opposition: An "Other" Introduction to Literary and Cultural Theory* (Washington, D.C., 1991).

missed any political definition of rhetoric and instead reduced contemporary rhetorical study to some kind of apolitical tropology. "War of the Words" made a similar move by again ignoring political definitions of rhetoric and reducing rhetorical inquiry to formalist analysis or, at best, a version of legitimation study that focused on "'moral' (but not political) questions."[13]

But why should rhetorical study be so limited? Who else insists that rhetorical analysis never asks "why" but only "how"? Why should rhetoric and politics be so absolutely separated? Among other things, this separation completely ignores the long tradition from the Greek Sophists onward that conceptualized rhetorical theory and practice as integrally connected to politics. Moreover, depoliticizing rhetorical theory hinders inquiry into one of the most important contemporary topics in critical theory and cultural studies: the relation of rhetoric to ideology. Such an inquiry asks a number of pressing questions:

How does ideology consist of beliefs and practices constituting interested positions within a cultural conversation at specific historical moments? How does an ideology attempt through trope and argument to convince individuals of the objectivity and universality of its interpretation of the real? How does a crucial part of an ideology's interpretive rhetoric involve producing subjects within socio-political positions consistent with the ideology's world view? How does an ideology function agonistically to represent its adversaries' positions as the exact opposite of how they represent themselves? Is this rhetorical process the only way to salvage the notion of ideology as a false consciousness representing the real in *camera obscura*? Is ideology always and only constituted in a rhetorical contest that is historically specific and politically situated?[14]

---

[13] Zavarzadeh and Morton, "War of the Words," p. 19.
[14] Mailloux, memo (11 November 1987), p. 4. Cf. Kenneth Burke, "Marx on 'Mystification,'" in his *A Rhetoric of Motives* (1950; rpt. Berkeley, Calif., 1969), pp. 101–10; Michael Ryan, *Politics and Culture: Working Hypotheses for a Post-Revolutionary Society* (Baltimore, 1989); Charles W. Kneupper, ed., *Rhetoric and Ideology: Compositions and Criticisms of Power* (Arlington, Tex., 1989); Stephen Bygrave, *Kenneth Burke: Rhetoric and Ideology* (London, 1993); Andrzej Warminski, "Ending Up/ Taking Back (with Two Postscripts on Paul de Man's Historical Materialism)," in *Critical Encounters: Reference and Responsibility in Deconstructive Writing*, ed. Cathy Caruth and Deborah Esch (New Brunswick, N.J., 1995), pp. 11–41; James A. Berlin, "Social-Epistemic Rhetoric, Ideology, and English Studies," chap. 5 in *Rhetorics, Poetics, and Cultures: Refiguring College English Studies* (Urbana, Ill., 1996), pp. 77–94; Robert Wess, *Kenneth Burke: Rhetoric, Subjectivity, Postmodernism* (Cambridge, 1996); and Chap. 4, above.

All of these questions, I argued, were excluded by Zavarzadeh and Morton's apolitical definition of rhetoric.

This exchange over rhetoric was provocative and useful for my own rhetorical purposes, but unfortunately for those purposes it was very much a sideshow to the main event. By the time of "War of the Words" and my response, rhetoric was no longer the center of departmental discussion. In fact, by the following semester, in the proposal voted on by the department, the term "cultural rhetoric" made only a very minor appearance. Instead, the "problematics of reading" and "modes of inquiry" were the prominent concepts, and the major was officially designated as English and Textual Studies. In April 1988 the department voted 20-7-1 to replace the old English major with the new ETS curriculum. (See the Appendix for a description of the three curricular categories approved at that time and for a list of specific courses developed later.) [15]

Although my specific rhetorical proposals were not adopted, I participated in the rhetorical process of invention and negotiation that created this new major, and I hope I am understood when I say that I am proud of what my colleagues established. The new curriculum was a collective accomplishment, with all the strengths and weaknesses that implies. A result of innovative thinking and difficult compromises, the new curriculum presents one of the first detailed alternatives to the traditional coverage model for English studies. Across all three categories of courses, the ETS major provides one example of how recent developments in critical theory and cultural studies can be institutionalized.

THE MISFORTUNES OF RHETORIC

But one troublesome crux remains: why did "rhetoric" lose out as an organizing term? My answer may seem simplistic: The proposal of rhetoric by a rhetorician beginning with politics did not convince an audience whose conceptions of rhetoric began with either language or composition. My original proposal to use the study of rhetoric as a redefinition of

---

[15] In spring 1989 Bill Readings and Steven Cohan proposed a grid of twenty-seven course titles, along with descriptions, which became the basis for the detailed curriculum eventually developed by the department and outlined here in the Appendix. The Syracuse University general catalogue publishes a general description of each "introduction to" and "studies in" course, and specific course descriptions (with the standard course title and changing subtitles) appear each semester in the English department newsletter. For an early campus account of the new major, see Don Sena, "English Studies Plans Course Overload [Overhaul?]," Syracuse University *Daily Orange*, 17 April 1989, p. 1+.

our enterprise was initially an attempt to convince my colleagues to work with the term "rhetoric" as a focus of curricular discussion. My political definition of "cultural rhetoric" was an illustration of how one might enter the debate over what rhetoric could mean and how it could be studied.

For several reasons, this strategy didn't work. First, those colleagues most amenable to accepting "rhetoric" as a useful piece of vocabulary were located in a new Writing Program that was institutionally separate from the English department. Though they remained officially within the department (as dual appointments), their daily practices, their own conversations, their own institutional interests were now centered in the Writing Program. The challenge of creating a university-wide, four-year composition curriculum almost from scratch gave these potential rhetorical allies little time to participate in the debates over the English department's undergraduate major.

Not realizing I was already at a rhetorical disadvantage, I focused my attention on the Theory Group, an informal collective consisting of eleven to thirteen faculty who were the strongest advocates for curricular change. Early in the fall semester of my first year, I discovered an important fact about the rhetorical context for curricular debate in the department: the most significant difference was not, as I had thought, between anti-theory traditionalists and the Theory Group but between two kinds of poststructural theorists in and outside the group. Crudely put, the rhetorical divide was between the theorists who emphasized language and the play of signification and those who emphasized politics and the materiality of discourse. On one side were the so-called language theorists, including deconstructionists, Lacanians, narratologists, and semioticians; the other side encompassed the so-called political theorists, including postmodern Marxists, materialist feminists, and one Foucauldian rhetorician. In arguing for rhetoric as an organizing term, I tried to convince my theory colleagues to view their positions as different stances on rhetoric: one side began with language and was oriented to rhetoric as trope; the other began with power and was oriented to rhetoric as argument. Unfortunately, I could not persuade my fellow theorists at least to try working with these (admittedly reductive) labels for their theoretical positions.

In a sense, I failed rhetorically because of the very definitions of rhetoric I was attempting to thematize. That is, I wanted arguments over the definition of rhetoric to serve as a way for articulating positions within the curricular debates, but it was the dominant definitions of rhetoric currently in place that helped defeat my attempt. Specifically, I lost out in the institutional politics of naming partly because many people in the

department viewed rhetoric through a narrow understanding of composition study. Unfamiliar with the rich theorizing and sophisticated research in this emergent discipline, some did not take rhetoric as disciplinary knowledge seriously and viewed composition simply as the intuitive
art of teaching writing, something "they" did over there in the Writing
Program. Another, more debilitating, definition of rhetoric circulated in
the Theory Group: the equation of rhetoric with the formalist dynamics
of the text, including the kind of dynamics often associated with American deconstruction and its view of textual tropes working to subvert textual arguments. Both the "political theorists" and the "language theorists" agreed about this nonpolitical definition of rhetoric.[16] I convinced
neither side of the viability of my more political definition of cultural
rhetoric, and, most important, I did not convince even my closest allies,
the politically oriented theorists, to accept the definition of rhetoric as a
useful area to stage our debates. Rhetoric oriented toward language (and
not power) seemed the only rhetoric they could accept as such.

THE RECEPTION OF ETS IN THE CULTURE WARS

As I look back at the institutional politics of SU's curriculum effort, I realize how much I speak from a position very much within its ongoing
rhetorical history.[17] The Syracuse reception of my rhetoric proposals
continues in a very attenuated way. The SU Writing Program, not surprisingly, was the only place where something from my original proposals explicitly stuck: The new Ph.D. developed there has recently been

[16] Here my labels are especially misleading since it could easily be argued that some
"language theorists" were actively reconceptualizing the category of the "political." For
more on the diversity of theoretical talk overheard at Syracuse during the late eighties and
early nineties, see two collections of papers delivered on campus: Bill Readings and Bennet
Schaber, eds., *Postmodernism across the Ages: Essays for a Postmodernity That Wasn't Born Yester-
day* (Syracuse, 1993); and Stephen Melville and Bill Readings, eds., *Vision and Textuality*
(Durham, N.C., 1995).

[17] My position within and relation to that history has changed significantly over the last
few years. One important change occurred when, having achieved my goal of helping establish a new curriculum, I decided not to accept a second three-year term as department
chair. And another took place when I left Syracuse to teach rhetorical theory and cultural
studies at the University of California, Irvine, where I became an advisor to the composition program and, not incidentally, returned home to Southern California. For a recent account of rhetorical studies in the UCI Department of English and Comparative Literature,
see Gary A. Olson, "Rhetoric, Cultural Studies, and the Future of Critical Theory: A Conversation with J. Hillis Miller," in *Philosophy, Rhetoric, Literary Criticism: (Inter)views*, ed. Olson (Carbondale, Ill., 1994), pp. 115–43.

officially approved as a degree in "composition and cultural rhetoric." The fact that the Writing Program understands "cultural rhetoric" differently than my more political definition does not bother me. "Cultural rhetoric" might after all help to open up a space at Syracuse where issues of culture, politics, pedagogy, and rhetoric can be negotiated and theorized.[18]

Now let me turn to the reception of the ETS major. Several members of the original group pushing for curriculum reform have now left Syracuse, but the great advantage of institutionalizing new disciplinary movements is that a program like ETS is less dependent for its survival on specific individual professors and, in the short run, can rely upon institutional inertia to prevent an immediate abandonment of progressive reforms, the same inertia ironically that in other departments helps traditionalists defend outworn curricula. The first full year of ETS course offerings (1990–91) resulted in positive evaluations from students, and the number of department majors, which had grown dramatically during the previous five years, remained stable despite a sudden drop in total university enrollment.[19]

Outside Syracuse University, the diverse reception of ETS was symptomatic of wider cultural debates. The local newspapers published accounts of the curricular changes, ranging from rather straightforward news stories with a slightly positive slant (primarily because department administrators were given the most space in explaining the theory and practice of the ETS major) to polemical opinion pieces condemning the changes for all manner of cultural, intellectual, and political sinning. In summer 1990 when the national discussions, dubbed "the Culture Wars," often focused on reading lists and canon debates, the Syracuse *Post-Standard* published two articles, Fred Pierce's "SU Curriculum Challenges 'Classics'" and James McKeever's "SU Takes a New Look at the Classics." The overall tone of the first can be gleaned from the opening sentences: "Starting this fall, you won't have to read Shakespeare, Chaucer or Milton to be a Syracuse University English major. You might, however, have to dig through tomes on Marxist theory, obscure feminist texts, or even Stephen King's horror novel, *Carrie*."[20] Pierce quotes Charles Watson, the

[18] See Syracuse University Writing Program, "Proposal for a Doctorate of Philosophy in Composition and Cultural Rhetoric" (spring 1996), especially the discussion of the title under "Distinctiveness of Degree," pp. 4–6.

[19] For a detailed account of the general university situation, see Kenneth A. Shaw, "The Chancellor's Report: Restructuring Syracuse University," 17 February 1992, special insert section in *Syracuse University Magazine* 8 (March 1992).

[20] Fred Pierce, "SU Curriculum Challenges 'Classics,'" Syracuse *Post-Standard*, 19 July 1990, p. A1.

English department's director of undergraduate studies, as claiming that "what you read is not now as important as how you read it."[21] Instead of explaining Watson's comment, Pierce quickly moves on. He gives a bit more space—but not much—to John Crowley, the chair who succeeded me and who saw the curricular reforms through the school and university curriculum committees.[22] But Pierce takes a passing reference by Crowley as an opportunity to connect the Syracuse reforms with the Western Civ controversy at Stanford University, where two years before "similar—but less extensive—curriculum changes" brought forth from William Bennett the charge that those changes amounted to "'an attempt to junk Western civilization.'"[23]

A month later a second *Post-Standard* article on ETS seemed to be a direct reply to worries expressed by the first reporter and the few "dissenters" he identified. Speaking of the majority, James McKeever reports that many Syracuse English faculty "say those who respond to the changes by focusing on the 'fate' of the classics are trivializing the new curriculum."[24] In the new ETS curriculum "literary classics will still be read, but in a different light." They "will be studied not only for their artistic merits, but in the context of the political, cultural and historical forces that shaped their work—and the work of lesser-known writers" (C1). Other faculty quoted in the article note the way that ETS reflected changes in the humanistic disciplines, and they remark on the inevitability of controversy as such intellectual transformations take place.

But the nature of that controversy as represented in the national media had shifted by the following year, with the emphasis in the Culture Wars moving from struggles over the canon to battles over "political correctness." Beginning in late 1990 and continuing through President

---

[21] Pierce, "SU Curriculum," p. A1. Pierce limits Watson to that single sentence. Carol Parlin was a bit more generous in her report three days earlier, when she quoted Watson on the same topic: "The purpose of a literary education is no longer to have a student get a sort of Regents-exam familiarity with the standard classics. . . . We're much more interested in the process of interpretation and in the literary and cultural status of texts than in taking for granted and mastering a list of so-called literary classics. In a general sense, the new curriculum will refuse to take for granted the status of a classic just because it has traditionally been called a classic"—Watson quoted in Carol A. Parlin, "English Dept. Curriculum Restructured," Syracuse *Record*, 16 July 1990, p.1.

[22] See John W. Crowley, "Unmastering All We Survey," *ADE Bulletin* 100 (winter 1991): 31–34.

[23] Pierce, "SU Curriculum," p. A1. For accounts of the Stanford controversy, see Herbert Lindenberger, "The Western Culture Debate at Stanford University," *Comparative Criticism* 11 (1989): 225–34; and Mary Louise Pratt, "Humanities for the Future: Reflections on the Western Culture Debate at Stanford," *South Atlantic Quarterly* 89 (winter 1990): 7–25.

[24] James McKeever, "SU Takes a New Look at the Classics," Syracuse *Post-Standard*, 30 August 1990, p. C1.

George Bush's June 1991 commencement address at the University of Michigan, PC-bashing remained a topic of passionate debate within the cultural conversation about the present and future of U.S. higher education. This impassioned rhetoric registered on the local scene in November 1991, when the Syracuse *New Times* ran a piece entitled "The Corruption of SU English: New Curriculum Discourages Independent Thinking," which claimed that multiculturalism had "infected Syracuse University's Hall of Languages," home of the English department. The professors there—"primarily aging refugees from the frustrated neo-Marxist flower child movement of the 1960s"—were abandoning "the idea of inspiring students to think in favor of telling them how to think." Traditionally, the article explained, "courses were primarily concerned with introducing students to the evolution of literature, the difference between art and rhetoric, and how to speak and write clearly, accurately, even honestly." Now, "a new breed of English professors" was changing all this—presumably with the agenda to ignore literary history, collapse the distinction between art and rhetoric, and encourage unclear, inaccurate, and dishonest (sophistic?) speaking and writing. "Joining the deconstructionists, these dedicated followers of fashion prepared the department for the political correctness . . . that was already stifling independent thought in some of the nation's other colleges."[25]

These local receptions near the university were not unimportant for the wider reception of ETS within the broader Culture Wars. I turn now to that larger context to provide still another example of reception study, not only to illustrate the rhetorical interconnection of local and national debates about the humanities but also to argue once again that the

[25] Spider Rybaak, "The Corruption of SU English," Syracuse *New Times*, 20–27 November 1991, pp. 8–9. As the nineties progressed, the reception of the ETS curriculum was tied explicitly to the controversies about "political correctness." Shortly before the publication of the *New Times* piece, the Syracuse English department had been visited by a documentary crew from British television, and the ETS major became a prime exhibit for a rather sensationalist "exposé" about U.S. universities, aired in London as "War of the Word" during December 1991. See the appropriately titled commentaries in London newspapers: Simon Hoggart, "All Present and Incorrect on Campus," *Observer*, 15 December 1991; and Hugh Hebert, "Inside the Universities of Uniformity," *Guardian*, 18 December 1991. For a less negative local account of PC and ETS, see Renée Gearhart Levy, "PC'ed Out," *Syracuse University Magazine* (December 1991): 29–35. On the debates over political correctness more generally, see *PC Wars: Politics and Theory in the Academy*, ed. Jeffrey Williams (New York, 1995); *After Political Correctness: The Humanities and Society in the 1990s*, ed. Christopher Newfield and Ronald Strickland (Boulder, Colo., 1995); Harold K. Bush, Jr., "A Brief History of PC, with Annotated Bibliography," *American Studies International* 33 (April 1995): 42–64; and John K. Wilson, *The Myth of Political Correctness: The Conservative Attack on Higher Education* (Durham, N.C., 1995).

philosophy/rhetoric and Plato/Sophist oppositions do indeed remain
pertinent to an understanding of contemporary cultural politics.

The more general reception of ETS involved as many understandings
and misunderstandings, compliments and insults, careful articulations
and silly caricatures as other episodes in the Culture Wars of the last few
years. One of my favorite misinterpretations of the Syracuse ETS major
came from the ex-chair of a more publicized stronghold of cultural left-
ism, Duke University. In *Journal of Advanced Composition* the editor entitled one interview: "Fish Tales: A Conversation with 'The Contemporary
Sophist,'" a title quite appropriate to the story I'm telling. When asked
about the future of disciplinary reform in English departments, Stanley
Fish commented in this interview: "If the change, when it comes, goes in
the same direction that Syracuse has pioneered, then it might be just as
accurate to call the department 'the department of rhetoric,' with a new
understanding of the old scope of the subject and province of rhetoric."[26]
I would like to think Fish was historically accurate here, but in fact, as we
have seen, the Syracuse English faculty specifically rejected the name of
rhetoric, and the unit most sympathetic to rhetoric as an organizing term,
the Writing Program, slowly separated from the English department during and after my tenure as chair.

But if I could hold onto my wishful thinking just a bit longer, I might
argue that, indeed, some self-representations of the Syracuse ETS major
suggest interesting possibilities for its future reinterpretation in terms of
rhetoric. Take a look at the categories of the new major (see Appendix).
In one sense, rhetoric makes an appearance only as a subcategory under
theoretical inquiries; in another sense, it is everywhere in the new major.
Unnamed as such, rhetoric nevertheless provides a framework after all,
or at least a way of understanding the framework in which differences are
marked in the new curriculum. What is it but *rhetorical contestation* that is
being referred to in this passage from a collectively written document explaining the new major:

> In literature departments at the moment, arguments about the formulation
> of [disciplinary] questions are as intense as arguments about their answers.
> The traditional curriculum, however, does not call attention to these issues
> or to the different positions from which textual study proceeds. Faculty may
> disagree profoundly; and even though students may find out about those

---

[26] Gary A. Olson, "Fish Tales: A Conversation with 'The Contemporary Sophist,'" *Journal of Advanced Composition* 12 (fall 1992); rpt. in Stanley Fish, *There's No Such Thing as Free
Speech* (New York, 1994), p. 285.

disagreements by chance as they move from course to course, the curricular structure implies that it is more important to master certain predesignated works organized by genres, periods, and authors, than to inquire into the grounds of such categories or into the ends and means of reading. Ideally, a new curriculum would shift this emphasis without simply reifying a fashionable methodology or settling for a vapid pluralism as a way of defusing disagreements. At Syracuse, we have tried to construct such a curriculum, one that foregrounds differences among modes of critical practice, acknowledges its own provisionality, and looks to its own further transformation.[27]

This passage describing the new curriculum seems fully involved in a rhetorical perspective. A curriculum that aims to foreground "differences among modes of critical practices" appears to have made rhetoric its framework even while tending to ignore it explicitly.

But more historically convincing than Fish's interview comment and my wishful thinking are some remarks by Gerald Graff in *Beyond the Culture Wars: How Teaching the Conflicts Can Revitalize American Education.* Graff interpreted the ETS major as an illustration of his "teaching the conflicts" model, which I discuss more fully in the next chapter. However, let me note here that the ETS curriculum contrasts with Graff's model in some important ways. For example, ETS juxtaposes differences (in modes of reading) throughout the curriculum as a whole but does not necessarily thematize those differences in department-wide conferences or in a single course as in Graff's proposals. Thus, ETS emphasizes performing the conflicts in recognizable ways rather than explicitly teaching them, though such teaching might also occur in individual classrooms and advising sessions.

But to learn more about current debates over the academic humanities and about the ETS major's reception within those debates, we need to look at less sympathetic readers of the Syracuse curriculum. In the *New Criterion,* a journal of the cultural right if there ever was one, James Tuttleton wrote a review of Graff's *Beyond the Culture Wars* in March 1993. Near the end of the review, Tuttleton takes up Graff's discussion of the ETS major at Syracuse. First, Tuttleton gives a long quotation from Graff's book: Graff writes that "no teacher at Syracuse is *forced* to enter the departmental dialogue. . . . [B]ecause the program is organized as a dialogue, any teacher's refusal to enter can be interpreted by students as

---

[27] Steven Cohan, John W. Crowley, Jean E. Howard, Veronica Kelly, Steven Mailloux, Stephen Melville, Felicity Nussbaum, Bill Readings, Bennet Schaber, Linda Shires, and Thomas Yingling, "Not a Good Idea: A New Curriculum at Syracuse," unpublished essay, December 1987; copy available on request (sjmaillo@uci.edu).

itself a meaningful choice (not necessarily a discreditable one)." Graff then includes and Tuttleton reproduces part of a letter to Graff, in which I said that under the Syracuse plan

> a faculty member simply continuing to teach his course in a traditional, iso-lated way does not undermine the curricular "conversation" because the cur-riculum causes his action to be read as a move in the conversation. Since students will be helped to "read" their courses side-by-side, when they take a traditionalist course they will be able to read it through the grid of the new major.[28]

Now, I think my rhetorical point here was simply that the ETS grid of courses helped students understand the different ways of reading within the department and that the grid allowed them to interrelate these dif-ferent interpretive rhetorics more easily than they had been able to do in the old curriculum. Be that as it may, Graff followed the quotation from my letter with the realistic comment: "It remains to be seen how well the conception [of a curricular conversation] will translate into practice, but the principle seems to me sound."

Then Tuttleton comments in his turn:

> Sound? It is a recipe for punishing the independent thinker. First, the de-partmental boss tells the lone professor that he is not *forced* to collaborate; then his non-cooperation is noted as intentional; then there is the insinu-ation that his non-cooperation is possibly discreditable; students are then instructed by the cooperators in how to view the traditionalist and his non-cooperative course. I have no doubt about the fate of the lone non-cooperator: first, the salary cut, then discriminatory course assignments, then the impossible schedule—and before and above all else, chairmanly and departmental contempt.

Tuttleton ends his hypothetical scenario about the probable results of the new Syracuse ETS curriculum: "Since the Department is now a Com-mune for promulgating left-wing sociological arguments, with a view to politically correct indoctrination, the lone professor can be expected to undergo group 'Re-Education' and 'Rehabilitation'" (34).

There is something of the same anti-PC rhetoric in a 1990 article called "Syracuse University and the Kool-Aid Acid Curriculum," which

---

[28] Mailloux quoted in Gerald Graff, *Beyond the Culture Wars* (New York, 1992), p. 187; quoted in James W. Tuttleton, "Back to the Sixties with Spindoctor Graff," *New Criterion* 11 (March 1993): 33.

combines Tuttleton's vehement political censures with its own blunt theoretical objections. Taking all his information about ETS from Pierce's Syracuse *Post-Standard* article, Nino Langiulli attacks what he calls the "Marxist, relativist, and historicist" assumptions of the new curriculum and argues that given those assumptions, "there could be no basis for preferring Shakespeare, Milton, or Chaucer, to Alice Walker, Roger Rabbit, or, indeed, the Simpsons. The added implication for anyone addicted to the habit of drawing inferences," Langiulli continues, "is that there are no great books, no great authors, no issues which are transhistorical or transcultural. Still further, there is no human nature and no civilization; only books and authors captive of their times, only issues which are transient and culture-bound, and, therefore, only the vagaries of race, gender, and ethnicity."[29] Langiulli's fear of relativism is typical of the Culture Wars, as is his reductive move in the politics of naming, where all advocates of the ETS curriculum get indiscriminately lumped together under the label "postmodern Marxists." But his particular version of the move becomes more meaningful when seen in relation to some of his more scholarly work.

In the Syracuse article, Langiulli facetiously writes: "We must be excused for raising the issues of consistency and non-contradiction, when we have been told by post-modern Marxists that they have learned to live with ambiguity—not to say contradiction and inconsistency" (6). Then he follows this up with claiming that for "our blessed postmodern Marxists" at Syracuse, "anything means everything and everything means anything" (7). Langiulli attributes this "doctrine" to Derrida (7) and then repeats it using the exact same phrase in his book, *Possibility, Necessity, and Existence*, on the Italian philosopher Nicola Abbagnano. Comparing Abbagnano's and Derrida's interpretations of possibility, Langiulli notes the ambiguity of the central concept: "Aristotle's classical treatment recognizes this ambiguity. After attempting to defend the principle of non-contradiction (the principle of meaning, the basis of truth, and the starting point of 'first philosophy') against the Sophists especially, Aristotle says, 'It is possible for the same thing to be *potentially* two opposites, but not actually' (emphasis added)."[30] As Langiulli explains, Abbagnano builds

[29] Nino Langiulli, "Syracuse University and the Kool-Aid Acid Curriculum," *Measure*, no. 88 (September 1990): 5; further references appear in the text. In passing here, I note the irony (for my book, not the ETS curriculum) that the newsletter publishing Langiulli's article goes by the name of one of my favorite sophistic tropes and was founded by the pragmatist Sydney Hook.

[30] Aristotle, *Metaphysics* 1009a35, quoted in Nino Langiulli, *Possibility, Necessity, and Existence: Abbagnano and His Predecessors* (Philadelphia, 1992), pp. 51–52.

on Plato and Aristotle's notions of existence and possibility to establish a primary sense of the latter term, an originary, univocal level of unambiguous meaning that Langiulli requires of a successful philosophy of possibility. In contrast, Langiulli sees Derrida as coining the term *différance* to describe the "otherness and disconnection" at the very "bottom of things," an otherness and disconnection "so absolute that there is never univocity but only equivocity—no origins and no ends." Whereas Abbagnano "looks into the face of possibility and sees finitude," Derrida "looks into the face of possibility and sees infinitude." Using the phrase he used to condemn the Syracuse ETS curriculum, Langiulli says of Derrida's *différance*: "Distinctions dissolve into one another so that anything means everything and everything means anything" (52).

But the rhetorical echoes of Langiulli's diatribe against the ETS major do not stop here. In the very next paragraph, in "a digression on a digression," Langiulli wonders why "many literary critics claiming to be disciples of Derrida and the deconstructive method do not follow him into the absolute free play of sense/nonsense but stop short in their interpretations of 'writers' and 'texts' at the banalities of race, ethnicity, sex, and, of course, class" (52). In his Syracuse article, Langiulli makes an analogous move from criticizing the curriculum's purported interpretive relativism—anything means everything, everything means anything—to condemning its reductive imposition of a single political meaning and value. That is, as Langiulli goes on at great polemical length about the ETS major, he shifts his target from the philosophical relativism he sees in its structure and content to the political indoctrination he deplores in its pedagogical process and educational effects. He notes at one point that the new ETS courses "are curiously reminiscent of those given as 're-education' in such places as Kampuchea, Ethiopia and, until its deliberate demise, Jonestown, Guyana" (6). The article ends sedately: "As the students of Syracuse imbibe this sweet new curriculum, laced as it is with the poison of multiculturalism, let us hope that the body count remains low. If we do not find the will to resist this suicide of the West being carried out in the labyrinths of America's academe, our students will find themselves on line to drink from the vats of a Kool-Aid acid curriculum—one that is intellectually trivial and ethically lethal" (8).

Now, Langiulli's rhetorical move here is typical not only of the cultural right within curriculum debates but also, as we will see, of the left as well. Michael Bérubé has usefully characterized one version of this foundationalist gambit that transforms charges of epistemological and ethical relativism into attacks on intellectual intolerance and political correctness. Bérubé writes: "Here's the strategy in a nutshell: First, accuse the academics of relativism. When the academics reply that they don't actually consider all opinions equally valid, that they take strong exception to student-goons, who demolish shanties, hold mock slave auctions, and scrawl swastikas on university structures, then follow the accusation of relativism with the accusation of political correctness."[31]

Relativism leads to nihilism which leads to fascism: this logic appears often in current debates over teaching the humanities and originates at several different points on the political spectrum. I am especially interested in how it appears as a contemporary repetition of ancient and modern attacks on sophistic rhetoric. I realize that a reduction of the Culture Wars and curriculum debates to a restaging of Plato versus the Sophists might be among my most blatant oversimplifications. As mentioned in Chapter 2, I am cognizant of various warnings that these ancient debates are simply not pertinent now. But it seems to me that it is precisely a perception of the impertinence of postmodern sophistic rhetoric that seems to be causing a good deal of the intellectual and political controversy within today's heated public discussions. Obviously, the current Culture Wars differ from debates in classical Athens, but differences as well as similarities can be usefully assessed by demonstrating the way restagings of Platonism versus sophistry are both continuous and discontinuous with their ancient antecedents.

This rhetorical fact—of repetition with a (sometimes radical) difference—can be seen both in the explicit namings that go on in the more popular cultural debates as well as in the less obvious connections these debates have to the sometimes technical and specialized arguments made by participants in their scholarly work directed at more restricted professional audiences, as I have just tried to show in the case of Langiulli. Let me expand this claim into two points important for a fuller understanding of what might be called the rhetorical density of any cultural conversation. First, technical academic discussions have multiple and complex interconnections to debates in the mass media outside the university. We might figure these connections as rhetorical transfers from one cultural site to another, movements of arguments, narratives, tropes, phrases, and names from one medium (department memos) through

---

[31] Michael Bérubé, "Public Image Limited: Political Correctness and the Media's Big Lie," *Village Voice*, 18 June 1991; rpt. in *Debating P.C.: The Controversy over Political Correctness on College Campuses*, ed. Paul Berman (New York, 1992), p. 130. Also, for a more detailed analysis of the cultural debates outlined in this chapter and Chap. 2, see Michael Bérubé, *Public Access: Literary Theory and American Cultural Politics* (London, 1994).

other media (catalogue course descriptions and scholarly journal publications) to others (daily newspapers, radio interview shows, and monthly news magazines) to still others (television documentaries, national party platforms, and congressional hearings) and back again. It would be odd indeed if during such travels the cultural rhetoric on any side of a particular issue did not become radically transformed in various ways for various purposes as it moved from one site to another, from one medium to another. Whether such transformations clarify or distort, oversimplify or purify, these translated pieces of cultural rhetoric play prominent roles in the debates at the sites of their destination.

Thus, and this is my second point, cultural rhetoric study cannot simply dismiss caricatures of theoretical or political positions by either the cultural right or left if such translations play significant roles in determining the dynamics or outcomes of various cultural confrontations. What such study can do is clarify the rhetorical interconnections, for example, between academic and popular levels of debate. Out of such clarification comes not necessarily a solution to conflict but at least an opportunity for intervention. Such rhetorical analysis is another form of reception study, in this case the reception of academic theories and vocabularies in the more general cultural conversation outside the university.[32]

To again make my rhetorical point concrete, let me return to the reception of ETS. I have tried to suggest that behind Langiulli's condemnation of the Syracuse curriculum is the same Platonic-Aristotelian suspicion of sophistic relativism that fueled his rejection of "the extreme consequences of the thought of Derrida, Deleuze, Foucault, and Lacan" in his scholarly book.[33] Similarly, Tuttleton's condemnation of ETS relates to an appeal made in his literary scholarship to this identical tradition within Western philosophy. The appeal is explicit and emphatic in the final chapters of his book *Vital Signs: Essays on American Literature and Criticism*, "Jacques et moi" and "Some Modern Sophists." In order to

---

[32] Cf. Michel Foucault, *The Archaeology of Knowledge*, trans. A. M. Sheridan Smith (New York, 1972), esp. "Archaeology and the History of Ideas," pp. 135–40; and Edward W. Said, "Traveling Theory," chap. 10 in *The World, the Text, and the Critic* (Cambridge, 1983), pp. 226–47.

[33] Langiulli, *Possibility*, p. 53. Also see Nino Langiulli, "On the Location of Socrates' Feet or the Immanence of Transcendence," *Telos* 96 (summer 1993): 143–47, where he interprets a line from Plato's *Phaedo* as a reply to "the ancient liberal view represented by the Sophists—the view that reality, morality, and esthetics are only matters of opinion since there are no transcendent points of reference" and then uses this interpretation as "a reply to contemporary sophists, a.k.a. anti-foundationalists or contemporary liberals" who "in order to vindicate humanity . . . maintain that there can be no foundations and philosophy as the search for them . . . is either futile at worst or poetry at best" (143).

ground his attack on the contemporary Nietzschean claims of "a number of pontificating Sophists," he argues for "the ancient analysis of the nature of truth and how it can be linguistically represented."[34] For Tuttleton, "there is no better account available than that in Plato and the *Metaphysics*, the *Posterior Analytics*, and the *Peri Hermeneias* (*On Interpretation*) of Aristotle" (326).

Just as the ancient Greek Sophists were refuted—"I regard them as sufficiently eviscerated in the great dialogues of Plato, in Socrates' innocent questions, and in the stunning *Metaphysics* of Aristotle" (314)—so too does Tuttleton see himself as extending the Platonic-Aristotelian tradition in a vigorous refutation of "the contemporary Sophists" who "have it that the inevitable gap between the word and the thing itself, between the signifier and the signified, proves that reality is inaccessible through language" (322). This linguistic skepticism is "the latest form of nihilism" (318) and, combined with a tendency "toward interpretive chaos" (340), constitutes a form of sophistic relativism: "Once the critic breaks with essentialism, anything goes" (348; cf. 330). But—and here we approach a more direct connection between his foundationalist philosophizing and his political objections to the ETS curriculum—for Tuttleton all this postmodern sophistry leads, as with Langiulli, from absurd theory to dangerous politics. "Once we verbally invert everything—by saying that black is white, up down, central marginal, aberrational normative, and so on—perfection will arrive," says Tuttleton's contemporary Sophists. "This seems hopeless and a desperate council" to Tuttleton (328), who argues further that the politics of these Sophists is not simply that of emptying out the theory supporting the moral and social traditions of the West but of filling up that emptiness with whatever personal or ideological agenda they see fit (339).

Even more specifically, Tuttleton resorts to the once tried and true rhetoric of the Cold War to make his case against "the current academic Sophists" (349), whose "deconstructionism has proved immensely fruitful to the political left in trying to foment that chaos in the domain of values that is said to be necessary to launch the supposed forthcoming revolution" (344). Tuttleton thus sees himself exposing this "covert intention" (345) of poststructuralist sophistry, which opens the way for political opportunists with a Marxist agenda and encourages a "sinister assault on liberty" (346). Tuttleton claims this potential assault is actualized in the Syracuse ETS curriculum, which, to repeat, he sees as "promul-

---

[34] James W. Tuttleton, *Vital Signs: Essays on American Literature and Criticism* (Chicago, 1996), pp. 338, 326; further citations are in the text.

gating left-wing sociological arguments, with a view to politically correct indoctrination."[35]

It is perhaps ironic that some of the strongest attacks on the Syracuse reforms have come from exactly those ideological positions both Langiulli and Tuttleton identify with ETS itself. Soon after the department formally accepted a general description of the changes, a *Chronicle of Higher Education* article ran with the title "New Curriculum at Syracuse U. Attacked by 2 Marxist Professors." Contending "that the planned curriculum is 'part of the crisis management of late capitalism,'" Donald Morton and Mas'ud Zavarzadeh are reported to "have beaten the traditionalists to the punch—call it a left hook—arguing that the changes are superficial and not radical enough."[36] Many of Morton and Zavarzadeh's 1986–87 department memos had already sketched out their objections, which later became the extended critiques of ETS published in their essays and books of the early nineties. Like those on the cultural right, these postmodern Marxists from the cultural left found the supporters of ETS to be woefully wanting in their theories and politics. But whereas Tuttleton and Langiulli worried about sophistic relativism leading to leftist ideological indoctrination, Morton and Zavarzadeh complained about relativistic rhetoricism maintaining the wishy-washy liberal pluralism of the traditional humanist status quo.

"Like all 'new' transforming curricula in U.S. universities," write Morton and Zavarzadeh, the Syracuse ETS major "is a 'transformation' which does not transform anything: it simply meets the educational needs of the changing (post)modern labor force of late capitalism."[37] The authors argue that "among the most important strategies for absorbing the opposition and maintaining the system is the strategy of pluralistic inclusion: the institution assimilates the discourses of its adversaries." And this was exactly "the strategy that was deployed to ward off radical change in the Syracuse English Department," according to Morton and Zavarzadeh (149). Moreover, a pluralistic leveling of discourses that explicitly *in-*

[35] Tuttleton, "Back to the Sixties," p. 34.

[36] Scott Heller, "New Curriculum at Syracuse U. Attacked by 2 Marxist Professors," *Chronicle of Higher Education*, 3 August 1988, p. A17. This article appeared alongside a longer piece by Heller, "Some English Departments Are Giving Undergraduates Grounding in New Literary and Critical Theory," pp. A15–A17, which described curricular and pedagogical reforms at Carnegie Mellon, Syracuse, and other universities. For a very brief follow-up, see Scott Heller, "The Curriculum," *Chronicle of Higher Education*, 21 November 1990, p. A17.

[37] Mas'ud Zavarzadeh and Donald Morton, *Theory as Resistance: Politics and Culture after (Post)structuralism* (New York, 1994), p. 136. Unless otherwise indicated, references in these paragraphs are to this text.

cluded led to a coalitionist politics that covertly *excluded*. Or, as Morton and Zavarzadeh put it, in a rather incisive rhetorical analysis:

> What happened in the Syracuse English Department happens all the time: the radical thinker is situated on an axis of alternatives such that she has the "free choice" either of working from within the system or being marked as an "extremist" who can therefore be "legitimately" excluded because she can be regarded as "self-excluding." In other words, the options come down to either being "persuaded" of the legitimacy of working within the system and thus accepting the existing structures, or finding that there is no space for radical change. "Persuasion" (the model of democratic conversation) is, in other words, an alibi for a pernicious system of surveillance and punishment built on the principle: "Be persuaded, or else . . ." (149)

I suppose I am being rather disingenuous in attributing to Morton and Zavarzadeh an "incisive *rhetorical* analysis," since "rhetoric" is the last thing with which they wish to be associated, as we saw in their 1988 "War of the Words" article. But "rhetorical" is exactly what their talk of persuasion amounts to, and, furthermore, their analysis illustrates precisely why rhetoric and politics go hand in hand and need not (even should not) be separated in theory or practice.

Nevertheless, a separation of rhetoric and politics is what Morton and Zavarzadeh continue to insist upon—in their depoliticized notion of rhetoric and in their limited representation of contemporary rhetorical study. For example, in their use of Theresa Ebert's distinction between "ludic (post)modernism" and their own "resistance (post)modernism," they continue to give rhetoric over to an apolitical formalism, now under the guise of a reactionary postmodernism with its view of the "unending 'playfulness' (thus the term 'ludic') of the signifier in signifying practices." As with Tuttleton and Langiulli, the rhetorical Derrida becomes the pivotal theoretical figure where poststructuralism goes wrong: In contrast to ludic (post)modernism's Derridean "understanding of *différance* as an effect of rhetoric," Morton and Zavarzadeh's resistance (post)modernism "articulates difference in the social space of economic exploitation and labor." But whereas Tuttleton and Langiulli see *différance* as providing the theoretical excuse for imposing a repugnant Marxist agenda upon the humanities, Morton and Zavarzadeh see *différance* as a strategic device for taking away the ground of the "real" necessary for any liberatory political project like Marxism.[38]

---

[38] Zavarzadeh and Morton, *Theory, (Post)Modernity, Opposition*, pp. 106–7: see also Zavarzadeh and Morton, *Theory as Resistance*, p. 7. This view of Derridean deconstruction

Morton and Zavarzadeh's persistence in depoliticizing rhetorical study extends from their theoretical formulations to their historical narratives. In their story, "the rhetorical turn in the humanities has successfully diverted inquiries from the politics of intelligibility to the tropics of knowledge."[39] Such an account is misleading but instructively so. Shouldn't the authors have recognized that contemporary rhetorical studies often resists separating rhetoric and politics, language use and social materiality? Aren't they aware of earlier proposals for Marxist and materialist rhetorics?[40]

In their most recent critiques, Morton and Zavarzadeh continue to demonstrate the antirhetorical bias already apparent in their initial published attacks on ETS. Their *Theory as Resistance* uses in expanded form the same attacks on the "revival of the concept of rhetoric (through the deployment of the strategies developed in the writings of Jacques Derrida, Paul de Man, and their annotators and followers)" and extends the complaints to the "more politically relevant forms of rhetorical studies, following the later writings of Michel Foucault and Michel de Certeau." According to Zavarzadeh and Morton, the latter studies of "legitimation" ask "ethical" but not "political" questions and end up "representing all existing discourses as automatically legitimate simply by virtue of their existence and thus, by implication, as equal" (17–18). These criticisms of rhetorical study once again raise the specter of relativism, dangerous now not because rhetoricians dismiss objectivity but because they embrace it too naively:

> A rhetorician—in the name of the liberal ideal of pluralistic truth and the freedom of objective inquiry—can be as interested in the rhetoric of the Ku Klux Klan as in the rhetoric of the uprising in Los Angeles in 1992: all social phenomena are occasions for cognitive inquiry. . . . This, of course, fits into the dominant picture of what the academy is and tries to continue to be: a place where *all* inquiries are objective and equally urgent. (18)

Morton and Zavarzadeh are both right and wrong here. They are right in that rhetorical study has no built-in ideology; it can be effectively adapted

---

should be contrasted to Derrida's explicit rejection of rhetoricism—see Jacques Derrida, "Afterword: Toward an Ethic of Discussion," trans. Samuel Weber, in *Limited Inc* (Evanston, Ill., 1988), p. 156, n. 9; and Gary A. Olson, "Jacques Derrida on Rhetoric and Composition: A Conversation," *Journal of Advanced Composition* 10 (1990): 18–19.

[39] Zavarzadeh and Morton, *Theory, (Post)Modernity, Opposition*, p. 205.

[40] See, for example, Michael Calvin McGee, "A Materialist's Conception of Rhetoric," in *Explorations in Rhetoric*, ed. Ray E. McKerrow (Dallas, 1982), pp. 23–48; and Robert Wess, "Notes toward a Marxist Rhetoric," *Bucknell Review* 28, no. 2 (1983): 126–48.

to various political agendas. They are wrong in that no interpreter can treat all inquiries equally. Any rhetorician is situated within particular social, disciplinary, and institutional networks, acting within specific webs of desires, beliefs, and practices; and this situatedness makes some inquiries more urgent than others. Unsituated relativism is an impossibility, and thus it is not a danger that Morton and Zavarzadeh need worry about, for rhetorical study or any other inquiry.

Differences in ideology are, of course, another matter. Rhetoricians do come in various ideological flavors, and it is quite possible that rhetorical theorists currently tend to be more liberal than radical. Still, this need not be the case, as evidenced by the many recent proposals of critical rhetorics.[41] Moreover, the topic of language and ideology has gained increasing attention in contemporary cultural study and political theory. To pursue such topics within the human sciences, we need more rhetorical studies, not less. And, finally, as I have tried to demonstrate in this chapter, readings of today's Culture Wars make it obvious how important the relation of rhetoric to politics continues to be, both as part of the analytic frame and as a topic within the debates analyzed. These reception narratives can play a prominent role in a cultural rhetoric studies wishing to avoid the pitfalls of various orthodoxies on both the cultural right and left. Avoiding such pitfalls will remain a significant challenge for cultural criticism and humanistic inquiry in the near future. And it is to that future I now wish to turn.

---

[41] There have been calls for "critical rhetorics," "radical rhetorical studies," and "materialist rhetoric": see R. E. McKerrow, "Critical Rhetoric: Theory and Praxis," *Communication Monographs* 56 (1989): 91–111; T. V. Reed, *Fifteen Jugglers, Five Believers: Literary Politics and the Poetics of American Social Movements* (Berkeley, Calif., 1992), pp. 174, n. 5, and 176, n. 20; and Michael F. Bernard-Donals, *Mikhail Bakhtin: Between Phenomenology and Marxism* (Cambridge, 1994), pp. 159–78. Also see James Arnt Aune, *Rhetoric and Marxism* (Boulder, Colo., 1994); and William E. Cain, ed., *Reconceptualizing American Literary/Cultural Studies: Rhetoric, History, and Politics in the Humanities* (New York, 1996), esp. the essays by Dale M. Bauer, William J. Spurlin, and Michele Sordi.

RHETORICAL STUDIES:
FUTURE PROSPECTS

Any reflection about human hope has as much to do with the battle of ideas
as it does the battle for resources.
— Cornel West, "The Future of Pragmatic Thought"

Acknowledging that culture is a debate rather than a monologue does not
prevent us from energetically fighting for the truth of our own convictions.
On the contrary, when truth is disputed, we can seek it only by entering the
debate—as Socrates knew when he taught the conflicts two millennia ago.
— Gerald Graff, *Beyond the Culture Wars*

During June 1903 the British pragmatist F. C. S. Schiller wrote
somewhat playfully to William James about several labels for the new philosophy they were advocating. In a "table of contraries," he opposed their
"Good & Finite" pragmatism to "the Evil & Infinite" idealism of his day.
Under the former, he listed "humanism," "pluralism," "radical empiri-
cism," and "voluntarism," contrasting them respectively to such negative
terms as "scholasticism," "absolutism," "apriorism," and "intellectualism,"
concluding with such oppositions as "Britticism" vs. "Germanism" and
"Witticism" vs. "Barbarism." Later and more seriously, Schiller expressed
disappointment that in a recent book, John Dewey, a potential ally, had
not specifically used one of their most important positive terms—"pragmatism"—in describing his own new philosophical project.[1] In these letters, Schiller was writing to his American friend about the strategic importance of what you call what you do. That is, he focused explicitly on
the rhetorical politics of naming—within a specialized disciplinary field,
within an academic institution, within a larger cultural conversation be-

---

[1] F. C. S. Schiller to William James, 9 June 1903 and 25 September 1903, bMS Am 1092
(872) and (875), by permission of the Houghton Library, Harvard University.

yond the university. As I have tried to demonstrate, this rhetorical politics of naming was central to the outcome of my Syracuse rhetoric proposals and remains crucial to the ongoing reception of the ETS curriculum. In this final chapter, I pursue the topic further, moving toward the proposal of rhetorical studies as an organizing framework for reconceptualizing the human sciences.

RHETORICALLY DO THEY TEACH

In *Professing Literature*, Gerald Graff presents academic literary studies with a valuable rhetorical history of its past disciplinary life. In *Beyond the Culture Wars* he advocates "teaching the conflicts" as a rhetorical solution to the discipline's present curricular problems.[2] In both cases, he uses tropes of "debate," "conversation," and "dialogue" to rethink past and present institutional practices and structures. In this section, I discuss Graff's "teaching the conflicts" as one model for curricular and pedagogical reform. But my main purpose is to show how it relates to cultural rhetoric studies and how such studies can be used to reconceive English departments specifically and then more generally the institutionalized disciplines of the human sciences.

To demonstrate how his model is not just incidentally rhetorical in its tropology and argumentation, I will examine some of Graff's statements and use them to redescribe the Syracuse major in English and Textual Studies. My rhetorical reading of Graff's vocabulary and its juxtaposition to ETS will clarify the utility of his proposed framework and the advantages of thematizing its rhetoricity and, potentially, that of the ETS curriculum. Graff himself has already made some suggestive comments about the relation of his model to the Syracuse reforms. Remarking in "Other Voices, Other Rooms" that "knowledge and culture now look less like a unified package, capable of being formalized in a list of great books or cultural literacy facts, and more like a set of unruly and conflicted social practices," Graff notes that "departmental and curricular structure continues to express an earlier positivist-humanist paradigm" that fails to recognize these recent transformations in the shape of knowledge and culture or even acknowledge that there is a deep and widespread conflict between the old structures and the new assumptions. "This very conflict and the need to work through it," Graff argues, "demands a model of the

---

[2] Gerald Graff, *Professing Literature: An Institutional History* (Chicago, 1987); Graff, *Beyond the Culture Wars* (New York, 1992).

curriculum that is neither a cafeteria counter nor a core, but something more like a conversation."[3] He then cites the Syracuse ETS major as one example of this model of curricular conversation about the conflicts.

One of the most admirable characteristics of Graff's model is its oft-stated goal of helping students "become interested participants in the cultural conversation" over our society's aesthetic, ethical, and political values. Teaching the conflicts within the university is a way of introducing students into "the intellectual vocabularies" in which those conflicts are carried on, and a curricular structure aimed at enhancing such "academic literacy" must work against "a disjunctive curriculum in which students encounter each course as an isolated unit" and instead must put each course into a "conversational relation to other courses and discourses."[4]

Though the privileged trope of its self-descriptions tends to be that of contestation rather than conversation, the Syracuse ETS curriculum shares many of the rhetorical goals of teaching the conflicts. It introduces students to a vocabulary that would help them enter into debates over such topics as canon reform, cultural heritage, aesthetic value, political ideology, multiculturalism, and other topics of intense controversy within English studies and higher education more generally. The introductory course—ETS 141, Reading and Interpretation—attempts to initiate students into the basic theoretical vocabulary of the major, especially semiotics and discourse analysis. In the words of the university catalogue, ETS 141 involves "the reading of literary and nonliterary texts" and "juxtaposes language as a system of differences to language in its concrete social and historical uses." This first course provides a basis for further work in textual studies and makes it easier for students to use the curricular structure or grid to read the differences that matter most among the courses offered in the department. In Graff's more rhetorical terms, the grid can be used to place the various courses into "conversational relation."

From Graff's perspective, one of the advantages of the ETS major must surely be that the new curricular structure highlights the differences between the old model of literary historical coverage and the newer projects of critical theory and cultural critique. It does this, for example, by placing the traditional literary history courses under one subcategory of the historical mode of inquiry rather than using literary historical cover-

[3] Gerald Graff, "Other Voices, Other Rooms: Organizing and Teaching the Humanities Conflict," *New Literary History* 21 (1990): 817–39; rpt. in *Teaching the Conflicts: Gerald Graff, Curricular Reform, and the Culture Wars*, ed. William E. Cain (New York, 1994), p. 37.

[4] Graff, "Other Voices," pp. 23–26.

age as the overarching frame for all the courses (see Appendix). By re-situating traditional courses in this way, the curricular structure creates a "conversation" among diverse ways of reading and talking about literary and nonliterary texts. In such a curriculum in any given semester, "Shakespeare" might appear as a subtitle for several different courses such as ETS 411, Studies in Literary History to 1800; ETS 343, Introduction to Cultural Theories of Representation; and ETS 491, Studies in Feminisms. What gets emphasized in such contrasting uses of Shakespearean texts is the distinctive modes of inquiry or critical perspectives and the interpretive and often political stakes in reading texts differently. The point of such a curriculum, Graff notes in *Beyond the Culture Wars*, is to replace a major based on "'a traditional pluralism' in which different viewpoints are separately represented, with a framework in which each position 'acknowledges its allied or contestatory relation to other positions.'"[5] Again, "allied or contestatory" here might be read in rhetorical terms, for certainly the relations desired are those of direct and indirect dialogue, just the kind of "dialogic curriculum" that Graff advocates.[6]

Graff's rhetorical explanations of his conflict model can be used to read the ETS major more rhetorically than it reads itself, but what I really want to emphasize is how his proposal to teach the conflicts and the ETS major might both be viewed as curricular models for institutionalizing the study of cultural rhetoric. Besides whatever persuasiveness my earlier chapters might lend to my argument here, I see several specifically institutional reasons for adopting cultural rhetoric studies as a framework for rethinking literary studies specifically and the humanities and interpretive social sciences more generally. Simply put, the study of cultural rhetoric has significant relations to several emergent proposals for changing the practices and structures of the human sciences: it has important intellectual connections with the cultural studies movement, transdisciplinary inquiry, and interdisciplinary projects like feminist, ethnic, and postcolonial studies; it has pedagogical connections to such proposals as Graff's "teaching the conflicts" model; and it has institutional connections to composition as a discipline. Let me elaborate briefly on each of these points.

[5] Graff, *Beyond the Culture Wars*, p. 186, quoting *The English Newsletter: Undergraduate News from the English Department, Syracuse University* 1, no. 1 (March 1990): 3.
[6] This rhetorical reading of Syracuse's ETS major goes somewhat against the grain of its institutional history. As we saw in the previous chapter, the Syracuse English faculty did not accept "rhetoric" as an organizing term for their innovative curricular reforms when they produced them in 1986–89.

As I noted in Chapter 3, cultural studies has become the most influential new alternative to literary studies as a paradigm for English departments. Some departments have explicitly embraced cultural studies in the titles of their new graduate programs, and many others have incorporated cultural studies arguments into their proposals for revising their curricula. Even more pervasive are the number of published attempts to promote a redefinition of traditional literary studies as a study of cultural texts more generally. There is continuing debate about the definition and purpose of cultural studies,[7] but most of its advocates within English departments propose expanding the study of literature into an investigation of many kinds of cultural productions, including noncanonical literature, nonliterary written texts, and other media such as film and television; and they promote an analysis of the relations among these different cultural practices and the sociopolitical formations in which both their objects of study and the studies themselves are situated.

In Parts One and Two, I proposed taking an explicitly rhetorical slant on this emergent field of cultural studies. Such a slant begins by conceptualizing the object of study—culture—as a heterogeneous, interconnected tangle of rhetorical practices extending and manipulating other practices and structures—social, political, and economic. A study of cultural rhetoric attempts to read the tropes, arguments, and narratives of its object texts (whether literary or nonliterary) within their sociopolitical contexts of cultural production and reception. Such an enterprise can figure its work as investigating the rhetorical dynamics of cultural conversations at particular historical moments, through certain institutions, within specific material circumstances.

This rhetorical enterprise must necessarily be interdisciplinary, strategically borrowing from many different subdisciplines focused on interpretation, communication, and symbol using, broadly defined. The study of cultural rhetoric can also be transdisciplinary, investigating the conditions, purposes, activities, and results of the disciplinary production of knowledge, especially within academic institutions such as the U.S. university. Thus, the study of cultural rhetoric links up with two currently growing fields within the human sciences: the rhetoric of inquiry movement and the study of professionalized disciplines, their histories and contemporary organization.[8]

---

[7] For discussion and bibliography, see Lawrence Grossberg, Cary Nelson, and Paula A. Treichler, eds., *Cultural Studies* (New York, 1992); and Isaiah Smithson and Nancy Ruff, eds., *English Studies/Culture Studies: Institutionalizing Dissent* (Urbana, Ill., 1994).

[8] On the former, see John S. Nelson, Allan Megill, and Donald N. McCloskey, eds., *The Rhetoric of the Human Sciences: Language and Argument in Scholarship and Public Affairs* (Madi-

A politicized study of cultural rhetoric also needs to relate its agenda to work in such fields as feminist, ethnic, and postcolonial studies.[9] By defining "cultural rhetoric" as the political effectivity of trope and argument in culture, I am trying to build into cultural rhetoric study from the very start an investigation of political questions, such as those involving the ideological production of communal solidarity and conflict and the symbolic mechanisms of domination and resistance within a multicultural society. I believe that rhetorical study generally should reclaim its (often ignored) political heritage and should install a concern with power into its project from the beginning rather than tagging it on at the end as an afterthought.[10] Michel Foucault's genealogical work is especially helpful in theorizing rhetoric politically right now. Let me give just one example.

In answering the question "What happens when individuals exert (as they say) power over others?" Foucault in a late essay distinguishes three kinds of relationships: objective capacities, power relations, and relationships of communication. By "objective capacities" he means power over things, abilities to "modify, use, consume, or destroy them . . . a power which stems from aptitudes directly inherent in the body or relayed by external instruments." Foucault distinguishes this form of power from the one with which he is most directly concerned: power that "brings into play relations between individuals (or between groups)." The exercise of this power is "always a way of acting upon an acting subject or acting subjects by virtue of their acting or being capable of action." Foucault then differentiates these power relations from relationships of communication, "which transmit information by means of a language, a system of signs, or any other symbolic medium."[11] In another place, he describes

son, Wis., 1987); and Herbert W. Simons, ed., *The Rhetorical Turn: Invention and Persuasion in the Conduct of Inquiry* (Chicago, 1990). For examples of the latter within English studies, see Graff, *Professing Literature*; James A. Berlin, *Rhetoric and Reality: Writing Instruction in American Colleges, 1900–1985* (Carbondale, Ill., 1987); and David Shumway, ed., "Episodes in the History of Criticism and Theory: Papers from the Fourth Annual Meeting of the GRIP Project," special issue, *Poetics Today* 9, no. 4 (1988).

9 See, for example, the chapters on feminist criticism, gender criticism, African-American criticism, Marxist criticism, and postcolonial criticism in Stephen Greenblatt and Giles Gunn, eds., *Redrawing the Boundaries: The Transformation of English and American Literary Studies* (New York, 1992).

10 T. V. Reed calls such work "radical rhetorical studies" and provides a useful list of examples, most of which I would include on any list of my own: Reed, *Fifteen Jugglers, Five Believers: Literary Politics and the Poetics of American Social Movements* (Berkeley, Calif., 1992), p. 174, n. 5; and see the other texts cited above in Chap. 7, nn. 14, 40, 41.

11 Michel Foucault, "The Subject and Power," in Hubert L. Dreyfus and Paul Rabinow, *Michel Foucault: Beyond Structuralism and Hermeneutics*, 2d ed. (Chicago, 1983), pp. 217–20.

this relationship more satisfactorily as involving "technologies of sign systems, which permit us to use signs, meanings, symbols, or signification."[12]

Foucault does not mean to define these three kinds of relationships as separate domains, for in his view the three "always overlap." For example, he says that "communicating is always a certain way of acting upon another person or persons," and "the production and circulation of elements of meaning can have as their objective or as their consequence certain results in the realm of power." The study of cultural rhetoric might elaborate theoretically and illustrate historically exactly how relations of power and communication overlap. Indeed, my earlier definition of cultural rhetoric could easily be rewritten in Foucauldian terms: cultural rhetoric involves power relations that "pass through systems of communication."[13]

Foucault's rhetoric (like that of Graff's model and the Syracuse ETS major) tends to favor tropes of "conflict" in its theoretical and historical work. Further rhetorical use of the Foucauldian vocabulary should probably be balanced by figurings of rhetorical exchanges or cultural conversations in terms of more collaborative or cooperative metaphors.[14] Still, rhetorical conflict, especially in times of historical crisis, seems much more pervasive than rhetorical cooperation. The battle metaphor—especially in its masculinist forms—might be somewhat overused at the present moment in critical theory, but it does usefully convey a sense of the many tensions and conflicts in various contemporary cultural sites. Not the least important of these sites is U.S. higher education.

These academic conflicts are most evident in debates over curriculum reform and pedagogical practices. Again, the study of cultural rhetoric

---

[12] Michel Foucault, "Technologies of the Self," in *Technologies of the Self: A Seminar with Michel Foucault*, ed. Luther H. Martin, Huck Gutman, and Patrick H. Hutton (Amherst, Mass., 1988), p. 18.

[13] Foucault, "The Subject and Power," pp. 217–18. For other attempts to adapt Foucault's work to rhetorical studies, see works listed in M. Lane Bruner, "Toward a Poststructural Rhetorical Critical Praxis: Foucault, Limit Work, and Jenninger's *Kristallnacht* Address," *Rhetorica* 14 (spring 1996): 169–70, n. 6; and also Sonja K. Foss, Karen A. Foss, and Robert Trapp, eds., *Contemporary Perspectives on Rhetoric*, 2d ed. (Prospect Heights, Ill., 1991), chap. 8; Martha Cooper, "Reconceptualizing Ideology According to the Relationship between Rhetoric and Knowledge/Power," in *Rhetoric and Ideology: Compositions and Criticisms of Power*, ed. Charles W. Kneupper (Arlington, Tex., 1989), pp. 30–41; my *Rhetorical Power* (Ithaca, 1989), chaps. 4 and 5; Bruce Herzberg, "Michel Foucault's Rhetorical Theory," in *Contending with Words: Composition and Rhetoric in a Postmodern Age*, ed. Patricia Harkin and John Schilb (New York, 1991), pp. 69–81; and, above, Chap. 6.

[14] See my *Rhetorical Power*, pp. 146–47. My point here is at least partly responsive to Stephen Yarbrough's perceptive critique of my reliance on a Foucauldian notion of power; see his "Force, Power, and Motive," *Philosophy and Rhetoric* 29, no. 4 (1996): 344–58.

gives some helpful hints for thinking about these issues. Rhetoric provides a way of analyzing the controversies within contemporary culture wars and curriculum debates, as I attempted to demonstrate in the previous chapter. But just as important are the possible rhetorical "solutions" to those conflicts, such as Graff's dialogic curricular proposals. Graff suggests that since English studies no longer has a generally stable consensus on some of its most basic issues of canon, methodology, curriculum, and pedagogy, perhaps the best mode of disciplinary organization is to thematize the conflicts. As he and William Cain put it, "the best solution to the conflicts over the canon, the curriculum and the culture is to teach them. Teach the conflicts themselves." They go on to argue that the "classes conducted in the university at any moment make up a potentially coherent conversation, but it is not experienced *as* a conversation by most students, who encounter its different voices in separation from one another. . . . If the academic conversation were made less disjunctive and more coherent, we suspect that more students would see the point of acquiring the information needed to participate in it."[15]

Whatever the validity of the authors' hopefulness, they are certainly persuasive when they claim that a curriculum that explicitly relates the different, conflicting voices to each other will have a better chance of achieving the end they seek: curricular effectiveness through student understanding. Teaching the conflicts as a model for curricular and pedagogical reform would be a definite improvement over the disorganized practices and contradictory structures on the current academic scene. What I would like to emphasize here is that these descriptions of Graff's conflict model already exemplify one very rhetorical way of framing and addressing problems in curriculum and pedagogy. Adding to Graff's proposal an explicitly self-conscious rhetorical vocabulary might further promote a new effective collaboration within a discipline lacking consensus on important topics and goals.[16]

[15] Gerald Graff and William E. Cain, "Peace Plan for the Canon Wars," *The Nation*, 6 March 1989, p. 311.

[16] For other curricular proposals that give a central role to rhetoric, see Gary Waller, "Working within the Paradigm Shift: Post-Structuralism in the Undergraduate Curriculum," *ADE Bulletin* 81 (fall 1985): 5–12; and Jonathan Culler, "Imagining Changes," in *The Future of Doctoral Studies in English*, ed. Andrea Lunsford, Helene Moglen, and James F. Slevin (New York, 1989), pp. 79–83. Also see Richard A. Lanham, *Literacy and the Survival of Humanism* (New Haven, Conn., 1983); W. Ross Winterowd, *Composition/Rhetoric: A Synthesis* (Carbondale, Ill., 1986), pp. 323–53; Wayne C. Booth, *Now Don't Try to Reason with Me: Essays and Ironies for a Credulous Age* (Chicago, 1970), pp. 35–46; Booth, *The Vocation of a Teacher: Rhetorical Occasions, 1967–1988* (Chicago, 1988), pp. 105–28; Don H. Bialostosky, "Dialogics as an Art of Discourse in Literary Criticism," *PMLA* 101 (October 1986): 788–97;

All the connections sketched so far provide reasons for institutionaliz-ing the study of cultural rhetoric by name. A reform of English depart-ments along the lines proposed would most likely require a major re-thinking of the relation of English studies to other disciplines in the human sciences. However, what I am most interested in pursuing here is still another reason for English departments adopting cultural rhetoric study as a new framework: the connection of cultural rhetoric to the dis-cipline of composition.

English departments and composition programs have much to gain intellectually and politically by working as institutional allies within Amer-ican universities. However, to accomplish this alliance in the years ahead, these two changing disciplines must work out their agendas in view of each other. The best, perhaps the only, way for this to be done is through the development of local institutional agreements among groups in liter-ary studies, composition, ESL, cultural studies, literary theory, linguistics, creative writing, and other fractions of traditional English departments. No national, discipline-wide solution seems possible at the present mo-ment. Furthermore, these local agreements and alliances must be rhe-torically negotiated in full awareness of the controversial history of the relation between traditional English departments and their composition programs.[17]

In light of that often regrettable institutional past, I would like to sug-gest the following: literature faculty throughout the country should re-conceptualize their English curricula *not* in their own terms (literary his-tory, cultural studies, critical theory, or whatever) and then ask their understandably suspicious composition colleagues to join up. But rather English departments should adopt a term traditionally associated with composition study and use that concept as a way of rethinking their own theories, practices, and structures. Of course, the term I suggest that En-glish departments adopt is "rhetoric." More specifically, the notion of "cultural rhetoric" could be used as a means to renegotiate the relation-ship between English departments and composition programs as well as their joint relation to other disciplines throughout the university.[18]

---

and Bialostosky, "Liberal Education and the English Department: Or, English as a Trivial Pursuit," in Lunsford, Moglen, and Slevin, *Future of Doctoral Studies*, pp. 97–100.

[17] For something of this history, see Berlin, *Rhetoric and Reality*; and John C. Brereton, ed., *The Origins of Composition Studies in the American College, 1875–1925: A Documentary His-tory* (Pittsburgh, 1995).

[18] For some helpful recent discussions, see John Clifford and John Schilb, eds., *Writing Theory and Critical Theory* (New York, 1994); James A. Berlin, *Rhetorics, Poetics, and Cultures:*

If "rhetoric" became the organizing term for English studies, the future discipline could revise its practices by looking both backward and forward within its academic history. A rhetoricized English studies would remember its humanistic heritage in modern philology and textual scholarship, the two fields most directly concerned with textual transmission, another form of reception study.[19] The history of rhetoric could play a more prominent role, especially the strand that investigates the evolving relation among rhetoric, philosophy, and poetics. But a reformed English studies would also look ahead to emerging forms of cultural critique. Cutting across traditional linguistic and historical fields would be a new cultural studies with a rhetorical slant, moving the center of attention toward the topics and perspectives of new forms of sociopolitical investigations of culture. The study of cultural rhetoric would be the future site where the old and new intersect, consolidate, and transform if not each other then the larger field of which they form a part.

I am not suggesting, however, that all English departments give up literature as their primary object of study or even that they necessarily need to scrap literary history as the organizational schema for their curricula. But I am arguing that using rhetorical study as an organizing framework makes room for a much wider range of interrelated scholarly activities than using a narrowly defined literary studies. Work in this new rhetorical studies would not simply replace traditional interpretations of individual literary texts. Rather, it would incorporate such activities into a larger project of closely reading cultural practices, one that focuses on all the rhetorical events forming the cultural conversation at particular historical moments. Another way of putting this is to say that in cultural rhetoric studies the categories of "theory," "history," and "politics" receive as much prominence as the "aesthetic." It's not that the "literary" drops out of such a project; it's just that this rhetorical study always historicizes the literary, showing how a text works rhetorically *when it is categorized as literary* within particular episodes of the cultural conversation and how the literary/nonliterary distinction functions differently in different contexts of reception.

Though Graff's model of teaching the conflicts is not the only structure available for organizing the study of cultural rhetoric, it is, as I've tried to show throughout this section, one proposal that is especially

---

Refiguring College English Studies (Urbana, Ill., 1996); and John Schilb, *Between the Lines: Relating Composition Theory and Literary Theory* (Portsmouth, N.H., 1996).

[19] See D. C. Greetham, *Textual Scholarship: An Introduction* (New York, 1994).

compatible with a rhetorical vocabulary and framework. Thus, cultural rhetoric study might find teaching the conflicts a useful strategy for accomplishing its own dialogic purposes. But Graff's model itself would also benefit from a cultural rhetoric focus. Indeed, by explicitly emphasizing the rhetorical in its self-descriptions, Graff could more easily incorporate into his model composition research and teaching, to which he has given less prominence than literary studies in his histories and curricular proposals. In any case, I propose this section as another episode in a curricular conversation between teaching the conflicts and rhetoricizing cultural studies, and now I turn to a larger argument regarding the utility of rhetoric as an organizing term.

RHETORIC 2000: THE NEW PROSPECTS

Rhetorical study today offers us a unique opportunity. It has the potential to lead scholars and teachers into a new interdisciplinary, transdisciplinary, or even postdisciplinary future. What exactly are these new prospects of rhetoric? I begin my answer with some general claims about universities and the role of the humanities.

As producer and conduit of knowledge, the university has often had an ambivalent relationship to the society that supports it. While supplying the basic intellectual tools for carrying out established cultural functions, the university has also been among those institutions providing a space for criticism of societal principles and practices. Central to these conventional missions of transmitter and producer, supporter and critic are the disciplines organized under the name of "humanities."

The humanities provide the basic core and the cutting edge of the university today. These fields study and develop the linguistic practices (foreign languages, rhetoric and composition, oral performance) and cultural knowledges (literature, philosophy, history) forming the core of the traditional university. That is, humanities disciplines analyze the fundamental techniques of communication used by other components of the whole educational system and the larger society, as well as criticize those techniques and the cultural web of beliefs in which they are practiced. It is this critical function, so necessary for the production of new knowledges, that establishes the humanities as an important site of cultural critique and intellectual transformation.

In their current shape within U.S. higher education, schools of humanities bring together these analytical and critical functions, these core

and transformative activities, to focus on new areas of interest throughout the academy and broader culture: interests that might be called "critical literacy" or, better, "cultural rhetoric." These studies investigate traditional and emerging rhetorical techniques and contexts, including the
new *technologies* of communication (the electronic media revolution) and
the multicultural and global *conditions* of communication (cultural diversity within a democratic society and cultural difference in a transnational setting). The examination of language and its effects is central to
cultural rhetoric study. Language can be understood broadly as any means
of signification and narrowly as specific vernaculars relevant to national
and transnational interactions. If language is understood broadly, then
one crucial research focus of cultural rhetoric is electronic media, which
is being conceptualized and applied in a range of humanistic disciplines,
from the postmodern theorizing of cyber-culture to the pedagogies of
e-mail and web sites in writing courses. In addition, the study of cultural
rhetoric interprets the use of specific languages within ethnically diverse
democracies and across different national cultures. It plays a central role
in analyzing and criticizing the multicultural conversation in which the
members of this diverse democracy will participate throughout the next
century.

Now if there is something in all this that smacks a bit of facile booster-
ism, I attribute that effect to the institutional origin and rhetorical intention of the preceding claims. I first wrote something very like these
words during the summer of 1995 in my role as associate dean when the
dean of humanities asked me to help draft a brief profile for our School
that could be used to explain to the higher administration, mostly scientists, the current nature of the humanities and the role its departments
will play in the future of research universities. Frankly, this was an internal press release that aimed to persuade nonhumanists to give the School
of Humanities more money in the years ahead.

Whatever its rhetorical success or failure in that context at the University of California, Irvine, I offer it here as part of my rough, imperfect attempt to sketch the new prospects of rhetoric. In the future, rhetorical
study will help organize and reconceptualize the humanities and the interpretive social sciences, meeting the intellectual and political challenges of its historical moment, as it has done at other times in its history.

But as we approach the end of this millennium, rhetorical study is in a
rather different historical position than previously. I have already alluded
to the rapid changes in technology and cultural demographics we have
experienced. But another transformation in our rhetorical context can

also be named—the intellectual effects of the postmodern—in reference to which I make this rather crude prognostication: The next decade or so will be a period of consolidation and possible reconfiguration within the humanities and between the humanities and the interpretive social sciences. I say "consolidation," not "downsizing," because I am not here referring to the economic situation before us—though that must certainly be taken into consideration when making predictions. No, I use the term "consolidation" to refer to the intellectual dynamic of academic disciplines in the years immediately ahead. I predict we will see more and more methodological and substantive reintegration, in which no new initiatives of thought comparable to poststructuralist theory will gain wide currency. This means that we will participate in a period of consolidation in which the so-called humanistic tradition will come to intellectual terms with postmodernism in both a more open and a more covert way than it has heretofore.

And it is precisely in this period of consolidation that I see rhetorical studies playing an increasingly active role. It is the field of rhetoric that offers both an analytic of cultural change and a hermeneutic of intellectual transformation. By an "analytic of cultural change," I mean, among other things, a useful, nuanced rhetorical account of how new ideas are resisted, accepted, and translated within the cultural conversations inside and outside the university. By a "hermeneutic of intellectual transformation," I mean an interpretive strategy for tracking rhetorical traditions in the movement *of* and as a topic *for* the history leading to our postmodern present. That is, though some of its enemies and advocates argue that poststructuralist thought is a dramatic break with the so-called humanistic tradition, much of that thought was developed during this century from within a reinterpretation of the very humanistic tradition it supposedly rejects. This, of course, is only news to those who have not read Nietzsche, Heidegger, and Dewey, seminal thinkers for contemporary critical theory, or much of that contemporary theory itself. I'm thinking especially of the critical engagement with or even reversal of Platonism in Derrida, Irigaray, Deleuze, Foucault, Lyotard, Rorty, Fish, Butler, and many, many others.[20] Rhetoric, especially sophistic rhetoric, plays a prominent role in the development of these thinkers' theories, which have in turn significantly affected the new forms of cultural studies.[21] As-

[20] See, for example, Steven Shankman, ed., *Plato and Postmodernism* (Glenside, Pa., 1994); and Catherine H. Zuckert, *Postmodern Platos: Nietzsche, Heidegger, Gadamer, Strauss, Derrida* (Chicago, 1996).

[21] See my "Measuring Justice: Notes on Fish, Foucault, and the Law," *Cardozo Studies in Law and Literature* 9 (spring/summer 1997): 1–10.

sumptions about this historical agon between Platonic philosophy and sophistic rhetoric form a significant part of what I am calling contemporary rhetoric's hermeneutic of intellectual transformation.

Thus, it is my claim that rhetorical study today offers the academic human sciences both a way of critically analyzing their current evolution (an analytic) and a way of historically interpreting the postmodern humanism or, if you like, posthumanism that is emerging in this coming period of consolidation (a hermeneutic). Rhetoric also provides tools for rethinking the relation between what have been seen as radically different methodologies, humanistic and scientific. That is, rather than seeing, for example, the humanities and the behavioral sciences as offering competing modes of inquiry into rhetoric, rhetoric can be seen as offering a framework for analyzing these fields generally and for remapping their similarities and differences more specifically.[22] The new prospects of rhetoric, then, include the opportunity for using a flexible analytic of cultural change, a powerful hermeneutic of intellectual transformation, and a practical framework for transdisciplinary studies.

By placing specific interpretive acts within the cultural rhetoric of particular times and places, rhetorical hermeneutics moves from critiquing foundationalist theory to doing rhetorical history. Indeed, I would like the reception studies I have done throughout this book to stand as concrete instances of hermeneutic theorizing. Or, one final time, I want to claim that rhetorical hermeneutics, as the intersection of rhetorical pragmatism and cultural rhetoric studies, attempts to use rhetoric to practice theory by doing history. But alongside this specifically disciplinary project, I hope to have at least begun an argument for a larger role for rhetorical studies beyond the academy.

A new rhetorical studies can help reconceptualize and reorganize the human sciences within the future university. As it does so, it needs to remember the calls for action by an earlier generation: "Rhetorical studies are not in themselves the solution to social, political, or personal problems. They are, however, by their nature and functions relevant to the tasks of social betterment."[23] The academic humanities struggle today

---

[22] See Jack Selzer, ed., *Understanding Scientific Prose* (Madison, Wis., 1993); Alan G. Gross, *The Rhetoric of Science*, 2d ed. (Cambridge, Mass., 1996); and Alan G. Gross and William M. Keith, eds., *Rhetorical Hermeneutics: Invention and Interpretation in the Age of Science* (Albany, N.Y., 1997).

[23] Douglas Ehninger et al., "Report of the Committee on the Scope of Rhetoric and the Place of Rhetorical Studies in Higher Education," in *The Prospect of Rhetoric*, ed. Lloyd F. Bitzer and Edwin Black (Englewood Cliffs, N.J., 1971), p. 210.

with their critical relation to the society in which they reside. The Culture Wars are with us still, and rhetorical study has a crucial function to play in those wars. While continuing debate over the future role of public intellectuals, cultural rhetoricians should analyze, discuss, and respond forcefully to the political challenges now facing the professionalized humanities. These, then, are today's challenges; these are the new prospects of rhetoric.

Major in English and Textual Studies, Syracuse University

Requirements

Lower Division

    ETS 141   Reading and Interpretation I: From Language to Discourse
    ETS 241   Reading and Interpretation II: Practices of Reading

Upper Division

Courses are divided into three groups, according to whether their mode of inquiry or conceptual orientation is primarily historical, theoretical, or political. Students are required to take two courses from one of these groups, two courses from a second group, and one course from a third group. The three remaining courses are major electives, which can come from any of the three groups or from among other courses not included in any group, for example, creative writing workshops or upper-level composition studios.

Historical inquiries assume that texts bear meaning as they are produced and read in specific historical formations. Courses taught under this rubric will study, for example, periods and periodization, reception aesthetics, modes of historical inquiry, and specific histories of genres.

Theoretical inquiries, instead of taking the possibility of textual meaning for granted, investigate the conditions under which texts can be said to bear meaning, as well as the questions of whether and how such meaning can become available to a reader. They include courses in psychoanalysis, deconstruction, hermeneutics, rhetoric, and poetics.

Information taken from *The English Newsletter: Undergraduate News from the English Department, Syracuse University* 1, no. 1 (March 1990) and no. 2 (November 1990).

Political inquiries assume that texts are bearers of political meaning: that is, they mediate power relations. Courses taught under this rubric will focus, for example, on the politics of canon formation, the writings of "marginal groups," and the institutional mediation of reading and writing, and include courses in modes of ideology critique, Marxism, cultural rhetoric, and materialist feminism.

In the following list, fifty-four courses are represented. The 300-level number in each pair represents an "Introduction to" course while the 400-level number represents a "Studies in" course. For example, under the "Rhetoric" division of the general "Theory Group" courses, there is a listing "362/462 Hermeneutics," which stands for two courses: 362, Introduction to Hermeneutics; and 462, Studies in Hermeneutics.

HISTORY GROUP

I. Literary Histories

311/411   Literary History to 1800
312/412   Literary History, 1700 to Contemporary
313/413   Periodization and Chronology

II. Histories of Symbolic Forms

321/421   History of Forms
322/422   History of Ideas
323/423   History of Myths

III. Discursive Histories

331/431   Discourses
332/432   Reception Aesthetics
333/433   Language

THEORY GROUP

I. Theories of Representation

341/441   Psychological Theories of Representation
342/442   Semiotic Theories of Representation
343/443   Cultural Theories of Representation

II. Poetics and Formal Analysis

351/451 Theory of Genre
352/452 Theory of Forms
353/453 Style and Language

III. Rhetoric

361/461 Tropes and Figures
362/462 Hermeneutics
363/463 Discourse Analysis

POLITICS GROUP

I. Culture, Power, Knowledge

371/471 Ideology
372/472 Canons
373/473 Institutions

II. Resistance and Power

381/481 Race and Discourse
382/482 Imperialism and Nationalism
383/483 Class, Culture, and the Power of Discourse

III. Gender and Sexualities

391/491 Feminisms
392/492 Gender Studies
393/493 Sexualities

INDEX

202   *Index*